Brainwashed: Fighting for the Enemy

An American Soldier's WWII memoir
as a Hitler Youth and German Soldier

By

Herman Esfeld and Edna Esfeld

Brainwashed: Fighting for the Enemy: 2

Dedication

To all WWII survivors,

to the "Bug" lovers,

and

to my Oma and Opa Esfeld in heaven,

to my mother Ida who gave me my freedom early on,

and to my sister Nora.

I love you.

--Edna Esfeld

Preface

by Herman Esfeld

Life has many winners. War only lucky ones. I am one of the lucky ones. This story is for my two daughters, Nora Brzezinski and Edna Esfeld, my stepdaughter Christine von Eyss, my grandchildren Krista and Matthew, step-grandsons Daniel and Adrian, and all my offspring. Anyone else is welcome to read it too.

My heartfelt thanks goes out to my lovely wife Ruth for her patience during my long hours of writing.

I hereby applaud the literary work my daughter Edna did as co-author. It massaged many of my words into exciting and suspenseful reading material.

I have tried to recreate events, locales and conversations from my memories of them. In order to maintain their anonymity in some instances I have changed the names of individuals and places, I may have changed some identifying characteristics and details such as physical properties, occupations and places of residence.

Foreword

by Edna Esfeld

War is not the answer. A sincere thank you to my father. For the past seven years I've been writing and transcribing his letters and the taped conversations we made, and researching more facts about our world's worst war in which over 50 million people perished and millions of more lives were sacrificed in terms of their quality of life—from serious injuries to loss of parents, home and other family members, and who have had to carry the scars of that war throughout their lives.

As the child of parents who were both World War II survivors, I feel deep gratitude for my father's unrestricted outpouring of his experiences during the war at my dinner table one afternoon after having kept it bottled up for seventy-five years. And I dearly thank his second wife, my stepmother Ruth, who patiently watched him writing away every day for an entire summer. His story opened my eyes to the deep wounds, tenderness, and humbleness in him that I had never seen before. For that I too am humbled. My father's experience confirmed my belief that love, knowledge, and forgiveness are the hardest things to understand and come by in life; and the greatest to bear from a war.

I must thank first and foremost my late auntie Yachana (a.k.a. Norma Henrietta Esfeld, my father's younger sister), an elementary and middle school teacher for forty years, who was my mentor and soul-mate. It was she who planted the seed in me to write my father's story. During that memorable evening at the dinner table, she told me, "Edna, you've got to write this down. And get a tape recorder!" My father and I were lucky to have her around at the birth of writing his story for her excellent memory of those six long years of war the family lived through. I was lucky to have an unselfish aunt who gave her whole life to teaching children, and others, compassion and tolerance. I love you and miss you so much, my dear Yachana.

I must thank an established author Dr. Eva Shaw, my on-line writing teacher who gave me the courage to continue to write no matter what. You never let me down in your classes, Eva.

With many special thanks to my ex-partner, Linda Edwards, a bookworm and journalism major, who came across the book *Small*

Wonder, about the VW pre-, post-, and present years. Through the last seven years you stood by me with encouragement and provided material to write this story. Your last minute editing, in the middle of your busy tax season, demonstrates your hard work ethics and optimistic outlook on life that is admired by me. I am grateful for our friendship.

I thank my therapist, Sharon Burnett Ph.D., M.F.T., whom I saw for over fifteen years. She helped me through times I thought I could not handle as a young woman, and supported this book with open arms. She also threw out another seed for a book about children of WWII survivors.

A big thanks to my German/American friends Silvia Martini and her husband Michael for their German to English translation of parts in this story that were deemed impossible to interpret by others.

There are a couple of friends, new and old, I wish to thank that have encouraged me, sometimes in subtle ways, to write. Especially Jayne, since you are my biggest fan from your kind words and encouragement. You've supported my poetry for over thirty years. Our everlasting love and friendship help fill my blank pages often.

We thank our e- book designer Rita Toews. You made the last mile to the finish line easy and fun.

And lastly, my father and I want to thank one of the toughest editors, actress, and established author of several books, Elaine Partnow. Your expertise, professionalism and thought-provoking style has made me appreciate even more what the writing world can do. For a first time author, I hope I have become a better writer from your jabs, and editing, but more importantly, a bigger fan and student of this wondrous world of history and knowledge in print.

Part I

Detroit, Michigan
1927-1937

Chapter 1

The Last Holiday

"All children of the earth,
Rise up to see, all the best they can be,
And forever they shall heed
To only the good in thee."
---Edna Esfeld

Herman's mother found his father lying on the cold concrete floor of their garage with his head rested on an embroidered pillow directly underneath the tail pipe of their Ford sedan. It was a typical frigid Michigan morning in January. His father routinely warmed up their car to drive his mother to her weekly bowling game. Later the autopsy confirmed Herman's father had died within minutes from carbon monoxide asphyxiation from the trapped exhaust fumes. There were no visual signs of trauma to his head or body. Only under extraordinary circumstances would he have left the engine running with the automatic garage door closed. Henry Esfeld was sixty-eight.

It was 1970 and Herman's father had retired three years earlier.

Twenty-nine years of dedicated service at Ford Motor Company in Detroit Michigan, his retirement was a milestone in his industrial life of automobiles. Henry and Frieda had built a modest red and white aluminum-sided two-bedroom, one and a quarter bath home on less than an acre of property. It had an attached one car garage. In the backyard the hundreds of tropical lime colored Michigan Backer ferns that grew three to four feet high seemed out of place in this cold mitten shaped state. Thirty foot spruces swayed by the winds shaded the backyard. They lived amidst a forest. Their quaint home sat across a small street that paralleled one of the biggest natural lakes in the heart of Michigan: Houghton Lake.

"Herman, I could smell the exhaust while I was getting ready in the bathroom," Herman's mother cried on the phone in her perfect English. "I called for Vati (father) to see if he had come inside. I didn't hear him answer. So I ran to the utility room and opened the door. To my shock the garage door was still closed. I pushed the button to the electric door opener and saw Vati lying on the ground not moving. I called him again and he didn't move. So I called the ambulance."

It was the first time he ever recalled hearing a quiver in his mother's voice.

The day after that harrowing phone conversation, Herman took his wife and their two daughters and drove the four hour trip up north in silence. It was hard to believe they were headed to the place where the entire family had enjoyed so many wonderful memories over the decades for such a solemn purpose.

There are only two places where the sun can shine directly into the house: a window and a door. The view from the house to Houghton Lake was squeezed between a row of summer cottages and permanent custom homes. From there one could see blasts of bright blazing sunsets, like the color inside a blood orange. The sun's rays bounced upon the shimmering water, piercing through the front sliding porch door and landing to rest on the dining room table. Every afternoon Frieda would carefully pull the drawstrings from the floor length silk drapes to cut the blinding glare and, hopefully, reduce the heat and humidity Michigan summers produced. It was chancy to let the sun shine directly on the mahogany wood table she'd brought all the way back from Germany twenty years before. The handmade

German lace tablecloth that graced the table was invaluable.

During the last family visit up north in winter of 1969, Herman noted, after he unpacked the car, an unfamiliar attitude from his mother.

"Vati, did you pull the shade outside?" she asked him in her native German tongue.

It was that quick robotic tone Mutti (mother) used that caught Herman's attention. Why, he asked himself, did she ask Vati that? Did he have to be reminded of the simplest things? He watched as his father shook his head in silence, a gesture he'd seen a thousand times, and then shuffle to the porch and pull the bamboo shade closed.

"The window coverings inside the house are not enough protection," Frieda said.

On that trip, Herman had been excited to talk with his father about the automobile industry, especially the latest on new inventions in technology and engineering. Herman worked in the manufacture of door hinges and handles. His father had retired from design and process engineering. The top three American carmakers from Motor City had been creating jobs all across America at a fast pace.

"So, how's business, Herman?" Henry quipped.

"Oh, it's getting tough with the competition from Japan," Herman said, happy his father had asked him.

His father calmly shook his head in disgust. "Well, I always knew that would happen," he said in a lowered voice. "We just have to keep our heads together and figure out a new way to compete with them." Even as a kid his father's constant positive outlook had made a lasting impression on Herman.

Being a precisionist and a handyman, Herman's father kept his garage impeccably clean. It amazed him how his father organized their single car garage from floor to ceiling, everything from chisels, saws, hammer, nuts and bolts, to garden tools and gloves on the spotless painted drywall. Each tool was carefully hung with neatly written English name tags underneath, as if each one told a story of Henry's hands at work. The sparkling lawnmower stowed under the workbench, which Henry built from scratch, looked like one straight out of a Sears catalogue. The red Ford Maverick looked as if he'd just driven it off the show room floor. Not a speck of dirt could be found in his garage.

Herman's articulate mother also liked neatness. She swept what didn't need sweeping and organized closets and kitchen cabinets. She kept her pantry filled with foods such as dried figs, prunes, nuts and dates, granola, bottles of vitamins and oatmeal and natural baking ingredients, all the things found in a health food store. That was something his parents both had in common: neatness.

Henry liked to stay home. He didn't like to go out much except to play cards. Not even to dinner. He also didn't celebrate Christmas. Growing up in Germany Henry's mother never celebrated the Christmas holiday with gifts and all the holiday fanfare. So every Christmas he would send Herman's younger sister Norma to go out and buy his wife a Christmas present. Frieda eventually found out and she became furious.

When Frieda wanted to go out to dinner, see a concert or movie, Henry wouldn't go. One Christmas Frieda wanted to see Marlene Dietrich, who was appearing live in Detroit, but Henry wanted to stay home so she took Norma instead.

Only two times when they lived on California Street in Detroit did Herman's parents have a big argument. He saw his father become so angry, on both occasions he smashed a TV tray. Frieda stood in the kitchen crying.

The last Christmas they'd spent together Herman had observed his father sitting quietly in his blue velvet recliner, not particularly unusual for him. As everyone unwrapped presents he could see his father's baby blue eyes moisten as he watched his grandchildren feverishly tearing apart the paper. He thought it odd, knowing his father didn't ordinarily show emotion. Perhaps it had to do with the several strokes his father had suffered right after retirement, though none had impaired him physically or, it seemed, emotionally. When dinner was served Herman soon forgot.

His mother loved to set her dining table with their fine china and silver serving dishes, especially her favorite silver dinnerware engraved with the letters "F" and "E" laid out on white cloth napkins.

"Nora and Edna, please set the table," Oma (grandmother) said.

The plates, silverware, and glasses were kept locked in the mahogany buffet and in the glass door china cabinet Henry and Frieda were lucky enough to bring back from Germany. Herman's two daughters carefully took out each piece and placed it in its proper place on the table.

"Dinner is served!"Mutti called out.

Everyone started to gather around the dining table. But where was Vati? Herman wondered.

"Vati," Frieda called out. There was no word.

"Vati!'' she yelled, *"das abendessen wird serviert wird* (dinner is ready)." When he didn't answer she asked Herman to get his father.

Without a word Herman walked down the narrow hallway to the bathroom. No Vati.

"Oh my Gott! Vati," he heard his mother from the kitchen.

When Herman came back he saw his mother looking out the window that faced the backyard. He walked up to take a look and there he saw his father relieving himself behind a tree.

His father always sat at the head of the table and this time it was no different. Herman sat on his left, his wife Ida next to him, and Herman's younger brother Ronald on Vati's right, with Ronald's wife next to him. Their sister Norma sat in the middle. Herman's two daughters sat on each side of their Oma, who sat at the other head of the table.

"Okay, now let's make a toast," his mother said. "*Prost*! To our health. To happiness," the adults said in German.

"God is great, God is good. Let us thank him for our food," Herman's youngest recited.

Herman proudly poured a fine German white wine he'd brought from Chicago into the crystal wine glasses. Twice a year Herman and his wife, along with eight or so of their German friends, caravanned from Jackson to Chicago to stock up on special German liquors and other alcohol. They acted like college kids on spring break. On some trips they made a whole weekend out of it. They'd be packed in six or seven cars and drove the six and half hour trip southwest single file on highway I-94. Their destination was a special German liquor store downtown that imported everything from Germany. They left with car trunks laden with tax free booze. Herman and his friends laughed and joked at how the bottom of their cars scraped the long road at every bump on the way back.

Herman poured the dinner wine with a smile on his face, not knowing it would be his last holiday dinner together with his father.

One year later Herman, his family and their close friends stood on frozen soil while the pallbearers lowered his father's casket into the ground. They buried Henry at a cemetery off the main highway by Houghton Lake among the wondrous woods, as his father had wished. Pines, furs, birches, and maples older than Herman's father, thirty to forty feet high, grew over and around all the gravesites.

Early 1950's, Detroit. Our traditional holiday cheer.

Chapter 2

Houghton Lake

Herman thoroughly enjoyed his northern visits to his parents in winter, spring, summer and fall. In Houghton Lake, the largest inland lake in Michigan, the changing of the seasons created spectacular sights. From the branches of snowcapped pines trees drooped foot long icicles that quickly melted in the early spring thaw. Fields of wildflowers, like purple lupine and custards of dandelions, filled the countryside like a Monet painting. The lake became a postcard backdrop of the Michigan sunsets that grew brilliant in summer.

Ever since his parents had retired, Herman took his wife and two daughters here for summer vacations. They stayed in a rustic lakeside cottage which was next to a series of other cottages. A long single lane dirt road led to the edge of the lake. The road was edged by dry grass and wild weeds that fused into their natural surroundings among the dead pine needles. Each cottage had a kitchenette with one and two bedrooms situated within a short walking distance to the lake. The lovely setting, the amenities, and the affordable rates made these resort dwellings very popular in the Fifties and Sixties, especially for a startup family like Herman's. He liked being frugal.

"Come on, there's nothing to be scared about," Herman yelled to his two daughters as he tried coaxing them to swim far out into the lake that stretched seven and half miles long and four and half miles wide. The murky water did not faze Herman. Though you couldn't see it, the bottom was only seven feet deep.

On one vacation, before his youngest daughter could swim, he picked her up and threw her head first into the motel pool. She was five at the time. He'd never seen anyone jump out of a pool as fast as she did.

"Dad!" She yelled so that everyone heard. "I hate you." Everyone around the pool laughed, including Herman.

His parents' best friends and their neighbors in Detroit since before the war joined them on many occasions. Out came the drinks and imported liquor. They drank and toasted and ate like no tomorrow. Coffee klatches were at three in the afternoon served with his mother's homemade mouthwatering German butter *kuchen*, a coffee cake, or a plum torte cake and with coffee so strong it could part waters. Their friends' two grandchildren were around his daughters' ages. So Herman's summer vacations in Houghton Lake were like one big family reunion.

One vacation afternoon Herman's mother held a black and white photograph in her hand while everyone relaxed in the living room.

"See this picture, girls? These men standing next to your Opa (grandpa) are very important men."

Herman didn't have to look at the photograph. He knew who they were.

"This one is your Opa. Do you know who Henry Ford was?" my mother asked. "He created the first automobile in Detroit called the model T." In the photo sat nicely dressed men side by side on the couch.

"These distinguished men, including your Opa, helped build the first Volkswagen factory."

Herman gently put down his coffee on its saucer. His new and sparkling 1969 cream colored VW beetle with a sun roof sat outside on the driveway. Beetle was the nickname given to the Volkswagen when they were first introduced to the U.S. in 1949. The Volkswagen became the most popular imported car in America. Herman taught his two daughters how to drive it when they were fifteen and ten at the parking lots at the high school and community college: there were several hours of bump, stop, and bump, stop.

"Mutti, was that a real fox on your winter stole?" Herman asked, changing the subject.

"Before it got shot, Herman," she said jokingly.

"Can we see it, Oma?" asked his youngest.

"It was expensive. Vati bought it for me" she said.

During the Depression Herman and his parents lived in Detroit. His mother, a connoisseur of fashion, had the latest in long gowns, ruffled skirts, and accessories, such as the grey fox fur stole she had stored away with the taxidermy head of the fox attached. She wore that stole so much it started to get bald spots.

1938. Dr. Porsche's original engineers. L-R front: Henry Esfeld, Joe Werner, Reidel, Walter Kuntze, Hoehne. L-R back: Stephan, Luik, Rechenback. (One other engineer named Meyer is not in photo).

Chapter 3

The Three Tiers

In 1920 Herman's grandfather told his son, "Henry, you will be better off to go to an engineering school. Get an education in this field because it will be the way of the future."

With his father's persuasion, Henry followed his dream to come to the United States; he arrived in New York City alone by ship five years later. Frieda's parents had insisted she stay behind until she heard from Henry. They wanted to make sure that he was serious about wanting to marry her. Henry sent for her right away. While he waited for her he found work repairing laundry trucks. This was right before the Great Depression and good jobs were starting to become scarce. When his mother arrived they hopped on a train from New York to Detroit where they stayed with Henry's uncle and his wife. Soon after, Henry got an engineering job at Ford Motor Company. Only a few years later Herman was born at Providence Hospital on

West Grand Boulevard in Detroit. An unusual building for a hospital,

Herman's mother picked an elegant hospital, with its castle-

like structure, high arched ceilings and tiled floors. Sadly the one

hundred year old hospital was demolished in 1975.

June 1927. Frieda, Herman's mother, bringing Herman
home for the first time from Providence Hospital in Detroit.

1930 Detroit Mich. Herman's father Henry Esfeld.

In 1914, during the First World War, Herman's grandfather was chosen to be a mechanic on the giant German airships called Zeppelins. Once one of the tied anchor ropes broke loose from the blimp and hit his grandfather, causing him to lose an eye. He was subsequently discharged from the army. With his disability income, he started a farm to raise hogs.

When Henry turned fourteen he began an apprenticeship in the ship building business working on submarines. Soon he received his degree in design engineering from Bremen Technology College in the city of Bremen where he went to work for an automotive company called Borgward.

But almost from the start, Herman's father had aspirations of going to America. He had heard and read of Henry Ford's automobile where, in Detroit, the first assembly lines produced the successful Ford Model T. There were opportunities for engineers and advancement in the automotive industry there. His uncle, who was working for Ford Motor Company, wrote to him and said, "Henry, this is where you belong."

Herman's mother was born in the small town of Bremen, ten miles south of his father's town. They met on a blind date at a restaurant arranged by a mutual friend. Henry called on Frieda the very next day and asked her out again. He was infatuated with her beauty. Frieda had pretty blue eyes and wavy short-cropped black hair, the fashion at the time, and revealed a style and grace like no other woman he had seen. During their second date Henry so smitten, he asked Frieda if she'd like to go to a motel with him and stay the night.

She immediately said, "No. That is too fast. You don't ask a woman to bed on the second date!" Lo and behold, it took one and a half years before they would be together.

They were already engaged when Frieda's parents learned of Henry's intentions of coming to the United States. Frieda's parents disapproved of Herman's mother and father marrying in Germany before going to the United States. So they gave her one condition: they insisted that Henry must first go to America and get a job. Then, if he doesn't change his mind about marrying her, she could go to America and marry him there. Frieda wanted to marry in Germany and have a traditional wedding with her family and friends.

"Oh, I was disappointed," Mutti would say. "But in those days, you did what you were told and made sacrifices in hopes for a better life."

Herman's mother took English classes at night and learned the language quickly. She went to legal secretary school and eventually worked for an attorney in Detroit. Herman considered his father fortunate to land an engineering job at Ford Motor Company in the 1930s when millions of people were unemployed.

Germany had its own depression. It was during these times that, in 1931, a man named Dr. Ferdinand Porsche opened his first engineering shop in Stuttgart, where the center of the automobile industry had started. He wanted to build the world's smallest and most affordable car for all people.

Porsche heard about Henry Ford's assembly line for the Model T. Now that his design, which looked like a bug, was finished, Porsche sailed to Detroit to see how cars could be mass produced. He toured the Ford factory twice in October 1936.

Because Henry could not write English and since his spoken English language was subpar, it was clear he would not be able to advance further into a managerial position at Ford. "We should go into our own design and engineering business," he said to a German-American engineer he'd befriended. An innovator at heart, Henry wanted to create something. He looked for and loved challenges.

Henry had heard that the famous race car designer Porsche wanted to speak to and recruit German Nationalist (Germans living in the United States without citizenship) workers from the factory in Detroit. Even though Henry and Frieda had become American citizens, he hoped that Porsche was amenable to speaking to him as well.

He told a colleague, "I've heard at the plant that Dr. Porsche has the idea of building an automobile factory from the ground up in Germany."

On a spring day in 1937, just when major league baseball was starting up, the phone rang at the home of a Ford company co-worker named Joe Werner. Henry got to know Joe while working at Ford. He was a jovial person with an outgoing personality. Henry and Joe got along well.

On another day shortly after that phone call a short plump man in his 50s dressed in a fine business suit and accompanied by another younger man both stalked the engineering department at the River Rouge Plant. The whistle of the factory horn blew like a steam engine train, signaling the end of the shift; it could be heard a mile away. Ford Motor Company had three shifts so that the assembly line could run twenty-four hours a day. Herman's father, a lean man with a slight gut and wearing a white dress shirt and tie, had just finished washing his hands and was walking out of the lavatory when one of the well-dressed men, who sported a jet black curly mustache, came up to him.

"I'm told you speak English and are German/American," he said in German.

Henry thought he might be from the UAW trying to recruit him to join. In those days, the unions were just getting organized and were fierce in their recruitment efforts.

"Yah", he said.

"I am looking for engineers with your background and experience to recruit for a position to build a factory for a new automobile in Deutschland," he said. "I am Dr. Ferdinand Porsche."

Henry, a bit stunned, stared at the gentleman who stood expressionless. The factory assembly machines hissed and grinded to a shuttering halt.

"What is your name?" Porsche asked.

"*Ich bin* Henry Esfeld," he said.

"I would like to hire you on a contract basis and you will be paid the same as here."

"What are you going to build?" he asked.

Porsche had already built the fastest midsize luxury cars, such as the Mercedes Benz roadsters SS and SSK.

"A factory for an automobile that will be affordable to the masses. I am expecting to have my new engineers relocated to Germany by this September. I would like you and five others to come first. Your moving expenses will be paid for. My secretary will contact you and give you the details." He reached out to shake Henry's hand.

"Thank you, Dr. Porsche. Nice to meet you."

That evening he came home excited. "You would not believe who I met. Dr. Ferdinand Porsche, the well-known luxury car and race car designer from Deutschland. He came to me just before I was leaving and propositioned me to go to work for him."

"Yah, und what for?" Herman's mother asked.

"To help build a different kind of automobile, small and affordable for everyone. And, they are building a factory and an entire city for it."

"And where is he going to build this?"

She was used to having to probe information out of him.

"In Deutschland, near Stuttgart."

There was a gasp from Herman's mother. She contained herself long enough to ask the question, "And what did you answer?"

"Dr. Ferdinand Porsche is impressed with Ford Motor Company's Model T success and how it's being produced. He would like to copy the modern factories and assembly lines he's seen here in Detroit," he said. "Dr. Porsche said it is ready to be built. And Mr. Dyckhoff will be in charge."

Herman's mother listened with reluctance. "Who is Dyckhoff?

"He's the technical director and head designer of the factory to be built. He was an engineer with the popular car Opel. He'll be my immediate boss."

Frieda went to the sink to wash her hands. "How will we afford this?"

"Dr. Porsche said money is not a problem. All our expenses will be paid for, like transportation and housing. And I will be making about the same as here and a promise to advance. I will be in charge over other engineers," he replied.

"Where is this money coming from?"

"I'm told the National Socialist German Workers Party," he

said. "And they are going to build a new city around it."

Frieda and her friend, the wife of another of Herman's father's colleagues, felt this new German government could not be trusted. She listened and read all about the politics going on in Germany and she felt Hitler was going too far with his policies.

"Henry, I don't think it's a good idea," said a German friend and engineer at Ford named Mr. Weitzel. "I think you're making a big mistake."

"How could it be a mistake? This will be an affordable car for everyone. It will help Germany," Henry said. This was echoed by Porsche. Herman's father paid no attention to politics. Henry's love of engineering and design matched that of Porsche's obsession of the people's car. He sought greater challenges in his line of work.

Henry's father had written him a letter from Germany in 1936 saying, "Henry, things are wonderful here. Everywhere it's getting better. Come on back." After hearing how enthusiastic, ambitious and happy the German people lived, British people who were headed to Switzerland for vacation started traveling through Germany. The Brits were flabbergasted at what they saw.

Out of all the German/American engineers at the factory a handful warmed to the proposal. "It gives us a chance to see our relatives again," Henry said to Frieda. "You know, Muttie, I haven't seen my family since I came to the United States." Those were the same sentiments from his neighbor, who also accepted the proposal.

Porsche figured the factory would be ready for production by 1939. Then the American recruits could either stay or go back to the United States.

"Well, let's go then for the two years and get it over with and come back here. We have our three children to raise. Here in Detroit there are glorious opportunities for them," Mutti finally agreed. By now Frieda and Henry had a large circle of German/American friends among whom she was very popular because she was the only one who could speak fluent English. Now she was intent on listening to news from Germany. She liked to follow politics.

The Kuntzes were one of Herman's family friends. Mr. Kuntze, a tall, slender and handsome blond man, had designed and drawn out the factory floor plan. The original is still framed and hung in one of his grandson's home. The Werners, Kuntzes, Luwigs, and the

Rechenbachs, all part of their circle of friends in Detroit, accepted the contract offered by Dr. Porsche. These families were part of the earlier engineers to move back to Germany for the dream to build the first VW factory.

Within a few short weeks the first tier of six German/American design engineers packed up their families and sailed to Stuttgart, including Henry.

Joe Werner was reluctant to go, as was his wife. But they soon left with the second tier of men and their families, some from the GM plant. Their responsibility was to equip the factory with the needed machinery and tools.

The third tier followed with tool and die makers, mostly from Chicago. All in all, three tiers, around twenty German-Americans ended up back in Germany by September 1937.

Chapter 4

Preparations

Where is Fred? I asked myself. We had been best friends from the beginning of grade school, and I was looking for him to say goodbye.

"Herman, are you packing or daydreaming again?" yelled my mother. She first learned English by going to the movies and always took me along with her. Eventually she and my father took English classes at night.

"Herman, do I have to come in there? I did not hear you," yelled my mother.

"No, Mutti," I said. My mother, a strict disciplinarian and a loving German-bred woman, nurtured me through my adolescence. She doted on me and taught me how to groom myself, dress nicely, and to properly fold and pack my clothes. "No wrinkles," she'd say. It was from my mother that I learned about the finer things life had to offer.

I didn't feel like answering. I wanted to finish going about my packing quietly. A close game between the Tigers and White Sox on our radio distracted me. I knew where we were going and sweat rolled off my forehead when I thought about my last vacation in Germany a year ago. Upon my return, one of my grammar school classmates asked, "Did you see any German warships?" asked classmates.

"Yes, Muttie, I am almost finished," I yelled. I wondered if she knew about the knots I had felt in my stomach when we came back from that last vacation.

I need to say goodbye to Fred, I thought to myself. Fred, as an only child, was a little stuck up and didn't get along too well with the others our age. He didn't like sports, let alone the girls in our school. I, on the other hand, always had a girlfriend. It felt good walking them home from school and I was proud to carry their books. I always politely asked the girl if she wanted to be kissed, which got me in trouble with the other boys. The bullies jealously caused me to take a different and longer route home to avoid getting a thrashing from them. One time, when I was seven, I got really hooked on a girl about two years older than me. I thought she was as pretty as the deep blue

sky. When I think back, I think how mature she was. She would

politely listen to my babbling; but I never got a kiss from her. How

sweet puppy love can be.

As I continued to pack I couldn't keep my mind off the

conversation between my parents about moving back to Germany.

"But, Frieda, this is a good opportunity for us. And besides,

you will be close with your family once again, and I with mine," my

father said, trying to convince my mother about the move.

I had become apprehensive about going back. On our last

vacation, in the summer of 1936, we took my newborn brother and

sailed back to Germany. We spent three whole months visiting my

relatives. For the first time I met my grandparents, uncles, aunts, and

cousins. I began to speak a little bit of German for the first time.

Since school summer vacation in the U.S. was three months

and only six weeks in Germany, my mother felt during our last few

weeks of our vacation in Germany my time would be better spent if I

were enrolled in a German grade school, like an exchange student.

Besides, I didn't have any kids to play with that were my age because they were all in school. Well, that did not work out very well. There were bullies in my class who started to tease and harass me. They pummeled me, pulled my hair and spit in my face because I was an American. And all the class laughed at me.

"*Du bist iene shwein du Americano* (you are an American pig). *Du kanst nicht hier bliben* (you cannot stay here with us). *Du kanst nicht gute Duetche sprecken und* (you can't talk good German). *Wir glauben, dass Sie nicht wissen, welche Soccer ist* (we believe you don't know what soccer is)."

I defended myself, "Yes, I do. I play soccer back home at our lake near Detroit. I also play baseball." But the torment continued.

"Ha, ha. *Sie spielen eine Sportart nichts zu tun, was wir hier genießen in Deutchland* (you play a sport unrelated to what we enjoy here in Germany). *Sie sind ein idiot aus America* (you are an idiot from America)!"

The teacher just shrugged his shoulders and said nothing about the torments flung at me. Finally after I had enough of this harassment I told my mother. Thankfully, she took me out of that school.

That experience left a bitter taste in my mouth. When we sailed home, I was afraid of what my classmates' reactions might be in the States if they found out I had spent twelve weeks in Germany. I knew, from overhearing my parents' conversations, that there were still negative feelings towards Germany leftover from World War I. I was glad to be back swimming, playing baseball, and thinking how I wanted to be a Boy Scout. To my surprise, I was relieved to be treated like a hero by everyone when I returned home to Detroit that fall.

I did not know that less than a year later I would be facing the same dilemma.

Chapter 5

Reminiscing

We had lived at about five different places around Detroit before we left for Germany. When we lived on Rutherford Street, located in the town of Dearborn just west of the Ford factories, my father came home from work one day driving a brand new shiny black four-door Ford sedan. Coming to a screeching halt in the driveway and honking the funny sounding horn wildly, he shouted to my startled mother, "Frieda, look what I bought. A brand new Model A just off the assembly line!" It replaced the venerable old Model T.

"Now you have to teach me how to drive," my mother said. In no time at all my mother passed the driver's test with me sitting like a prince on the red velour-covered back seat with a big gleaming smile.

A few months before we left to help build the VW factory, we settled on Kentucky Avenue, south of Six Mile Road, in a two-story red brick house with a formal dining room, three bedrooms and a small bathroom upstairs. Most all of the houses on my block looked the same. They were tract houses, all situated close together with white painted front porches. Rows and rows of these middle class dwellings lined the streets. Our house was one of the few with a single car garage.

This neighborhood was so friendly that it was easy for me to get used to living there. At school, I had the loudest voice in class. During roll call I bellowed with enthusiasm, "Herman Esfeld!" After a long pause, the startled teacher said, "Now, class, that is the way I want you to speak up. Like Herman just did."

In the summer we frequented the tree-lined shores of Cass Lake, just north of Detroit, surrounded by towering oak trees and wooden country cottages from which we would run down to the shore to swim and sunbathe. There I played soccer and enjoyed picnics put on by the German-American soccer club. I'd daydream at the sight of the spacious mansions built nearby at St. Claire Shores. Someday, I thought, we would live in one.

There were at least ten other lakes to choose from, but Cass Lake was closest to home and our friends. My mother would let me swim and play in the lake the entire day. Several times I came home with sunburn all over my body. Years later, in my 60s, I was twice diagnosed with melanoma cancer: but it was caught in time.

My mother was so loving that on one of my birthdays I was listening to one of my favorite programs on the radio when during a commercial I heard an announcement that said, "Herman, if you are listening, please go look for your present down in your basement in the coal bin." Stunned, I immediately ran downstairs and found a brand new bicycle. She had arranged that surprise.

When my brother Ronald was born six years later, all the attention I had been getting from my parents stopped. I had to quickly adjust to not being the only child. Because he was born two months early, my mother was instructed to rub oil all over him a few times a day. A short time later a Jewish doctor, Dr. Tatelis, convinced my parents to circumcise Ronald. And he did it right on our kitchen table as I stood and watched from a safe distance away. I felt helpless as poor Ronald wailed and wailed.

The day before we were set to leave for Germany, I felt anxious. Walking down the street I looked for the old gray haired man who sold ice cream at the soda shop. "Ice cream, young man?" he asked from behind the canteen counter. My two favorite things were a scoop of cold, semi-hard chocolate ice cream on a cone and a long vigorous swim in the lake on a humid Michigan day. I grabbed the cone. "Thank you, sir." I walked away, stuffing myself madly and thinking of how I was leaving for Germany, this time for two years.

"Hey, I'm looking for my buddy Fred. Have you seen him?" I asked the old fellow.

"No, sonny boy. Not today." He called everyone sonny boy.

On my way home I hoped to find my best friend Fred to say goodbye. Tomorrow we were leaving for Germany. But he was nowhere to be found. When I got home, my father had just turned on the radio and it was my luck that the Detroit Tigers were on. It was a three-game series against the Chicago White Sox in Chicago. "Strike three, you're out!" the umpire barked over the radio. I could hear the fans roar from their seats, which made me wish I could be behind home plate, first row back.

"I can't find Fred," I said defiantly to my mother.

"Oh?" replied my mother rather nonchalantly, which of course made me more impatient to find him.

"I thought I would say goodbye to him before we leave," I said.

"You can write to him," my mother replied.

I thought of all the girls I had known at school that I would have to leave behind, especially the ones with whom I sneaked a peck on the cheek, and I stomped away.

The next day came too quickly for me when we left early in the morning for the port of New York. It was a mild humid day in May 1937, after I finished the fourth grade from Fitzgerald High School, my father, mother, six-year-old brother Ronald, and two-month old sister Norma boarded the train in Detroit.

As we passed through Windsor and Ontario, Canada, I thought about when we went to the Chicago World's Fair the year I started grade school at the Lutheran Church in East Detroit. The Fair was held adjacent to the white shoreline of Lake Michigan, the biggest of the Great Lakes. Since my father was an auto design engineer, it was little wonder that we spent a lot of time gawking at the automobile exhibit called "Dream Cars." There was also an exotic diesel locomotive from Germany among the train exhibits.

I wondered what I was going to experience living in Germany. Would I be able to continue with my guitar lessons? At home I took a bus and transferred to a streetcar to get to my lessons which were six miles from home. Sometimes I'd stop on the way at a drugstore where I had my first toasted tuna salad sandwich. Would I be going to movie matinees like I did every Saturday by myself, walking the one and half miles each way? It was a favorite pastime of mine. I saw westerns with cowboys like Tom Mix and the Lone Ranger, Shirley Temple films, musicals like *Indian Love Song*, and detective movies, too. I had become independent and quickly learned how to get around in the growing bustling city of Detroit. It helped me develop a good sense of direction, an advantage that proved to serve me well later.

I didn't know exactly what may lie ahead. I knew one thing for certain: that day, The Detroit Tigers beat the Cleveland Indians.

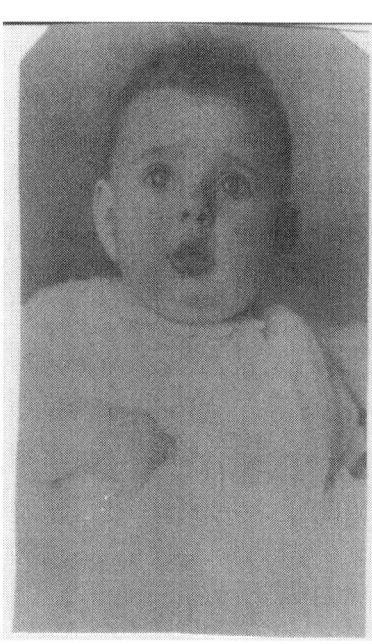

1933. Above L: My late brother Ronald. R: 1937. My late sister Norma, aka Yachana. Below: 1936. Detroit. My brother Ronald and me.

Chapter 6

Stuttgart

"Never was a place so imminent,
so vivid as a first goodbye,
first hello, that first kiss."
-- Edna Esfeld

We boarded a ship named Bremen, the famous German luxury ocean liner built in 1929 that had sparked the building of the very large and expensive express liners of the 1930s. With her long and low modern streamlined body, she became the fastest ship crossing the Atlantic, which she did in four days, seventeen hours and forty-two minutes, holding the westbound record until 1930 and the eastbound record until 1935. It took us six days from New York to the German port of Bremerhaven on our 1937 Atlantic crossing.

We had sailed the same ship twice before: once in 1936, when we went to Germany to visit my mother's relatives in Achim and my father's relatives in Kirchweyhe; that was the summer Germany hosted the Olympics in Berlin. With my German relatives, we listened to the Olympics on the radio, because there were no televisions at the time.

We heard Hitler's refusal to congratulate the American black sprinter Jesse Owens when he won the gold medal. I remember that my mother shook her head in disgust and said, "Sign of trouble." But my mother's sister and her family believed in Hitler; they believed that, with hard work, he could bring them back into European life and prosperity.

The other time we went was in 1927 when I was only eleven months old, and my mother chided me later on in life that I liked to sneak a peek too close to the ships rails. She'd yell, "Herman, don't get so close to the railing." I had just learned to walk and with me was my first friend, a little girl my own age. My father was not with us on that first trip, and we celebrated my first birthday in Germany without him. We had gone because my mother had received a letter from her sister stating that she was pregnant for the first time. She also said things were changing for the better there and that their parents were getting older, too. I remember seeing my mother crying one time in the kitchen. She told father how much she missed her family.

My father told her, "Take the boy and go back to Germany to see your parents and your sister Katie, and your old friends. Then you can decide whether you want to stay or not. I will be in Detroit waiting

for you." My father was a thoughtful and caring man.

1927 summer. Me on right at eleven months on the ocean liner going to Germany for vacation with my mother alone.

This 1937 journey was being paid for by the German

government, all the way from Detroit, Michigan to Stuttgart, Germany.

We brought along a lot of clothes packed in what were called steamer

trunks; you could stand the trunk on its end, open it, and hang dresses,

suits and coats in it, like a little closet. When it was closed it was four cubic feet; a leather band wrapped around it with a lock to secure it.

Foot lockers held our smaller items. We even brought our Sears

Coldspot refrigerator and a large Emerson console radio, both stored in

the freight room. But left behind were all our other home furnishings,

household goods, my brand new bicycle, and the car.

From the moment this once in a lifetime offer was extended to

my father by the plump and zealous Austrian-born Dr. Porsche, whose

lifelong dream was to build a car for "every man and not just for the

wealthy few," the idea resonated throughout my family's daily life

with fervor, and continued through our entire journey to Germany.

What would become the biggest mass produced, affordable and

economic vehicle in the world--a claim made by Porsche--persuaded

my father to accept the VW contract, like putting a feather in his hat.

The weather that May sailing over the great Atlantic was

typically chilly. Waves weren't too rough and none of us got seasick.

All of us--me, my parents, my younger brother Ronald, and my three

month old sister Norma, who slept in a crib--slept in a spacious cabin

with a couple of bull's eye windows. Some days I would stare at the

Nazi flag, which had replaced Germany's national flag, hanging high on the jack staff to gauge the swiftness of the winds. On deck I would breathe in all I could of that stimulating fresh air.

Now, standing on the stained hardwood deck, the salty ocean breezes cleared my senses. We had stayed with my grandparents on our last vacation and I wondered if my grandfather still owned a cigar shop in Germany. I used to reach for a freshly rolled cigar from the canister sitting on the counter, stick it in my mouth and puff on it as if it were lit. It was not long before he laughingly caught me.

In the past, I'd been happy to go, but on this trip I became anxious. Would I be playing with any German kids? Having had such a bad experience the year before when my German classmates taunted me and the Nazi teacher completely ignored my pleas for help, I was curious about how I was going to be accepted by my peers this time. But I told myself it would be an adventure and we would be coming back home in two years anyway. Plus the Detroit Tigers took the Chicago Series with a 12-9 win in the last game. The excitement of that game dominated my thoughts.

The town of Bramerhaven, Germany's premier emigration harbor as well as trade, shipbuilding and fishing port, was where we disembarked. It was bustling with cargo being loaded and unloaded. Despite the business, to me everything looked small here compared to the U.S.

1937-My Oma, Ronald, Norma, Muttie, and Opa, with one of his cigars.

"Herman, hurry up. We will miss our train. Come along now. Grab your bag," my mother said in her German accented voice.

Stuttgart was a beautiful city surrounded on three sides by high rolling hills of green grass and dense forest made up of pine trees and spiraling oaks. Bright flowerbeds and vegetable gardens occupied the yards of the homes. Colorful palettes of flowers hung in baskets on poles along the sidewalks in the city and in wooden window boxes of houses and offices. Every corner and street was surprisingly clean, considering this was the center of Germany's auto industry and housed many parts plants and machine shops. Unlike Detroit, not one piece of paper, cigarette butt or candy wrapper could be found. I thought this was because trash boxes and refuse baskets were scattered all over the place. I had just turned ten when we arrived and I fell in love with Stuttgart.

"Mother, when do I go to school?" I asked apprehensively.

"Your school is closing soon for summer vacation. You will start in six weeks."

That meant I had until the middle of August to get acquainted with my new German neighbors. Our neighbors respected us. They knew my father had come to work for the new factory. We lived on the first floor of a triplex in the suburb of Zuffenhousen. A two-car garage separated each house. Not many German's could afford a car. But my father bought a car and we took weekend trips into the Swabian hills, which helped me get familiar with the Swabian dialect; it was quite different from standard German and harder to understand.

The Swabian tribe dated back to the first millennium A.D. They had come down from northern Europe and part of the Imperial Empire. Many were farmers. Their ancestors eventually settled in southwestern Germany. Stuttgart had tens of thousands of Swabians, which is why it became known as the "the Swabian capital." The city served as the backdrop for the creation of the VW plant and the Swabians were very proud of it. The city had been carefully designed for the plant workers and, with Porsche's support, had changed the city of Stuttgart from a backwater to a sophisticated urban setting.

Leaving my shy younger brother Ronald and infant sister Norma home in the care of a Swabian housekeeper my mother had hired the first night we arrived, she took me to explore the mountainous Swabian countryside, flush with greenery. She knew about the Swabians' hard work ethic and clean habits. When we drove into the city on shopping trips I took notice of men dressed in thicker than cow hide shorts called Lederhosen; these were leather breeches with suspenders. The women were dressed in full flowered skirts and puffy sleeves on an apron-like dress called a Dirndl. I'd see broad smiles across the faces of these strangely dressed people. Compared to America, their fashion was highly unusual to me.

"These people are friendly and respectful," my mother said. "Don't speak before you are spoken to. Always say hello with a firm handshake and look the person in the eye, and say the person's name." I obeyed.

It didn't take too long before I was speaking German fluently. One day I asked the little girl that lived next door to us if I could kiss her. We sat in my father's parked car in our one-car garage. Helga was her name and she ran afterward to tell her parents because she was excited to have been kissed by an "older" American boy. She was seven years old. Her parents were outraged that an American boy had kissed their daughter. All hell broke loose between her parents and mine. I found myself in trouble for the first time since we arrived in Germany. Luckily, a year later, both families became good friends, as did Helga and I. Thirteen years later, six years after the war ended, I got to kiss Helga one more time.

I wanted to go to the movie theatre where they were playing a Shirley Temple film with German subtitles. I had watched every

Shirley Temple movie in Detroit. My mother told me she couldn't go

with me anymore because she had to take care of my baby sister. "You

can go by yourself," she said. She showed a lot of confidence for a ten

year old like me. Besides, I had gone to the movies in Detroit alone so,

why not? So I hopped on the street car and looked for the landmarks

my mother had pointed out to me before.

When I got there I bought my ticket and I asked for popcorn,

like I always had back home, but here they didn't serve any food.

After the movie ended, trailers appeared of German military victories.

Thereafter, whenever I went to the movies, the film was always

followed by newsreels depicting the fatherland in militaristic form.

During intermission, films were shown of young people doing

something for the fatherland, like climbing mountains, which showed

off the stamina of the young. Only victories were depicted--never

defeats.

When I finally started school that August in 1937 I was uneasy

because of the experiences I had the year before while on vacation.

But this time, my mother went to the school and explained to the

principal and all the teachers (all of whom were male) that we are

American citizens and that I had four years of grade school behind me. She told them why we had come back to Germany for a short while.

Even though I could speak German, I could not read or write it, so I had to start in the first grade with six-year-olds. I was ten and a huge object of curiosity to the younger students, not to mention quite imposing to those smaller, struggling first graders. Determined and unfettered, I kept my nose to the grindstone. I had a lot of catching up to do.

The recesses on the school grounds were the most difficult for me in the beginning. I was the outsider, an American, a foreigner, and my peers ignored me. I didn't make friends on the playground. A few times I walked home crying, not from the harassment like I'd experienced on our vacation to northern Germany, but because I felt lonely and homesick. I yearned for my best friend Fred back in the States, listening to Ty Tyson announce the Detroit Tiger games on WWJ radio, playing baseball with my pals, and swimming in the lakes.

I did develop a close friendship with Walter, the eldest son of the Kuntzes, a German/ American boy like me but one year younger.

Like my father, Walter's father had worked for Ford Motor Company. They lived a few miles from us during our stay in Stuttgart.

My father worked tirelessly at Porsche's Stuttgart engineering bureau helping to design the departments. He came home exhausted every night and consequently didn't talk much. He worked like it was his favorite hobby though.

My Swabian classmates, teachers and parents were different than those in northern Germany. My teachers in Stuttgart were more restrained, compassionate and understanding. They were a hardworking proud people and appreciated that in others. So I quickly moved up in classes. I remembered a time in my geography class, which was one of my favorite subjects, when my German classmates and I were instructed by the teacher to identify certain nearby areas in a sandbox depicting the city of Stuttgart. The teacher, using a long stick as a pointer, would indicate certain features for the students to identify. When he pointed to a small creek meandering down the side of a hill, all was quiet.

"What's this?" asked the teacher.

I waited for a minute for someone else to answer. When no one did, I worked up the nerve and spoke up: I named the creek correctly in German. The teacher was so surprised that he blurted out, "Now look class, here comes Herman, an American, all the way from America, and he has to tell you natives the name of this creek that flows right in your own back yard." For the first time since I'd arrived in Germany, I felt proud. My classmates respected my hard work and eventually I was accepted by them.

There came a day on November 9-10, 1938 when I was eleven called Kristallnacht[1]. Two days after that fateful day my mother took me into the city of Stuttgart. We saw what we had heard on the radio: many Jewish homes had been invaded, their crystal and china broken; brown shirted SA[2] men had smashed windows and display cases of shops and businesses owned by the German-Jews.

The next day in school we students were told by our history teachers the meaning of these actions. "They (the Jewish) are a threat to the state and they have to be persecuted as enemies of Hitler's new

---

[1] Literally, Night of the Broken Glass.
[2] *Sturmabteilung,* also known as Storm Detachment or Assault Division, or Brownshirts, functioned as the original paramilitary wing of the Nazi Party.

German order," they recited. That was my indoctrination into the role the Jews played in German society.

I could tell my mother was aghast over the happenings on that night. She squeezed my hand so hard I thought my knuckles would break. Back from school the next day I told her what the teachers had said. She listened intently then replied, "Herman, don't believe all they say. I have met many Jewish people in my life, both during my early years in Germany and in America. They are all hard working, law-abiding, nice people. Our family doctor in Detroit, Dr. Tatelis, is a Lithuanian Jew."

1938. The first 'six' German/American engineers at Dr. Porsche's Engineering Works office in Stuttgart, Germany. My father, Henry Esfeld, is sitting at desk on right, with his nose to the grindstone.

Chapter 7

The Knock

Shortly after my tenth birthday there was a loud knock on our door. From our foyer I could see a tall and lanky blond haired man dressed in a brown shirt and pants and standing at attention. That looks like a military uniform, I thought, noticing his armband which bore a swastika--the same emblem I saw hoisted high on our ship when we sailed over.

He introduced himself immediately. "*"Ich bin ein Führer mit der deutschen Jugendgruppe. Sind sie Frau Esfeld?"* (I am a leader with the German youth group. Are you Frau Esfeld?)

"Ya," my mother responded quietly.

Then he commanded, *"Frau Esfeld,* your son Herman has to join the Jungvolk now."

My mother, a quick thinker, innocently and vehemently responded in German, "Oh, no. My son does not have to join because we are American citizens."

The man continued, "Doesn't matter. You have to buy him a proper uniform. There are two meetings each week, Wednesday nights and Saturday afternoons. You have to bring him to the first meeting. If you do not comply, you will be summoned by the court."

My mother hesitated before she nodded her head. The man clicked his boots together, his right arm forward, like a salute, said, "*Heil*, Hitler," and off he went. My mother closed the door. Later that evening I heard my mother and father talking about this group.

"The Nazi regime has required that every young boy at the age of ten enter in this youth group called Das Jungvolk. I have been told by our neighbors and friends that it is based on disciplining our children at a young age. I didn't like the sound of it then and I still don't, Vati," my mother said.

The Nazis had passed a law in 1939 requiring all Aryan children to join the Jungvolk and the Hitler Youth. If parents refused, kids would be taken away into orphanages or placed with other loyal families. Most parents welcomed the discipline and supervision established under Hitler's regime.

"Well, let's see how it goes. We will pull him out, if the time comes," my father said reassuringly. "But in the meantime, Herman can go out into the fields and woods with the other boys and learn about the outdoors."

Days later I found out more from schoolmates. It sounded a lot like the Boy Scouts in America except this group was compulsory. I had wanted to join the Boy Scouts back home in Michigan. Walter, too, had to join a year later. He went to a different meeting so we didn't see much of each other anymore. Years later Walter didn't have to do service in the German army because of his age.

That evening, in her perfect English, my mother yelled, "Herman, wash your face and hands with soap and warm water before you come to the table." I had to be ready and dressed in uniform. I was excited. I did not know what to expect when I put on my uniform for the first time.

I quickly found out there was no camp as such for the

Jungvolk. I met with my peers and the leaders on streets, at parks and playgrounds, and in public buildings, like schools. My uniform consisted of a white shirt with a black scarf held together with a brown leather knot. A black leather strap ran diagonally across the shoulder. My shorts were black with a black leather belt and a silver belt buckle. We all wore white socks with black shoes. I could hear my mother's words, "Don't speak before you are spoken too." I felt alone and alienated.

In this organization we were scolded harshly if we did something that was not in line or wrong. I could not speak my mind anymore. In Germany the people did what they were told as a custom. Back home in the States my life had been carefree and open. I always had the opportunity to do what I liked. But in Germany the people did what they were commanded to do by any person of authority in any kind of uniform. Eventually the Nazis used force and terror if they were not obeyed. So no one spoke much.

When my family took up residency in Stuttgart we had to report to police headquarters. Germany required every family with boys to report every address change to the city hall or police headquarters. This started back in the Weimar hierarchy in 1919 before WWI.

Everything in Germany was regimented. I did what I was expected and commanded to do. We all obeyed and did not ask questions. Gradually I got used to this kind of strict discipline. I was a typical impressionable youngster, ready to appease authority. No fool, Hitler recognized this vulnerability. By inculcating us with his ideas and disciplines when we were young and impressionable, he was able to mold us boys and girls into an army ready to sacrifice their lives on command in the name of the Fuhrer and the Fatherland. So began my upbringing in Germany.

The first year and a half I did not like the Jungvolk. We were taught to march, sing patriotic and party songs, and to camp. There were nationalistic songs with lyrics like, "Today Germany belongs to us and tomorrow the whole world." Another song went, "Wild geese are rushing through the night to the north with screeching cries. Our watch [guard] stands at attention." The metaphor meant standing guard against any enemy.

I'd come home angry because of all the blisters on my feet from all the rally marches on hard dirt and stone. One day we listened over our radio to a rally of the National Hitler Youth held in Nuremburg. My mother became flustered over the threats made during the rally.

"Vati, I don't like this," she warned many times. My father reassured her that we were only here for two years. Everything was going as planned at the factory with Dr. Porsche. All was normal.

Occasionally in the Jungvolk we would play war games, blue against the red. I did not like this game because the bullies in our group would take advantage of us smaller, weaker kids. Sometimes I would hide in high grass or a clump of bushes. The bullies would jump on us in what they called a *Haufen* pile, a heap of dirt and debris, and they'd shout demeaning slurs at us. I hated that. I would always stand back during these games or stay subdued.

We went on numerous camping trips during which we were told lots of stories. Of course, there were the usual ghost stories, but we were also told stories of the heroic sacrifices of knights in shining armor and soldiers dressed in royal uniforms who obeyed the hierarchy, all of whom were draped in velvet robes and barked out commands. The knights and soldiers defended their homeland against foreign invaders throughout the history of Germany. One story in particular stuck in my mind: it was about how the Germans and Austrians, with the help of a Polish king, defeated the king Attila of Mongolia at the gates of Vienna.

All these heroic stories were fascinating, especially for me since I was interested in geography and history. The stories were mainly about ghosts, though. I would come home and tell some of the stories to my little sister and brother.

My two year old sister said, "Herman, can I join your meetings?" I was glad she was too young. Besides, the girls belonged to the *Jungmadels* and were separated from the boys in their own groups.

In our semiweekly meetings, held in school rooms or public facilities or whatever was available every Wednesday night and all day on Saturdays in parks, we were slowly but surely being politically indoctrinated; we were taught to love the Fuhrer and the Fatherland. Gradually, I began to like the history of Germany. We were taught patriotic songs and popular ones, like beer drinking songs, and we sang them outdoors on Saturdays, weather permitting. The idea was to foster in us youngsters the love, devotion and loyalty to our leader, the Fuhrer, and to the Fatherland.

Singing was a big part of binding us young boys together, forming a sense of camaraderie amongst us. When we saw German soldiers marching through the crowded streets singing at the top of their lungs, their faces beaming with enthusiasm and pride, we were inspired. Now we too, were singing and marching with pride. I had especially strong lungs and a big voice. In time I started to enjoy singing and I sang with gusto. My mother once said, "Herman, your singing will shake the walls down."

Most weekends and on all national holidays I watched from school or listened to the radio as thousands of Hitler Youths paraded for miles through every town or city. Singing their hearts out, and in step, they sang:

Die Straße *frei den roten Bataillonen!*

Wir fürchten nicht die blaue Polizei

Hat auch ein Severing den RFB verboten

Marschieren wir im gleichen Schritt und Tritt!"

(The street clear for the red battalions.

We do not fear the blue [uniformed] police.

Even if a Severing has banned the RFB

we'll [nevertheless] march in step)

Black and white pennants and, of course, the red and white

swastika flag led each column. Drowned out by the steady roll of the

marching drums, the melancholic sound of the fifes, and the blaring

sound of the trumpets, I became emotionally caught up in this charged

atmosphere of patriotism. These were happy songs.

Other than my mother's usual question--"So Herman, how was

your class group today?" –there were no political conversations

between my parents and me. My father was way too exhausted to talk

after coming home from the factory and working those ten-twelve

hour days.

I chose not to tell my mother about the thrashings I took from

the bullies during our war games. Even though I wore excellent shoes,

which my mother made sure I had, I didn't tell her about my blistered

feet, either. Later, this affliction helped save my life.

By the time I turned twelve I had begun to like the Jungvolk. The brown-shirted Nazis in the Jungvolk groups made discipline fun. And it softened us boys to it. I felt willing to sacrifice my life in battle on command in the name of the Fuhrer and the Fatherland. Between Jungvolk and my teachers from high school, Germany's military attitude cemented my belief in the nation and in Hitler.

Chapter 8

A Sliver of Brainwashing

My father rushed home one day with a booklet in his hand. "Muttie," he said proudly, "we are now proudly part of a layaway savings plan. We will soon be one of the first to own a Volkswagen." The KDF auto was now named Volkswagen, or people's car.

"What are you talking about?" Muttie asked.

"All I have to do is give a small amount of my pay weekly and in return I receive a stamp in this booklet. After I fill up all the necessary sheets, I get a certificate of ownership. And the car of course."

"How much do you have to give?"

"As much as we can afford, but with a small minimum--and I cannot miss a week or I will lose all my stamps, and money."

Sure enough my father was one of the first to finish his booklets. We had owned a Ford Model A back in Detroit and he and my mother had become accustomed to a level of luxury that most

Germans had not experienced. Being raised on a farm, the only transportation my father had growing up was a horse and cart or a bicycle; so having his own automobile was especially important to him.

The periodic broadcasts Hitler made for the Volkswagen or KDF-wagen, were for *Draft durch Frueda* (Strength through Joy), an organization established by Hitler and the Nazi party that offered perks to factory workers and their families, such as discount vacations, bargain prices for theatre, opera and cruises; these were meant to convince the working class of Germany that life would greatly improve. Proclamations like: "This car shall carry the name of the organization which works hardest to provide the broadest mass of our people with joy and, therefore, with strength," and "This factory shall arise out of the strength of the entire German people and it shall serve the happiness of the German people" resonated on radio broadcasts and newspaper articles. The prediction was that every working person would own a "people's" car. But my father never got the car.

Then one day in May 1938 my father announced that he, along with other engineers from Porsche's design bureau, were invited to attend the cornerstone dedication ceremony for the factory site in the nearby town of Fallersleben.

"Frieda, there are expected to be tens of thousands of people there for the ceremony. We have been instructed to board a bus here in Stuttgart that will take us to a specially designated spot. There will be top dignitaries and Hitler himself."

I was dumbfounded. A chance to see the Fuhrer in person was remarkable to me, but my mother shook her head and didn't say a word. That same day Hitler made another boisterous and thunderous speech.

"I have never witnessed such a climactic and dramatic celebration over a new city and a new auto factory, Frieda," my father said. "It was spectacular."

My mother kept mum.

That night at dinner no one spoke. Even though my brother, sister and I were not allowed to speak while eating at the table, I heard plenty that confirmed my belief in our Fuhrer and in his promise that Germany would be victorious. But I had to keep my lips closed. My parents would not approve of this.

1937. Ground breaking ceremony. L-first row, Henry Esfeld with Otto Dyckhoff, third from right.

In June of 1939 the employment contract with my father, his colleagues, and Dr. Ferdinand Porsche ended. But completion of the Volkswagen factory was delayed. The production start-up, we were told, was caused by delays in the delivery of equipment, machine presses and tools. Porsche along with the top management of Volkswagen asked my father and the other German-American engineers and specialists to stay on until the job was done. They were still sorely needed, he told them. Plus he had requested a raise for all of them. My father and the other engineers decided to continue working. Absorbed in his work with the factory, my father and his colleagues were oblivious to the gathering of war clouds coming toward us at rapid-fire speed. Consequently, my parents made no immediate plans to return to the United States. I had just turned twelve.

Then the unthinkable happened. In September 1939 Hitler marched into Poland. This came as a surprise to most of the German people, including and especially to my family. Hitler had been saying he wanted nothing but peace in Europe and that he was a peaceful man. This "skirmish" with Poland, he said, would end soon and peace would be restored.

Soon it was necessary for my family to move closer to the Volkswagen Factory site. An entirely new city was to be built just for this factory; it would have theatres, parks, hotels, markets, apartments, and two -story duplexes for us and all Volkswagen workers and their families to live in. The factory itself was proposed to be a mile long. But first we had to live in the city called Braunschweig (Brunswick) for a few months because it was closer, only twenty-nine kilometers (sixteen miles) away, since housing for the factory workers had not yet been completed. It was here, in Braunschweig, that I had a sliver of my first experience of bombardment shortly after the invasion of Poland.

"Herman, get inside immediately! What are you doing?" Muttie cried out.

For a twelve year old boy like me, it was an amazing sight to watch the tracer shells the German military shot up snake lazily like a string of pearls against the dark cloaked night sky as they tried to hit an enemy plane.

"Muttie, it's like fireworks back home," I yelled back excitedly, jumping up and down and hoping to see an airplane get shot down. Occasionally I could see a warplane get caught in the crisscrossing white beams of the searchlights that were strategically placed at factories and military installations that housed 20mm and 47mm anti-aircraft guns. The heavier 88 mm and 122.5 mm guns would arrive later.

These British reconnaissance planes of the Vickers Wellington and Handly Page Hampton types flew over the city at night to test the German air defenses. Somehow the British spy planes always slipped away safely. I noticed, to my amusement and my mother's disgust, how the shells took so long to get up into the sky and wondered why they didn't continue in a straight line. It wasn't until much later that I learned in my physics class about the earth's pull of gravity.

In Braunschweig I once again had to report to a Jungvolk squad. It had now been two years since I put on my first uniform and by this time I was all gung-ho. Brainwashing was something no one would dare talk or think about in Germany, and was not used as a word until later in the Korean War. Coined by the U.S. military, and based on the methods the Chinese used on their prisoners of war, brainwashing had succeeded in me. It was a technique especially successful with young impressionable children.

From time to time, my mother asked my father when the factory would be finished. "Frieda," he would reply, "the factory is expected to be finished in one year."

Actually, the factory was almost complete when a sudden change came. They had completed the design for the Beetle, which was to become a major success, when it was ordered that the factory change over to produce and repair parts for airplanes--the V-1 flying bombs and anti-tank mines. At that point, Germany had been at war for over a year. Then the factory introduced the Kubelwagen, a rugged type of army jeep later to be popular with the British army.

In the summer of 1940 my family and I spent a holiday with my father's parents at their home in Kirchweye, a village ten miles outside the city of Bremen. My Aunt Grete, my father's sister, and her husband, Uncle Fritz, lived with my grandparents. They had two children, my cousins Hermann and Anita. Hermann was just two years younger than I. So we palled around a lot, kicking the soccer ball and swimming. The second day of our visit, I happened to glance over into the neighbor's yard and spotted a frail looking young boy who was playing all by himself.

"Hermann, who is that?" I asked.

"Oh, that's Otto Polak. He is a Jew. He goes to a school in Bremen for Jewish children only. The government has ordered him not to leave the yard and play with anybody else. He is about seven years old and lives with his grandmother, Oma Jacobson, who is a widow. We don't see much of his mother. She is very sick. And I don't know anything about his father." That was all my cousin Hermann could tell me.

For me, my cousin's neighbor and *Kristallnacht*, which my mother and I had witnessed, remained mysteriously in the back of my mind. My elders kept quiet about our Jewish neighbors and never talked about it. I never heard the term concentration camp.

1938. The letter addressed to my father for a pay raise from the Nazi's and VW factory. Nazi swastika stamp upper left hand corner.

Chapter 9

Our American Emerson Radio

I felt good about our final move because we could now live in the quiet countryside closer to a forest and away from the hustle and bustle of the big city. Walter and his family along with the rest of the three tier families also moved to the new city.

I thought we would be farther away from the threat of being bombed out by allied air forces. Our newly constructed quaint city, named '*KdF-Stadt*' by Hitler (Kraft durch Freude, Strength through Joy, abbreviated KdF) was located in northern Germany just outside the small picturesque town of Fallersleben. Again, our move was paid for by the German government.

The move to KdF Stadt (later named Wolfsburg) in late 1940 took only a day. The VW factory was completed and the first one hundred Beetles ran off the assembly line. I was there to see a few of the black curvy cars with my father. One by one, they clamored down the line with the first air-cooled engine. I was enthralled by where the engine was in the back, like in the trunk of an American automobile, and not in the front of the car like our Model A. in Detroit.

Because I was already enrolled in high school back in Braunschweig, I had to commute back and forth from Wolfsburg by bus. The high schools in Germany were two story buildings made with red brick. Universities were higher. The classrooms held from thirty to forty students with two students to a hard wooden bench, very different from the schoolrooms back in Detroit where each student had his own desk in rows of individual attached desks.

"Wie gehtz? Meine name ist Herrman. Und du"? (How are you? My name is Herman. And yours?). I was proud I could speak fluent German as I slid in beside a German boy my age.

"Ich bin Herr Friedrich." Soon Fred and I became study companions.

The long commute to my high school in Braunschweig left me little time for homework, so my mother with her endless courage managed to pull me out of the Wednesday night Jungvolk meetings that I was supposed to attend twice a week.

Below: 1938. First six German/American VW factory engineers: L-R, Hoehne, Kuntze, Werner, Reidel, Rechenback, Luik, and Henry Esfeld. Above:: 1940.Wolfsburg, Germany. First 100 VW's to roll off the assembly line.

Sure enough, a high ranking Jungvolk leader dressed in a brown shirt with a swastika arm band and brown pants came to our home one day. *"Warum wurde Ihr Sohn Herman nicht bei unserem Treffen am Mittwoch Nacht?"* (Why was your son Herman not at our Wednesday night meeting?) He asked my mother, short and to the point.

My mother, utterly disenchanted and outspoken, responded defiantly in German, "We are all American citizens. My three children were born in Detroit, Michigan. You have no jurisdiction over us."

"Das mach nitchts," (doesn't matter) he said. Yet for some reason the leader accepted my mother's plea and I was excused from the Wednesday meetings.

In one of the tiny villages near Wolfsburg there stood a single old church. We never attended this church, but my sister recalled going with neighbors once a few years later and how she was in awe of its architectural beauty. My mother believed that God loved everyone and cared over nature and all living things.

The housing for the factory employees and families like ours was built in rows on each side of the street. Some were attached and all were shaded by columns of large oak trees. When the factory site

was toured from the air, at Hitler's request, his entourage carefully

picked a picturesque setting with many trees, although the marshes

were a problem because of the vast amount of mosquitoes.

Our home had a full basement with one room reinforced with a

thick steel door. This was my first air raid type shelter. The entrance to

the main floor had a foyer, a half bath, living room, and a dining room

that led to an attached stone-laid terrace. The furniture we brought

over was arranged nicely by my mother along with a few new pieces.

A few pictures and paintings were hung on the walls and her beloved

lace was draped over a couple tables. It felt homey, like back in

Detroit.

Early mornings my younger brother and sister and I ate

breakfast in the kitchen nook before school. Upstairs were three

bedrooms and a full bath. A narrow pull down staircase led to the attic

with a room for the maid. We also had a one car garage. Not many

Germans had this.

At first I commuted the thirty kilometers each way six days a

week from Wolfsburg to my new high school in Braunschweig in a company bus. It took an hour. I enjoyed gazing out the window at the untouched stark green rolling hills dotted with small villages and farm animals grazing. Us kids on the bus would get bored and start a few pranks. One day we threw spit paper wads. Mine plus a couple others hit our bus driver in the head. My throwing arm from baseball was still working.

"Achtung! Sie, und sie und sie, aus dem bus!" (You, and you and you, off the bus), he commanded. I still had fifteen kilometers to go home and managed to get there by foot.

One cold wintry day the bus came to a halt. We were caught in a freezing snowstorm and barely made it to an inn. We were able to stop in one of the villages along the way home. There we slept on hard wooden chairs put together for the night. I thought I would freeze to death. Was it ever this cold back home in Detroit, I wondered?

Life was carefree for me when I was back home. But following my favorite baseball team, the Detroit Tigers, swimming every summer and playing baseball was behind me now, a faded memory. I had no correspondence with friends back home in the U.S. My time here in Wolfsburg was spent reading and doing homework. I had very little time for play. Most summer vacations I had to help out on the farms by collecting herbs that we dried in our high school attic; gathering the herbs was mandatory for us young boys for tea drinking.

I did manage to go to the movies in the winter. Germany was still making them. But they were becoming more militaristic too. One movie in particular called "*Der Bruch Pilot*" (*Max Pilot*), which I saw many times, conveyed to us young boys the invincibility and toughness of a German fighter pilot. I liked it because it showed from high above the ground the grasslands and hillsides of Germany. Every movie showed Germany victorious in the end. We never saw any defeats.

One morning after getting dressed for school, I came downstairs to find my father still home for breakfast. My mother and father sat at opposite ends of the dining room table, their food untouched. The radio was on and I could hear a dramatic tune that I had come to fall in love with from one of composer Richard Wagner's "Die Walkure." Classical music always preceded an important announcement, like a German victory. Whenever I heard this music it sent chills down my spine. It strengthened my belief in the invincibility of the new German "Third Reich."

In my mind back then, Hitler could do nothing wrong. Propaganda of victories like the annexation of Austria and Sudetenland, a part of Czechoslovki with a heavy German population, and eventually the successful invasion of Poland, filled my life daily. "Muttie, what is the matter?" I asked curiously.

"Norma," she whispered to my little sister. "Please go outside and watch out for the truck. Make sure they don't see you looking. Then come right back in when you see it."

Each time my parents turned on the American Emerson radio we brought over on the ship to listen to the BBC news broadcast stations from England (which was forbidden by the Nazis. Anyone caught listening to the BBC news meant death), my sister was in charge of making sure no trucks were in sight. Our radio had the airwave most German-made radios did not, and it could reach thousands of miles further. We could get first hand reports about captured countries. After the 9pm broadcast a secret code was given to the resistance that were listening. The sound trucks were sent to detect radios such as ours.

The scratchy noise that was a staple over our radio airwaves could not drown out the voice that started every BBC broadcast to the U.S. and other countries: "This...is London." A familiar voice came over the radio as my mother listened intently after the war broke out. The tone of the broadcast struck a kind of homesick feeling in her.

That morning, when I hurried off to school, I heard the news from a windowless sound truck with a rangefinder antenna on the roof. War had broken out with Poland. It was the beginning of September 1940 and the commentator continued to speak of German air raids consisting of twenty to twenty-five planes sweeping across the skies of London. They bombed the east end of the city for twelve hours straight. The correspondent was reporting from London where he lived. The news was quite frightening to my parents. This was the German invasion that became known as "The Blitz."

I wondered why my parents were not happy for their homeland. After all, in the early months of the war the German people were used to being bombarded with news of victories on land, sea and air by Hitler's armed forces. The solemn look in their eyes was unshakeable in my mind that day. I learned four days later through our radio that Britain and France had declared war on Germany. My parents' gloomy mood and apprehension lingered for many days. Upon hearing of the British blockade of all German shipping they felt trapped. Thus our long wait to go back to the U.S.A had begun.

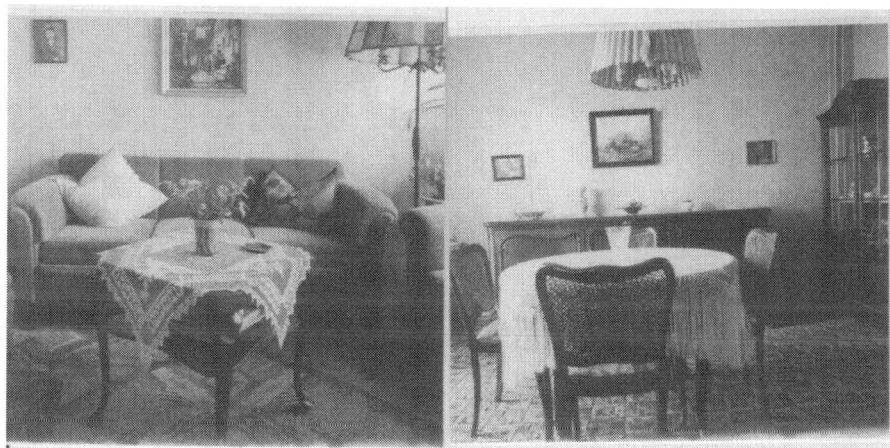

1940. Our duplex apartment in Wolfsburg.

Chapter 10

High School

In June of 1941 after I turned fourteen I became a member of the Hitler Youth (*Hitler Jugend*). These meetings were an automatic compulsory extension of the *Jungvolk* which I was in from age ten to thirteen. I had grown to five feet six inches tall and weighed one hundred and fifty pounds. Every morning I carefully groomed my dark brown hair, slicking it back like shellac and parting it to one side. My big blue eyes peeked out through round wired spectacles that neatly sat on my nose, reflecting my round face. My best friend Hans said my smile stuck to me like glue. I had no girlfriends, like back home in Detroit. There was no time--and besides, the girls here in Germany had their own high schools.

The uniform I had to wear was the same as in the *Jungvolk* only now I could wear a sheathed six inch long knife on my belt. On the blade was inscribed in capital letters: *In blut und ehre* (in blood and honor). My comrades and I felt proud, strong and brave.

Then came the moment when the Japanese attacked Pearl Harbor. The frightening announcement came over our radio on December 7, 1941 on a Sunday evening when my family and I were sitting at the dinner table. A moment of long silence came over us after the shock of the news. Stunned and distressed, my father, with the last bit of courage left in him, bent his head slightly down toward the table, saying quietly and earnestly, "Now, Germany has lost the war."

I panicked when I heard my father speak those words. I immediately replied with angst, "Vati, how can you say that? What you just said is treason. You could get arrested and shot!" He knew what the mighty U.S. industry could produce when it came to weapons of war used on the ground, in the air and on the seas. After that evening, my father never talked about the war to me again. And I, out of love and respect, kept my mouth shut. I did not want to believe he could be right, though deep inside the idea gnawed at me.

After the Pearl Harbor raid the United States lowered the age from twenty-one to eighteen for flying cadets. Young men fresh out of high school or with only one year of college were enlisting in the Army air corps or Navy flight training; within ten months, some were trained for WWII pilots. That isolationism that was once a national policy, the idea of staying out of foreign wars, became instant history in America.

The meetings I had to attend in the Hitler Youth now became more militaristic. Our day would start out with some marching and singing followed by discussing a political topic. Continued political orientation covered the assumed Jewish exploitation of German life in culture (theater, movies), business and banking, science (Einstein) and medicine. It also instilled in us young boys that the Aryan race was the master race, and how it had superior racial purity and meant to rule the world.

Our instructors taught us to fire small .22mm caliber rifles. To prepare us for the military service we were trained in aircraft identification, weapons handling and map reading with a compass. I liked map reading. It helped me later in my military life. And the brainwashing had achieved its goal; we were all ready to give our lives for our Fuhrer and Fatherland.

Our status as U.S. American citizens changed dramatically when the United States entered the war against the Germany in December 1941. All U.S.-born citizens could leave the country and be given safe passage to a neutral country in Europe. All naturalized citizens born in Germany, like my parents, were given a choice of either forfeiting their U.S. American citizenship and becoming German citizens again, or be interned in a camp with no certain future--similar to the Japanese-American situation in the U.S.

Two or three families of German-American nationalists that had come over with us in 1937 had decided to leave in 1939. They were afraid of getting into something a lot bigger and become trapped. Or perhaps they had foresight. One family trekked dangerously through Russia and over through the Pacific side to get back home.

For the first time since coming to Germany my parents felt a compulsion to escape back to the U.S. However, my father knew that to do so meant traveling over eleven hundred miles of mountainous terrain and swamps, which included getting through Russia, then get to Portugal where the British navy ships had a blockade against contraband. From Portugal he would somehow have to find a way back to the States. With a two year old, a six year old, myself and my mother, Vati felt it would be too dangerous. He was a cautious person and it was his concern for the safety of our family that kept us from escaping. Neither did he appreciate the idea of our living in an internment camp where we would have nothing but a miserable life of impoverishment. So he chose to sacrifice his U.S. citizenship and retain his position as director of the tool and process-engineering department at the Volkswagen factory. That decision, I believe, kept us out of a prison camp. Although my mother never signed any papers to that effect, she secretly kept her U.S. passport. Under Nazi law the rest of us, my mother, brother sister and I, automatically became German citizens. A new chapter in my life would begin.

In the hot summer of 1941, before the Pearl Harbor disaster and America's entrance into the war, I was fourteen years old and a loyal member of the Hitler Youth. Because of the persistence from my mother that we were U.S. citizens and her adamant claim that the Hitler Youth had no jurisdiction over us, I was excused from the Wednesday night meetings. I still had to attend the Sunday morning rallies. Gradually the Sunday Hitler Youth rallies sufficed to mold my mind along with the other youths in the belief that our Fuhrer, Adolf Hitler, could do no wrong and the war would end in a glorious victory for Germany.

"Heil Hitler. Im dritten Reich lebt seit tausend Jahren!" (The Third Reich lives for a thousand years) yelled my leaders right arms stretched out as far and high as they could get them.

The radio reports and other propaganda boasted of one German victory after another. Singing and dancing took place at every occasion, whether birthdays--especially Hitler's--weddings, beer and wine festivals, or political rallies, always signifying Germany's strength. Everybody was singing and celebrating. It became one big songfest. I swallowed it all easily.

During this victorious time I managed to visit friends of my family in Berlin. The most sophisticated city in Germany at that time, there were myriad multi-story apartment and office buildings. I went to museums, learned more about German culture, music, art, classical scholars like Goethe and Schiller and composers like Beethoven and Wagner. I took the S Bahn commuter train, which was elevated like Chicago's El, to Potsdam, once the seat of the Kingdom of Prussia, where I admired the beautiful plush gardens surrounding the imposing palace of King Fredrich the Great. Now it was decked out in the red and white swastika flags, Nazi flags, like on all the other public and government buildings in Berlin.

As Potsdam was a garrison city, I saw soldiers in colored uniforms marching in solidity, smartly and in perfect formation through the streets and singing at the top of their lungs. I returned home more impressed and enlightened with German history and culture. This was continually augmented over the next three years from my high school teachers.

The meetings in the Hitler Youth became increasingly militaristic. I was taught how to dig a foxhole and use camouflage. We learned how to identify every enemy aircraft. Although the German Luftwaffe (Air Force) had lost the air battle over Britain in February of that year, it was downplayed by the German propaganda, especially because of the victories the Luftwaffe had over the Russians in the summer.

By the end of 1941, I had become fully convinced that Germany was invincible and that the war would soon be won, in spite of my father's declaration that the U.S., with its mighty war machines, was now an enemy of Germany.

The construction of the VW factory and production of the KDF (the name given the car before it became Volkswagen) came to an abrupt halt. My father, being one of the first to save up for the car, had yet to see one. Porsche, under Hitler's orders, had agreed to build cars for the war.

The partially built factory was not ready for the massive air raids from the powerful U.S. There was not a single underground shelter in the entire factory. But in the apartment buildings there were steel doors to the basements and only one underground shelter in the city. I remember seeing my father come home with a worried look on his face about his tool and die shops and stamping press builders making their deliveries on time. He continued to block politics and the war out of his mind.

By the time I turned fifteen Germany had marched near toward Moscow and Japan had attacked Pearl Harbor. While the war was escalating, I was still collecting herbal plants. I had to start taking the train instead of the bus to school to conserve gas. We lived in a wooded subdivision and so I bicycled into town to the train station every day. Along the way I passed a huge barrack city that once housed thousands of skilled foreign workers, mostly Italian, for the construction of the VW factory. The barrack was now filled with forced labor people from German-occupied European countries. They were forced to work in the factory making war materials such as parts for military jeeps and tanks. They were given little food. Many died of starvation as the war went on. Because of food rationing, every household got stamps to cover meals, gas, clothing, and shoe wear.

One day while I waited at the station for the train to take me to school, I watched these bedraggled looking and mournful columns of human beings march by me on their way to the Volkswagen factory. I knew from riding my bike past them that these slave laborers where housed about fifteen minutes from where we lived and were taken from various German-occupied countries such as Poland, Czechoslovakia and Russia. Many were criminals, the first who were sent from Italy. None were ever Jews.

One older man stopped in front of me and a few feet away. "Could you give me some water, boy?" he groaned in a Polish-

German dialect. It startled me because I could barely hear what he had said. I knew I could get caught and punished by the Gestapo. The stench from the old man almost made me gag. I found myself with no pity, because in my Hitler Youth meetings I was taught by the Nazis that it was normal for our enemies to suffer like that. So I didn't move or say a word to him. I had to look away.

In 1942 the good fortune of Hitler's military campaign started to unravel. The surrender of General Field Marshal Rommel's Africa Corps and the defeat of the 6th German army at Stalingrad were signs of more struggles and less victories for the Nazis. Though these were clear signs of trouble, they were not acknowledged by me or my superiors. By that time, at the age of fifteen and a half, I was completely brainwashed by all the Nazi propaganda, and one hundred percent convinced of Germany's invincibility. The seeds had first been sown when our family arrived in Stuttgart, Germany and I had to join the "Jungvolk" in 1937 right after.

As a junior in high school, I was able to play soccer in the clean swept streets with my fellow classmates between our meetings and during holiday vacations. I was sixteen and my city had not been touched by bombs yet. I could only imagine what it was like from reports flooding in about victims straggling or fleeing from other bombed cites.

All the trips to downtown Detroit for Christmas shopping at Hudson's with my Muttie were a distant memory. Sometimes I'd think of how I sat on a Santa's lap one year and asked for a baseball glove. But the Detroit Tigers and baseball were alien here in Germany. They did not fit into my life anymore.

One day in 1943, shortly after Christmas when classes resumed, Hans and I could hear the solid beat of footsteps marching down our hallway, the noise of the clicking boots bouncing off the walls. A loud knock startled our classroom and gave me a quick shiver.

"*Aufmachen, bitte*" (open, please). It was our high school principal accompanied by a high ranking Luftwaffe officer. Instinctively all of us sprang up from our seats. We had been well trained by our teachers to greet higher authority as if in a regiment. In each classroom a member was chosen to be head of the class. He took roll call every day. Then he'd shout out, "*Achtum*!" Everyone jumped out of their seats when the teacher came in. Then the head student made a report on who was missing. This morning, as soon as the door opened, I held out my arm and greeted the officer with a loud, "*Heil Hitler*," a befitting greeting from us members of the Hitler Youth. My classmates followed suit.

"Children, this is Major Kraus of the Luftwaffe Commando who is in command of our powerful air defenses around Braunschweig. Say good morning to the Major," my high school principal gleamed.

"*Guten tag*, Major Krauss," the whole class said loudly in unison with the exception of my timid friend Hans who whispered good morning.

The Major addressed us with a few friendly words. I think he could sense the nervousness in us through our voices.

"I see all of you look healthy and happy," said the Major. "Learning is a requirement to all you young boys so you can grow up and become someone important and take care of your families. I too have a son around your age. He tells me about your soccer games and that the team keeps getting better. This is good." The Major's attempt to relax us did not succeed with Hans and me. I could hear our bench start to rattle from Hans's legs.

"As of this moment," he continued, "by order of our glorious Fuhrer Adolph Hitler, you students are now members of the Luftwaffe auxiliary and will be assigned to one of our heavy anti-aircraft batteries now ringing the city. You will be living in your own barracks among the other regular Luftwaffe personnel. Your teachers will commute to our battery emplacement and continue your lessons there. You will share warm meals together with the regular Luftwaffe soldiers in the mess hall." I had heard through neighbor friends that the German soldiers had hot meals like red meat, poultry, and more butter than the entire city. So that didn't sound so bad. The Major continued without interruption from my classmates.

"You will be allowed to visit your homes on weekends, at which time you may elect to take your laundry," the Major went on. "You are to report to your respective batteries one week from today. Here is a list of items you are to bring with you. Good luck. "*Heil Hitler*".

Thus all junior and senior high school students in Germany were mobilized into the Luftwaffe Auxiliary and put into harm's way. I looked at my classmates' stunned faces which reflected my own feelings as the Major turned and left with our school principal in tow. With mixed feelings I thought to myself, this could be dangerous.

When I returned home with the devastating news my Muttie exploded, her arms in the air and hands waving, "Why, you are mere boys!"

I looked at her more determined than thwarted and reminded her, "Muttie, as a Hitler youth they taught us to be mentally tough." I stopped short of saying we as Hitler Youths were prepared and ready to give our lives for the Fuhrer and Fatherland.

The night before I was to depart to my battery, I heard my Muttie sobbing behind her closed bedroom door. I thought it better not to disturb her. I tiptoed past, hoping she could not hear me.

When we arrived at our assigned anti-aircraft battery, we were greeted quite civilly by the top sergeant and shown to our barracks, which contained double bunks with straw-filled mattresses and a wood burning stove.

Then came the official greeting by our battery commander, who shouted, *"Heil Hitler der Jungen."* He was a young Captain, about twenty five with short blond hair, handsome looking, and walked well with a stiff leg as a result from a severe injury fighting at the Russian front. He greeted us warmly with a smile. He didn't shout or scream at us which helped us nervous boys relax a little. His endearing ways took the edge off my anxiety and made me feel at ease. He patted a few of us on the back every now and then. I had expected a stern Prussian type military reception scolding, and threatening to punish us inexperienced youths that I had heard so much about.

The captain then proceeded to outline the next day's happenings. First we were to stand in formation and swear the oath of allegiance to our Fuhrer Adolf Hitler and Fatherland. Then we had to pick a companion and dig our two-man foxholes just outside the perimeter of our base. Since Friedrick Oppermann and I shared a school bench, we decided to share a foxhole. These foxholes were shelters against bombing and strafing attacks. Next we were assigned the duties we were to perform in the battery.

Our battery was a double battery and consisted of eight 88mm caliber anti-aircraft guns which were spaced about one hundred feet apart and ringed with a six foot high earthen wall for protection against bomb splinters. The wall also contained the ammunition bunkers. Those eight guns packed so close together put up a lot of deadly shells in a concentrated area I was to find out later.

Selected to be gunner No. 1 on one of those 88mm guns, I had to sit on a metal stool in the back and on the right side of the gun barrel facing the breechblock where the shell was loaded and the firing-pin was located. Right in front of me was an eight inch diameter dial ringed with numbers and a single pointer in the center. Next to that was a hand wheel I had to turn with my right hand. I wore an earphone over my left ear to receive the numbers from the radar station which I then had to match with the pointer to the numbers on my dial by turning the wheel. This would move the barrel up or down into the correct position to send the shell, or bomb, on to its target. I wasn't the strongest at this young age so I was relieved no muscles were needed for this job. On the other side of me and the barrel sat gunner No. 2, another classmate of mine. His actions would rotate the gun in a full circle. I don't remember his name. We were the only

students out of a crew of seven. We were not considered strong

enough to handle the other jobs, like carrying the ammunition to the

gun, loading and pulling the lanyard to fire the gun. My training as a

flak helper would start the next day.

1943. Ronald, me and my sister Norma. A Hitler Youth lapel on my collar.

Chapter 11

My Initiation into the Luftwaffe Auxiliary

Our command bunker was dug only half way during that dark and cold night in the middle of January 1944 when at about eleven P.M. we were suddenly awakened by the wailing sounds of an air raid siren. Startled and being the first to rise, I leaped up out of my straw made mattress and yelled at my buddy.

"Fritz, wake up and get your clothes on. Grab your steel helmet and follow me out to our foxhole. *Mach schnell*." I couldn't scream any louder from my tightened gut. My schoolmate Fritz and I as well as the other students had just dug our first foxholes earlier that day, just in the nick of time.

We both jumped into the hole, crouched down facing each other, shivering from anticipation of the unknown. We sat still but my heart was racing like a hunted rabbit. Soon we heard a noise like a steady drum roll off in the distance; it was from the British 4-engine heavy Lancaster bombers. As they drew nearer, they got louder and louder. I suddenly thought back to my grade school chums back in the U.S. who threw paper airplanes across the classroom and drew pencil drawings of fighter planes. Who could have envisioned from the scale of those diminutive replications what they could actually annihilate in real combat? My classmates in Detroit could never have imagined me now in a German uniform, an ugly greyish one, taking cover from U.S. American allied warplanes.

Just then our guns started to fire with a blazon of red and yellow muzzle flashes into the sky and all hell broke loose. I strained to take a peek over our man-made mud wall to see the spectacle from any hits against the enemy. The sound of the roar that blasted from our only defense shook the ground under my feet. I wondered who the soldiers were manning the No. 1 gunner, a spot I soon would be assigned to, and if they could see well enough at night to aim for the enemy aircraft. They certainly did in the movies I went to.

I slapped my trembling hands over both my ears to block out the terrifying noise of the shelling and saw my buddy Fritz do the same.

"Fritz, isn't it loud?" I desperately wanted to steal attention away from it all. I looked at Fritz and saw he had his eyes closed. His lips began to quiver, a sign, I thought, of mortal fear. As my heart pounded faster I could hear myself telling myself, "Herman, be calm. Don't panic."

In that instant the eerie darkness was suddenly brilliantly lit by hundreds of white flares, each leaving a thin thread of smoke that lazily drifted down over the city. The Pathfinders, the herald twin engine planes called de Havilland Mosquitoes, had dropped these to show the way for the British bomber formations to come for attack. I later learned that these bundles of flares were called Christmas trees. Not the ones I was used to in Detroit.

The steady drone of the powerful British bombers grew louder and nearer. Our guns, positioned to aim at them, fired away furiously into the sky. Acrid smoke drifted slowly over our foxhole. So, that is what gun smoke smells like, I thought to myself.

I had my first glimpse of gunfire in the Wild West movies I loved to see back in the States, but certainly not this close up. What would Tom Mix do in a dangerous life-threatening situation?

Maybe if I had Tony Jr., his beloved horse, I could ride out into the crisp fiery sunset and save the Indians instead. Praying did not enter my mind. The memory of bedtime prayers I had done as a child with my mother was erased by the Nazi Party, which forbade us to believe in Jesus Christ although using the word "God" was encouraged.

My fantasy ended abruptly when my buddy and I heard a whistling screaming noise that rattled my ear drums. Bombs were dropping systematically all around us. In those few seconds my mind wandered back to the movies I was required to watch by my German youth leaders. I squirmed in my hard theater seat fixated at the big screen, filled with excitement hoping as I saw the bombs falling one by one, exploding indiscriminately, for a successful hit. Overwhelmed with disbelief and shock, I realized those hits were now aimed at me!

Suddenly Fritz jumped at me, flung his arms around me tight, buried his face in my shoulder, and cried out, "Herman, what are we going to do? Help me!" With tears streaming down his face he blurted out loud, "Mother, I don't want to die!"

I reassured him and said soothingly, "Fritz, there is nothing we can do. If a bomb hits us, then it hits us. Just let us hug each other." To this day I really don't know how I remained so calm.

Fritz quieted down some but periodically I could hear him whimper, like a wounded puppy.

Fear had finally made its way inside me, too. It stuck in my throat because I could not swallow. By now the bombs were hitting the ground with ear shattering explosions that shook the earth beneath us. The so-called bomb carpeting started at the edge of the village about a mile below us and rapidly moved up the earthen slope we were situated on. Then it stopped, with the last bomb detonating about 100 yards from the perimeter of our battery. My mouth felt dryer than a desert.

The bombing created an inferno like I had never seen except on the big screen. The numerous fires lit up the night sky in a crimson color. I could hear the wailing sirens of the fire trucks and ambulances moving about the city below. I thought of my family but I did not worry since they were thirty miles away. About an hour later, after the smoke had cleared enough, I could see the torched city below and witnessed the aftermath of people yelling and single handedly dousing what fires they could. I understood and welcomed more than ever the startup of all clear sirens that followed. Fritz and I were numb and half deaf but alive. We had survived without a scratch. That was our first baptism of fire.

School in my battery was closed the next day, mainly to get us students assigned to our positions and quickly trained in time for bombing raids that would surely follow. I was relieved.

Around this time, my mother found a farm located a few miles from our home in Wolfsburg where she could send my younger brother Ronald, who had just turned ten. A farmer had agreed to take him and a few other children to help tend the farm. Such assignments were part of a program that sent kids to nearby farms away from the cities to help out, since workers were scarce. Young men were hard to come by now since most, like me, were sent by the German army to the front lines. The food was much better, too. It also allowed my mother the chance--brave soul she was of risking her life, to hide my little brother—to have some relief. I know she was more determined than ever to keep Ronald out of the Hitler Youth.

My baby sister ran around the house cheerfully, helping my mother with the necessary chores, such as finding eggs, bread, and butter. She still watched out for the radio truck outside when my parents turned on their Emerson radio for the daily BBC broadcasts about the war. On one of my rare visits from military duty Norma told me about a time during a daylight air raid when they witnessed an enemy plane shot down. When she and Mutti crept back up the stairs from the basement air raid shelter they saw, lying in our own backyard, a yellow bag. They thought it might be a bomb.

"Norma, you do not go out there," Mutti cautioned. My curious little sister reluctantly obeyed. So my mother took my sister and ran to a wooden box type telephone outside near our building--every section of town had one--and called the neighborhood air raid warden. He came quickly on his bicycle. They peered out the window as he went by foot into the backyard and, without hesitation, picked up the strange object. He calmly stuffed it into his bicycle basket and left. My mother and sister both felt proud, like they had captured an enemy.

"Norma, we did the right thing," exclaimed Mutti. Norma was an adventurous, outdoor kid, kind of like a tomboy. She frequently climbed the shady twenty-five foot tall oak trees that covered our streets. She loved uncovering mysteries and it had been hard for her to restrain herself from grabbing that yellow package.

"Herman, we didn't hear anything more about it," Mutti said.

"Too bad, you fools. It was an inflatable life boat filled with gourmet food. You could have had a decent meal or two," I said. That took the air out of their balloons. They looked so dejected, I wanted to hug them both and not let go.

Fritz and I were chosen as gunners on one of the big and powerful 88mm anti-aircraft guns. I had to sit on a stool and turn a hand wheel that elevated the gun barrel up or down. I wore an earphone on my left ear through which I received numbers: 25, 26, 27, they'd come in methodically. There was a pointer on the face of the dial that rotated when the hand wheel was turned. My job as gunner number one was to line up the numbers I received with the corresponding ones on the dial in a matter of seconds. This raised or lowered the barrel. The gun sat so close to my left side that I could kiss it. A few feet ahead of my sitting position was the 88mm gun breach where older flakers loaded the shells to be fired. The other five guns and their positions were handled by regular "flak" soldiers, who were more experienced.

Because the shells were so heavy and could easily be dropped, us fifteen and sixteen year old boys were not deemed strong enough to perform the other duties. One of the instructions I received was to make sure, before going into action, that I stuff both of my ears with wads of cotton to protect them against the loud noise of the guns being fired. But I thought if I have my left ear blocked with this cotton I won't be able to make out the numbers I receive through my earphone. The earphone alone would give me protection. So I decided to leave out the cotton when the call of duty came again. It came soon enough.

The smoke from my initial bomb campaign experience was still rising lazily from the smoldering fires across the city when, a few days later, we were roused from our bunks again by the screams of the air raid siren.

"Fritz!" I screamed loudly. In my mind I had wanted to say, "This is it. We'll show 'em that we are soldiers, too." But the large lump of fear that stuck in my throat blocked the words. When I got to my post, I stared at the stool attached to my assigned gun, which was fully exposed to danger. At that moment I wished I could fly into the foxhole. Even though each gun emplacement sat an alarming twenty feet away from a protective earthen wall, there was no time to dwell on it. Fritz, gunner number two, and I jumped onto our stools and put on our earphones.

The split seconds of silence, like the falling snow, were welcome. I funneled my fears by paying attention to my job. I faintly heard the approach of the big British bombers, their engines buzzing like hungry bees hovering over sap. Soon our radar picked up their distance and height and the first numbers came through my earphone. I turned my hand wheel to line them up. I know I can do this, I thought to myself. In school I was excellent at and loved geography. I even named a creek in my first year of school in Germany. Back home in Detroit I walked everywhere, from movie theaters to school. I often took different routes home, going out of the way to avoid skirmishes with the jealous school boys.

The slow rise of the gun barrel seemed to take an eternity as I fidgeted, waiting. Any second the guns would fire. I pictured Tom Mix on his white horse raising his revolver to aim and fire away at the enemy and how impractical that would be now. I stiffened up in my stool, eyes glued to the dial. Then the inevitable happened. With a tremendous boom the gun fired simultaneously with the other seven in our battery. Boom! Boom! Boom! The noise was so thunderous that in that instant I could only hear a ringing in my left ear. To my horror I realized I could not hear the numbers coming through my earphone anymore.

"Fritz!" I yelled again. "I can't hear the numbers! I don't know where to point the gun."

The barrel of our gun remained pointed firmly into the dark skies above, the lingering flashes from the barrage lighting up the night like streaks of lightening. Out of the corner of my eye I could see that our gun was turning. Silently, I hoped that meant Fritz could get his numbers and do his job. I became paralyzed by the loss of hearing, but I knew I had to do something. I could not let my comrades down. I noticed that with each muzzle flash from the guns next to me I could see the angle of the barrels aim. I immediately started turning my hand wheel again in an effort to align my gun barrel with the others next to me. That split second decision made me feel at ease and so my confidence was restored, though my loss of hearing remained.

After the first wave of bombers went over us a change of tactics was ordered by the air defense command of our city. Instead of the AA (anti-aircraft) guns following each bomber formation until they passed over us and out of reach, the guns would be aimed in a certain direction to put up a so called "blocking fire" right in front of the oncoming bombers. Not only was it thought that this wall of shrapnel would cause more damage to the planes, but it would unnerve the pilots and bombardiers, causing them to veer off course or release the bombs prematurely. That tactic made our jobs as gunners much easier. Luckily my first mission that night as a gunner would also be my last.

After the all clear siren we rushed to our barracks where I found out that all of us gunners had the same deafening ringing in our ears. The next morning those of us with a more serious loss of hearing called in sick. I wrote my parents complaining about my hearing.

"If you are sick, you must go see the doctor. He will check you out and see what is going on with you. Go now," ordered my battery's first Sergeant.

We were taken to a military doctor who checked us out for ruptured eardrums that none of us had come to find out, which was a great relief. The doctor told us that the ringing noise would gradually go away. The ringing went away in my buddy Fritz's ear, as it did with the other gunners, who continued on in their posts. But it never did, in my case. I was too scared to go back to the doctor out of fear that I would be called a coward and that I wanted to shirk my duties to our Fuhrer and the Fatherland. As a result I was relieved as a gunner and assigned to duties in our battery command post. It was later determined that 60% of my hearing was destroyed due to damage to the nerves in the ear canal. My ear kept ringing and is still ringing to this day, 65 years later.

We were regularly updated on both enemy and friendly aircraft types. Aside from our classes in the morning our lives became more and more integrated with the regular Luftwaffe soldiers in the battery. When those who we were to replace were assigned to the front line, we said our goodbyes with heavy hearts.

Our assignments included guard duty and KP (kitchen police), where we peeled potatoes and cleaned vegetables. We learned how to fire a German rifle with blanks as ammunition. After all they didn't want us accidently killing a "friendly," just to give an alarm to scare off any intruders. Every Saturday morning we had a "GI" party which consisted of scrubbing the floors and cleaning the windows of our barrack with newspapers. They taught us to salute an officer with the new snappy outstretched right arm instead of the old right hand raised to the brim of one's cap. For exercise we had to march on the battery grounds while we sang, which we always did at the top of our lungs. If the sergeant wasn't happy with our performance he would order us to "Volle Deckung!" (hit the deck!).

Chapter 12

The Glass Plate

On my first tour of guard duty during an especially cold January night, lit only by a sliver of a moon, the kind of night when one imagines a lone wolf lurking quietly out of sight, I came to my last rounds just before daybreak. I passed the barrack where our commanding officer stayed. I glanced over and saw a sight that made me gasp for air. Hanging on a rope line in front of the CO's quarters was a pair of white women's panties. I stopped dead in my tracks to absorb the striking view. I had never seen lingerie before. Not even on my mother. She was outspoken and modest too. She tided everything up in our house and didn't leave anything lying around.

All kinds of thoughts raced through my fertile sixteen year old mind, intermingling with raging hormones that had lain dormant for too long a time. I wondered who our young handsome captain, who lost a leg on the Russian front, had got in there with him. Was it his wife, a woman of ill-repute, or a young beautiful girl?

I couldn't stop fantasizing after I noticed a woman's bicycle leaning up against the side of the barrack wall. My guard time was running out so I had to quickly move on to finish my tour. I worried that someone may have spotted me staring over at my CO's billet in the wee early morning hours. No, I thought, it's too early. I couldn't wait to get back to my classmates for breakfast to tell them my juicy story.

After relating the shocking sighting to them, not one said a word. Typical German behavior. They soon finished chewing on the customary hard crusted dark rye bread, washing it down with a coffee-like brew made from roasted ground barley grains. I surmised the wheels in their brains started to turn slowly. One by one the questions started.

"Who can this woman be, privileged to spend a night in our CO"s barrack?"

"Yes, perhaps even sleeping with him in his bed?" another asked.

"Then, what all happened in there to make this person have to wash her panties in the *middle* of a cold night and then have to hang them outside to dry for all to see?"

Our imaginations ran wild with the cool winds. Somehow, without a spoken word, every one of us kept a look out for this person in hopes of stealing a repeat glance when on guard duty. We were just a bunch of typical teenage high school boys frustrated from the saltpeter that was put into the food to suppress our raging hormones and dampen our sexual appetites.

A few days later the early morning cook told us he'd seen the young woman before breakfast. She was dressed in the uniform of the Luftwaffe's women's auxiliary Signacorps and was barreling like the dickens pass the kitchen barrack, down the hill, and into the city on her bicycle. Later I learned that these women were eighteen and older and served in the various Luftwaffe units as switchboard and telephone operators as well as drivers, secretaries, and other clerical jobs. Our cook could not tell how old or young "our" lady was. Nobody in our group ever saw her again. I was happy that my little tale had briefly lifted our spirits out of the gloom of our dangerous tasks and the anxiety of not knowing if we would be still alive from one air raid to the next. The raunchy stories and jokes we tossed around made up for some of the elusive joys of my early manhood.

In the deadened calm between the end of another night of air raids and the welcoming call from the all clear siren to allow us to go back to the barrack to finish our sleep, I heard the faint noise of a single airplane approaching. Then the landing lights of an airstrip located about three miles from us were turned on. The plane was one of the German night fighters returning from a mission and I could tell from the engine's sputtering sounds that it was in trouble. I watched it landing too low. Then it crashed into a ball of flames. It was a sober reminder that death can strike at any time anywhere. Poor pilot.

Unofficial reports had reached my unit that we already had our first casualties among other classmates. They were manning multi barrel 20mm and 37mm guns situated on top of buildings and flak towers in the city. We also learned that the 8th U.S. air force would be launching one-thousand bombers a day against targets all over Germany. Any day now we could expect the Americans to raid our city with their four-engine B-17 and B-24 bombers. We feared the B-

24 Liberator more than the B-17 Flying Fortress, which we called the Flying Coffin, because of its two- ton heavier bomb load. It was a tough plane to shoot down. Consequently more B-17s returned to base with casualties than the B-24s. The crews of the B-24 either went down with their plane or parachuted to their fate.

Because of my loss of hearing I had been assigned and retrained as a plotter located in the battery command post. My job was to mark the course of approaching bomber formations on a four foot square glass plate covered table located inside our bunker. Through a microphone, in my now perfect German, I called the information in to the air defense command in the city about four miles away.

The weather at the end of January had turned beautiful. There were an unusually high number of days of sunshine and blue skies, perfect for the American bombardiers to see their targets. And so they came, hundreds of B-17s glistening in the sun, leaving trails of white plumes from condensation behind them. It was a majestic sight with a deadly purpose. I had seen it before in Wolfsburg in a few newsreels. The intense German fighter pilot movies I was made to see were tame compared to the reality.

I started to become apprehensive wondering if they'd come for us. I decided to concentrate on my job of talking into my mike methodically and assuredly. Then I heard someone yell out, "They are turning towards us." Sure enough, a section of about fifteen to twenty planes had veered away from the main formation and were headed straight for our battery. By now my battery had increased to twelve 88mm guns, a formidable concentration of fire power. No wonder we were a menace to these American bombers. From their perspective, we had to be eliminated.

Our command bunker was purposely dug only halfway into the ground. The upper half was open so that one had a 360 degree view of the battery installation. Looking up from my position in front of the glass-topped plotting table I could see a good portion of the sky south and west of us, toward Italy and France. Judging by the increasing drone of the aircraft engines the American bombers would soon come into my view. I was getting the first reading from our telescopic rangefinder. I plotted these on the grid and conveyed the information by microphone to the air defense central command in Braunschweig.

Then I saw them. *"Da sind die Amerikaner, ach du liebergott,"* (Those are the Americans. Oh the love of God)," I hollered out at first sight of the U.S. bomber formations. The sound was far more real and awesome than anything in the newsreels. I could make out the bombers as B-17s, the Flying Fortresses, sturdily built to carry ten- ton bomb loads and the most difficult to knock out of the sky. On that cold January day the bombers shined in the clear ice blue skies, flying in tight formations, pulling their snow white trails of condensation behind them, four trails per plane, with silvery wing and fuselages reflected in the sun's rays. A frightening sight. I became mesmerized and lost my concentration on the immediate task before me. Christ, I thought, my father said the U.S. could mass produce war machines faster and more effectively.

Then the group of bombers headed straight for my battery. They were flying at around twenty-thousand feet; about ten-thousand feet lower than a commercial airliner. So, without any difficulty, I caught sight of the bomb bay doors underneath the belly of the craft opening slowly. In my controlled panic I yelled out, "Fellows, they are going to bomb us!" By now we were firing our guns furiously but we could not stop the bombs from dropping one by one, whistling their way down with a horrid noise. I wondered if this would be a repeat of that first night air raid by the British. I was afraid this time would be different. My comrades and I were easy targets, out in full view on a perfect sunny day.

Then the first bombs exploded, shaking and hammering the ground with the familiar staccato sounds of carpet bombs, one now racing upon a path of destruction toward my battery with perhaps death to follow. Mortal fear gripped my throat. It felt dry. I could not swallow. Had the glass topped table not prevented it, I would have thrown myself on the floor and curled up in a fetal position.

At that instant my battery CO, who had been outside observing the scene, came racing down the steps into our bunker hollering, "*Volle Decking!*" (take full cover). Everybody left their posts and lay down, hugging the walls. I instinctively crouched over the plotting table, pushing harder and harder with my arms. When the last bombs exploded just a few yards from our perimeter, I crashed through the plate glass from the force. Silence overcame all emotions in that instant and everyone in my bunker could hear a panicky voice coming over my microphone shouting, *"Sind sie getroffen?"* (Are you hit?)

My captain jumped up, grabbed my microphone and answered, *"Nein, wir sind ok. Wie sindt nicht getroffen. Glastisch wurde durch meine Plotter Unfall gebrochen."* (No, we are ok. The glass table was broken in accident by my plotter.) He then briefly explained how, with unflinching courage, we crew members of every gun, including my two classmates, gunners number one and two, kept on firing in the face of death. "They out-nerved the lead American bombardier, who apparently gave the famous command 'bombs away' prematurely," he exclaimed. I dared not say a word.

For another ten minutes my battery engaged in attacking a force of about three-hundred U.S. heavy bombers. Then the raid ended and I was abruptly out of a job. I felt miserable and wondered if I had failed. Was I a coward in the eyes of my classmates? But my captain came to my rescue. He did not reprimand me. Instead he praised my action for staying at my post, literally the glass plotter table.

"I ordered everyone to take full cover," he said. "But you stayed at your post. Breaking the plate glass was just an accident caused in the heat of battle."

I was grateful for my young captain who had empathy and compassion for us high school kids. Maybe it had something to do with his experiences on the Russian front and losing a leg there. My classmates and I began to like him more and more.

After that first bombing my anti-aircraft battery was never attacked again by the Americans. As to the courage it took to face down the enemy that can be attributed to the discipline and blind faith instilled in every German soldier from the first days in the Hitler Youth Corps. We were to follow the Fuhrer's orders and serve the Fatherland without any questions asked. Such is the power of persuasion.[3]

Some weeks later my battery was recognized for its valor by being invited to a farewell dinner for the CO of Central Command who was being transferred to another post. At sixteen I now had the

---

3. In a dictatorship it is called "brainwashing" and propaganda.

confidence of performing my duties as a Luftwaffe Auxiliary in the

defense of my homeland, Germany.

1944. Me in a Luftwaffe Auxiliary flaker uniform.

Chapter 13

The Devil is in the Sky

The following weekend, having survived my first daytime air raid by the U.S. bombers on Braunschweig, luck would find me again. My first leave finally came after just a little over six weeks of service. A few classmates and I were given a three-day furlough to go home to our families. I was ecstatic. I could not perform my job anyway. The replacement glass had not arrived yet.

Right after barracks cleaning, we stood at attention for inspection. Then my furlough and journey home started. Fritz, two other classmates, and I had to walk a mile from our battery at the southern edge of the city to the nearest streetcar which would take us to the train station in the city. I looked up to see the sun shining through a light cloud cover.

"A nice day for an air raid," I remarked wryly.

"Herman, don't paint the devil in the sky," Fritz said sternly.

Just as the four of us stepped off the streetcar the air raid sirens sounded full alarm.

"See what you did with your big mouth, Herman," said Fritz angrily. "Now I will miss my train to Lebenstedt."

"I will too, Fritz. Let's just get this over with."

We rushed into the station with about a hundred fellow passengers and headed straight for the air raid bunker located underneath the platforms. We heard the heavy flak guns open fire with a flurry and we knew the bombs would hit soon after. The ground shook violently from the explosions of bombs falling above us. When a bomb hit the entrance to our bunker and exploded with an earth shaking thunder, Fritz and I covered our ears and stuck our heads between our legs. The bunker immediately filled with dust and acrid smoke. A few women screamed while others cried, adding a new dimension to my early bombardment experiences. But Fritz and I stayed calm. We were by now seasoned soldiers, after all. As soon as the raid was over and the all clear sirens went off, we saw that the people who were sitting close to the open entrance were covered with debris and broken concrete; but no one was seriously injured.

When the smoke and dust cleared and we could see daylight, Fritz and I helped clear a path up to the platform where, right in front of us, there was a huge bomb crater still smoldering. A few yards closer and we would all have been dead. The train station was in shambles. Along with many gouges and busted up pavement, there were twisted tracks and smashed rail cars.

"No train is going to move in or out of this station," I managed to say. Fritz didn't say a word.

I was informed by the station master that in order to get to my destination to KdF Stadt (Wolfsburg) I had to catch the train in a suburb, but I have to walk to it because the streetcars had stopped running. It was about a four mile hike which took me through the city. For the first time I saw the devastation that previous air raids had done and I felt sorry for the homeless. I couldn't catch my train quickly enough and soon I was on my way home alone.

The train stopped at a few villages along the way. I could hear the townspeople talking in the nearby coaches. Then I overheard someone say, "Did you hear about KdF Stadt? It was bombed around noon." Fear grasped me again and my hands started to sweat. Were my mother, younger brother and sister okay? How about my father, who now worked as director of the engineering department and had his office on the top floor of the Volkswagen factory? I hoped it was just rumors.

When the train finally approached the end of the line in Wolfsburg, I leaned over at my window and I could see black smoke rising and forming grey clouds over the area by the factory. As the factory slowly came into my sight, I saw the tail end of a B-17 bomber sticking out the side of the end building, smoke still billowing out of the top offices located in the one mile length factory.

"That's where my father works!" I said to my fellow passengers. I didn't scream in public. The discipline I received taught me to hold back from doing anything like that. Hitler's motto to us Hitler Youth stated, "*Hart wie Kruppstahl, zah wie Leder, flink wi ien Windhund*" (Hard as steel from Krupp, tough as leather, and fast as a Greyhound). After three years in the Hitler Youth, I learned to hide my emotions.

When I finally got off, I looked around the station and with great relief I could see that the city and the suburb where we lived was not touched. It was a joyous moment when my mother opened the front door and I put my arms around her, my brother and my little sister.

"Where's father? Is he okay?" I hurriedly asked.

"Your father is fine. He survived the bombing in the air raid shelter below the factory first floor. He quickly came home to see if we were okay and then he went back to survey the smoke damage done to his offices. Luckily there were no fires in his area of the factory. He'll be home later," Mutti said without a wince.

That evening as we all sat around the dinner table together it felt like an eternity as the conversations between us went well into the night, elated and happy we had all survived that day.

"Vati, on the train home I saw the tail of an airplane sticking out of the factory, with smoke streaming out."

"Ya, Herman. It crashed right into my office. I could have brought home an American for dinner." We all laughed for the first time in a long time. My father continued and told us that he was busy with pleasing his superiors. What he did not tell us was that the Nazi regime interrupted the assembly line for the VW wagon to build the

Kubelwagon or 'military Beetle' and repair damaged airplane parts such as wings for the Luftwaffe, the German air force.

This initial air raid on the Volkswagen factory consisted primarily of incendiary bombs. These bombs could cause fires over a wide area with speed and cause more destruction from just one hit. There would be a total of three more air raids to follow a few weeks later with high explosive heavy bombs all dropped by American planes.

With sixty percent of the factory destroyed, production of parts for the deadly V-1 rockets came to a halt. I did not experience these attacks because I would embark on an odyssey of my own upon my return to the flak battery in the weeks and months to come. The city of Braunschweig would be hit by British and American bombers a total forty-two times, mostly with clusters of incendiary bombs also called Molotov bread baskets. My old home, the city of Braunschweig, burned for two-and a half days straight.

Chapter 14

My First Drink

Shortly after my furlough ended my battery was invited to a farewell dinner for the CO of the central air defense command of Braunschweig. He was being transferred to another post. My flak battery comrades were invited partly in recognition for our heroic action during that U.S. bomber attack and partly because we were closely located to the dining hall in the village below us. In case of an air raid alarm, my classmates and the other flak soldiers could run up the hill in time to take up our positions and be ready for action.

All us kids were seated at one table and were in a rare festive mood, curious and excited. Across the floor, where the CO and his staff would soon be sitting, I saw a sight that caused me to rub my eyes to make sure I was seeing right. With a nudge I said to Fritz, "Look, there at the table next to the CO's --a bunch of Luftwaffe auxiliary girls. Boy, do they look good. Those lucky stiffs sitting next to them…"

"Do you think our 'Fair Lady' is among them?" Fritz replied.

"What good would it do?" I answered dejected.

"There might be dancing, the band is warming up".

Then I noticed the wine glasses on the table and I turned to Fritz and asked, "How well can you hold your liquor?"

"You will see soon enough Herman. How about you?"

"Well, I've never had wine before and I'm curious to see how I like it," I replied.

With that the Luftwaffe band started to play in earnest. The CO was due to arrive any moment. We waited and waited but still he had not shown up yet. All of us in the room started to become impatient. We sat staring up and down at the women and talking up a storm.

Then a senior officer got up from his seat and announced, "The Commander has been delayed and will be late. Servers, please fill everyone's wine glasses so we can at least enjoy a drink before dinner."

We all greeted his gesture in unison with a big cheer. It was almost eight o'clock in the evening when I took my first drink of wine. I had no idea what effect drinking alcohol on an empty stomach would have.

"Prost, Fritz," I exclaimed, raising my wine glass to clink with his. I took a timid swallow of the red wine. "Not bad." He just nodded and took a big gulp from his. I glanced at the uniformed women. I felt my lips starting to warm up. The band started to play patriotic and marching songs.

By the time the CO arrived and dinner was served, Fritz and I had downed our first glass and gotten a refill. I was beginning to like wine. I had barely finished my meal when it hit me. The whole room started to turn around me. I had the spins. I felt a queasy feeling in my stomach. It got worse within seconds and I knew I had to get to a toilet fast before I puked all over the dinner table. With my hand in front of my mouth to keep me from vomiting, I reeled and zigzagged to the bathroom in front of all my classmates. As soon as I got there, with an animal like roar, I heaved and heaved until my stomach hurt and nothing was left.

"Herman, how are you feeling?" Fritz asked as he rushed to my aid.

"Worse than being bombed," I groaned. (Now I knew why, after drinking too much, people say, "I got bombed.") "I feel better in my stomach but terrible in my head," I babbled. Fritz tried to get me up off the bathroom floor but I collapsed like a sack of potatoes.

"I will have to get one of the other classmates to help me get you back to our barracks, Herman," Fritz said, walking out of the bathroom.

So my buddies picked up my debilitated body and, hanging limply between them, carried me on a tedious and almost impossible climb back to our sleeping quarters. Fritz took my clothes off and tucked me into bed. I was so grateful to have my classmates. I felt we were slowly bonding together like true comrades. After that episode I learned my lesson about drinking on an empty stomach. It took many years before I dared to drink wine again and enjoy it as I do today.

There had been several more bombing raids on Braunschweig at night by the British war planes and around noon by the Americans but no more raids on our battery before we were informed that we were to be relocated. The exact date and new location were kept secret, as was the extent of damages and progress made by the German military. I did learn at briefings from a Luftwaffe officer that synthetic oil and gasoline production facilities were now prime targets for the Americans; the previous targets had been aircraft production.

In May my classmates and I found ourselves en route to the large city of Hannover, about forty miles west of our previous post Braunschweig. On the outskirts of Hannover our battery, now reduced from twelve to eight guns, were set up to help defend the *Leunawerke* (Leuna works), Germany's biggest synthetic oil plant during WWII. The *Leunawerke* were located barely one mile on the other side of a wooded ridge and out of sight. The ridge offered our battery protection from strafing attacks by the feared twin-tailed and twin engine P-38 American Lightnings. Unbeknownst to us then, *Leunawerke* would come under heavy aerial bombardment and become one of the most dreaded flak zones by the Allies, since we were successfully downing enemy planes.

On the exposed side of my battery, two 30 caliber water-cooled machine guns were placed behind earthen parapets, or barricades. I was assigned to a different duty this time; I was an assistant machine gunner which meant I fed the ammunition belt into the machine gun. My machine gunner was a regular Luftwaffe soldier.

"Young man, I need you to pay strict attention when I am in need of more ammunition," he quickly explained. He then handed me the gun. "You must be ready because this gun is fast. Go now and shoot to get familiar with the noise."

I took the gun and shot a few practice rounds hoping for no strafing planes. They were the low flying fighter aircrafts that, during the weeks we were stationed there, attacked us high on the hill, even though the P-38s were constantly buzzing around us. My battery was in action numerous times for about four solid weeks during night and day attacks by British Lancaster and American B-17 heavy bombers that were targeting the refineries. This caused large fires to burn for days. From a safe distance I could hear the explosions, see the black smoke swell high into the sky, and smell the tainted oil. I could not see the factory itself, however, because of the ridge that served as good cover for us.

Located just on the other side of us and closer to the oil refinery complex was a battery of 122mm anti-aircraft guns, the largest caliber the Germans had in their arsenal. The complete shell with projectile was too heavy for a man to handle so instead it was laid on a conveyor belt and automatically loaded into the gun breach. The guns fired with a tremendous boom that rattled windows and shook the ground for thousands of feet around, though it didn't affect us.

On June 6, 1944, our battery heard the devastating news from the German high command that over 100,000 American, British and Canadian troops had landed on the French coast of Normandy, known as D-day. Despite the fact that it was expected, we all were still shocked. Things were going badly for Germany in many other areas, too. We heard from newspaper reports that the allies were advancing toward Rommel, the Russians were pushing the German Wehrmacht closer to Germany's borders, the German Navy was losing its submarine warfare, and the allied bombing campaign was decimating German cities, severely curtailing war material production.

Yet my convictions and those of my classmates clung steadfastly to the belief that our Fuhrer would lead us and Germany to a glorious victory. We didn't need any pep talks. We followed him

blindly. We were willing to sacrifice our lives and limbs for the Fuhrer

and the Fatherland. All the propaganda was working.

Chapter 15

Happy Seventeenth Birthday

The rumors of secret weapons in the works strengthened and sustained our beliefs that we would win. Germany had already advanced rocket science by producing and using the V1 rocket. It was responsible for the loss of thousands of lives in London, launched at England just after V-day. The first production jet fighters were making their appearance in the skies. The VW factory was busy producing stampings for the deadly V1 rocket. Smart bombs were also being tested. I heard talk among my peers: "Will an atom bomb be next? However, we had only heard of "heavy water" production, which was needed for an atom bomb.

For my 17th birthday in June, several weeks after V-day, I received permission for my parents to come and visit me at our barrack. It was for half a day in the afternoon when the threat of an air raid was minimal. It was only an hour train ride each way for my parents, so that worked out okay. I was happily looking forward to seeing them again after a month and a half apart. They arrived on a quiet, sunny day without any sirens going off. The first sergeant of the battery let us use the mess hall, where we had a little privacy. With a smile on her face my mother handed me a package.

"This is for your birthday, Herman. Go on and open it." I hastily unwrapped the package and there to my astonishment was a beautiful round double layer chocolate cake she'd made for me. I hadn't seen one in quite some time.

"Oh, thank you so much, Muttie," I exclaimed, giving her a big hug. "I will have to share it with my classmates. Especially with Fritz whose parents live in the country. They send him packages with those delicious smoked hams, sausages and cold cuts." It also was customary among us high school kids to share the contents of each other's packages. Then my parents proceeded to tell me what had happened in Wolfsburg the past six weeks.

"Your brother Ronald will be eleven in October. We found him shelter with a farmer out in the country where he can help with the chores. It's out of harm's way from the bombing," my mother said quietly in German. "Your sister Norma is seven now and I'm busy trying to keep her out of trouble, with all her pranks and antics. She trapped a cat in a metal garbage can with its tail pinched between the lid and the edge of the can. I heard a scream and thought someone had been shot. Then at the market, one of the neighbors looked at Norma and said to me, 'How could a nice lady like you have such a daughter?'"

My father then described the damage and devastation the Volkswagen factory suffered from a bombing raid from by the U.S. air force.

"I was sitting at my desk when the alarms went off. I rushed with the others down the steps and into the shelters that are deep in the bowels of the factory. I heard explosions and then I heard the collapse of steel from the roof falling. When it was over I could still reach my upstairs office, which received only light damage. My seventy-five engineers and I went back to work shortly.

"But," he continued, "What's there to do? More than half the factory is destroyed." He slowly shook his head, looking downward. Then he said somberly, "What the U.S. bombers had come for they accomplished." The making of parts for the dreaded V1 rockets and the repair of Luftwaffe bomber planes were their intended targets.

Mutti spoke up then. "A B-17 bomber was hit by flak directly over the targeted VW factory, forcing the crew to bail out. By telephone word spread quickly through Steimker Berg (a Wolfsburg suburb) that one of the crewmembers landed with his parachute in the top of a huge oak tree. Before I could get to her, your sister raced toward the scene about two hundred yards from our house. The poor man was tangled up in those branches and he was already dead. What a ghastly sight for a seven year old girl. Then the fire department arrived and removed the body."

As my parents' visit neared its end my father fell silent and did not mention anything more about the war or the drastic D-day invasion. He told me later, after the war, that he knew he could not convince me that it was only a matter of time before Germany would be defeated.

When we said our goodbyes my mother had tears in her eyes, "Herman, take care of yourself. Happy birthday." I hugged her tightly, then reached out and shook my father's hand. I surmised since nothing was mentioned about the Allies invasion at Normandy it was too much for all of us to realize how impenetrable this war had become.

A few days later the 8th U.S. air force command must have felt its bombers had destroyed enough of the *Leunawerke* refinery because not one drop of aviation fuel could be produced during the last leg of the war. When the bombing stopped our mission had ended. But later, in November 1944, an all out air attack over *Leunawerke* practically decimated the Luftwaffe fighters and ground batteries. My luck prevailed when my battery received orders to relocate back to Braunschweig in late June of that year. This time we were positioned closer to the city, positioned to protect the armament works that produced the heavy Tiger tanks, which were playing havoc with the allies and Russian armor.

I was relieved of my duties as an assistant machine gunner. My battery CO did not think it was necessary to defend against strafing attacks because the guns were shielded all around by high shaded trees, mostly oaks. I was trained with two other classmates to operate a new optical device called a predictor. It consisted of a three foot square metal box clad in dark leather. It would automatically measure the distance and angle of approaching aircraft and it relayed the information to the gunners. There were three of us gunners, including my buddy Fritz, who had to turn and aim the optics toward the advancing enemy planes. Our position was surrounded by a four foot high parapet made from sandbags for protection against bomb shrapnel.

The most frightening experience of one of the bombing raids during this time was a napalm incendiary attack on our anti-aircraft guns. These bombs reminded me of flame throwers used in battle during the Middle Ages except they were a hundred times more powerful because of the chemicals used to cause a fire on impact. As the bombs exploded around us we watched in terror as some of the barracks were set ablaze.

"Get down, everyone!" I screamed. Within seconds after we crouched low inside our sandbagged wall the burning napalm splattered on top of our director operator. Luckily, none of the rest of us was hit. Instantly, I jumped up with more force than I ever thought I had and yelled, "Get some sand on it. *Mach schnell*. It thrives on oxygen." So the three of us, with our bare hands, shoveled dirt on top of the napalm and were able to snuff out the napalm flames and then continue with our duties.

"Look, the fires are creeping toward our barrack!" I yelled in dismay. None of us could leave our post to save our belongings because the air raid was still going on. We watched in horror as our barrack burned when a lone four engine B-24 Liberator bomber came flying slowly but directly over our battery, trailing black smoke from one of its engines.

"It's flying awfully low," I managed to half sing. Our guns by now were firing furiously with the barrels pointing straight up as the crippled bomber flew over. Fascinated, and eagerly waiting for one of our shells to make a direct hit and bring the plane down, the three of us watched the thick black smoke streaming out of the left inboard engine. Sometime later my CO was informed that the B-24 had crashed and my battery was credited with the kill.

Soon the monotone wail of the siren finally signaled the end of the raid. Every member of the battery rushed to fight the fires. We desperately tried to save as many personal belongings as possible. We school kids managed to get all ours out before the flames engulfed the entire barrack and burned it to the ground. Dejected but thankful we all escaped alive and unhurt, we sat on a patch of grass clutching our sparse belongings, wondering what would happen next.

My battery chief walked toward us and told us, "You boys can go home. But report back in three days. By then we will have a new shelter erected to house you temporarily."

It was wonderful to be home again and to be with my parents and little sister. But my little brother was still away in the country, helping on the farm. Now I had a chance to see the damage done to the Volkswagen factory by the U.S. bombing raids.

"Fortunately, only one bomb struck our big power plant, causing minimal damage," my father told me matter-of-factly. "Had it not been a dud and exploded as it was intended to, all of Wolfsburg would be out of electricity. There would be no power for household stoves and no steam for heating since the power plant here at the factory is Wolfsburg's sole power supplier." Even though the factory was left unrepaired to convince allied reconnaissance of destruction they wrought, production continued. My father's office and his engineering departments, located on the top floors, escaped with little or no damage. Hitler had promised that the factory would be bigger and would out-produce the Ford assembly plant.

Shortly after I returned to the battery we received orders to move to a new location 32 miles southwest of Hanover and 15 miles southeast of Wolfsburg to a town called Salzgitter, known as the salt spring city. Salzgitter lies in the foothills of the Harz Mountains. Even though we passed numerous medieval fortresses and castles my mood was gloomy in anticipation of what would happen next. Low grade ore was being mined and transported around the ridge of Salzgitter. In 1944 the British navy blockaded shipments of high grade iron ore from Sweden in the North Sea along the coast of Norway and Denmark; Sweden was Germany's biggest exporter of the ore. The steel produced at Salzgitter was from the low grade iron ore mined nearby. Our mission was to help protect a new steel mill called the Reichswerke (Reichs Works) that was built by Hermann Goering and the Nationalist Socialist Party (the Nazis).

By now it was early August of 1944 and school had started again. Classes were held in the battery mess barrack. The activities in the steel mill were noisy, what with the clanging of machinery, hammers, and banging of railcars being shunted. Then at night the whistles blew warning the workers of the pouring of another batch of super-hot molten steel into ingot forms, which created a shower of sparks. I could see the smoke rise with an orange-red like glow, lighting up the sky for miles.

"Look, Fritz," I exclaimed one night while on guard duty. "What better beacon for enemy planes to hone in on and drop their bombs."

"Here you go again. Painting the devil on the wall," he repeated. But the bombing was left to the Americans at daylight and sporadic harassment bombing from the British at night.

Shortly after my classmates and I moved into our barrack we all awoke one morning scratching our bodies like mad.

"What the devil is going on?" We all cried out.

"They are bedbugs," one knowledgeable buddy of ours said. "During the day they hide in dark places. At nightfall they crawl up the wall and along the ceiling. When the warm draft from a human body floats up they drop on you, looking for hairy places to hide. Then they start to bite to suck your blood for food."

We all went rushing to sick bay for help with the itching and scratching, but to no avail. We were told we would have to be "debugged" with DDT and our barrack fumigated.

"Take your clothes off and put them in individual sacks for decontamination," we were told. "Go take a shower and get in line at the de-bugging trailers. Then report back for duty."

We had to carry our straw-filled mattress outside and put them in a pile to be burned. Then we stood in line to be sprayed with DDT powder. All the while I could see yellowish smoke pouring out of the barrack's doors and windows from the fumigation. The bedbugs never bothered us again. I found out later that before we arrived our barrack had been occupied by a group of forced laborers from one of the eastern European countries. We weren't the only ones infested.

Because my class had missed so many days of schooling during the last six months due to air raid activity, I had difficulty concentrating on my studies, which negatively affected my grades. So far, though, no serious bombing raid by the allies had taken place in Salzgitter. However, my battery was called out for action on an almost daily basis. It began to wear out us sixteen and seventeen year olds.

Chapter 16

No Daylight in Sight

One hot day in August of 1944, after nine long months filled with heavy bombing, I was finally released from anti-aircraft duty and sent home. I was elated to be going back to my family in Wolfsburg. I missed high school and those hard wooden bench seats. I yearned to be among my peers. My buddy Fritz and I were the only seventeen year olds among our high school classmates at the time we returned to class. I don't recall why Fritz was one year behind in high school but I knew there was a valid reason why I was.

In Germany, high school (*Oberschule* for boys and *Lyzeum* for girls) consisted of eight school years. After four years of elementary school, if a ten year old boy or girl chose to continue schooling at a higher learning level, an exam had to be taken. If they passed, a tuition fee had to be paid each year for eight years until graduation at age eighteen. When we arrived in Germany in 1937, I had to work myself through four years of elementary school to learn how to read and write German. It took me one school year to become proficient enough to pass the entrance exam and enter high school at the age of eleven— one year older than my classmates.

Dressed in our freshly pressed auxiliary *Luftwaffe* (air force) uniforms, our sparse belongings stuffed in satchels draped around our shoulders, Fritz and I said our goodbyes.

"Well, Fritz…" I started to say.

"Herman, don't say it."

"I wanted to tell you that we will meet again soon. Besides, you promised me a sausage and ham breakfast from your farm."

"Okay, Herman."

We shook hands and gave a quick embrace.

"Fritz, you take care now. Keep your chin up and good luck."

"You too, Herman, and don't always paint the in the sky."

We walked toward the station to catch our trains home, Fritz in one direction and me in the other. That was the last time we saw each other during the war. After the war ended in 1945 I learned from Fritz's parents that he survived but was captured by the British Army and sent to England to work in the coal mines. He spent three years there as a prisoner of war. We didn't make contact until a few years later.

During the two hour train ride home I overheard a few of the passengers talking in hushed voices and for the first time heard the term "concentration camp" mentioned. Sometime later I would hear more about these camps and what went on in them. Right now I had to await orders to report for duty as a member of the *Reichs Arbeits Dienst,* * also known as RAD. I was anxious to get back home.[4]

---

[4] Six major frontline units consisting of Reichs Arbeits Dienst troops were formed in the last months of WWII, three of which are known to have seen limited but fierce action. The six units of mainly RAD troops known to have been formed were as follows: RAD-Division z.b.V.1/Infanterie-Division Albert Leo Schlageter, RAD-Division z.b.V.2/Infanterie-Division Friedrich Ludwig Jahn, RAD-Division z.b.V.3/Infanterie-Division Theodor Körner, RAD-Division z.b.V.4/Infanterie-Division Güstrow, Gebirgsjager-Brigade Steiermark, and Gebrigsjager-Brigade Enns.

Chapter 17

Reichs Arbeits Dienst (RAD)

I had heard through talk among my schoolmates this RAD organization provided support for the *Wehrmacht*, the German armed forces, such as food supplies for the frontline troops, road reconstruction and repair of damaged airstrips. When I was younger, I'd see these young men dressed in a bland, light brown military uniform, a small peaked cap with dark brown piping atop their heads, marching in parades or at political rallies. I also spotted them digging ditches for irrigation back in Braunschweig. Instead of a rifle, they shouldered a spade, polished to a high shine. I felt compelled to ask them what they were a part of but at that time I could not speak German well enough to do so.

Adolf Hitler named the political party he founded in the 1920s in Munich, Germany, The National Socialist German Labor Party

(NSDAF). In his speeches he always emphasized the word "labor" with the German workers. The Volkswagen Factory exemplified this.

The DAF (The German Labor Front) limited the rights of the worker by prohibiting any strikes or disruptive demonstrations, contrary to the labor unions established in the U.S. American factories. In 1938, one year after my family arrived in Germany and the annexation of Austria by Hitler, he famously said, "This German car will also make a wish come true, a wish harbored by so many hard-working underpaid Austrian people."[5] He believed that in order to create a strong Germany every young man had to have an appreciation of what hard, physical labor meant and felt like. This idea also was to serve as an equalizer between young men from all walks of life.

When I arrived back home I was greeted with shocked looks and a gasp from my mother and little sister Norma. My father was absent, working endlessly at the VW factory.

"Herman, we thought you were dead! The last we heard you were still in Braunschweig. The American's bombed the city so badly we could see fiery smoke in the skies, nothing but ashes everywhere

---

[5] From the book *Small Wonder*.

and papers flown about. They say this time was the worst hit. Thank God you are alive!" my mother exclaimed.

Norma jumped up and down when she saw me. She could barely talk, she was so excited. I thought she was happy to see me again since she did that dance once before when I had come back home.

"Herman, I had to run into a bunker for the first time. That's too scary." Norma was six years old now and attending school.

"Ah, Norma. The bunker will keep you safe. You have nothing to worry about." I knew better, of course, but I wanted to comfort her.

"But Herman, there was so much smoke around I couldn't see anything. I don't ever want to go back there again!"

But my little sister had to go one more time into that city bunker. The school children had only ten minutes after an air raid signal to run home or to the city bunker before the bombs dropped. The Nazis would spray smoke all around for their cover. Her second and last experience in a public bunker, Norma made sure she stayed close to the door so she could see the light. Afterwards Norma made it home safely and we all huddled together, my mother, my little brother

Ronald, Norma and me, in our basement shelter until the all clear sirens sounded. When the war ended Norma told us it had become a game between the school children to see who could make it home first. Fortunately, the trees that lined and shaded the neighborhoods in Wolfsburg also shielded the city from the sky. Otherwise our home might have been reduced to ashes.

After Hitler came into power in 1933 he made six months of service in the RAD compulsory for every man at age eighteen. Working at manual labor took place under strict military discipline. Similar to the Hitler Youth, I was coerced into political indoctrination, which was intensified to erase any lingering doubt about blindly serving the Fuhrer and giving life and limb for the Fatherland when called into the Wehrmacht. But by the time I had to report for duty in early September 1944, the service in the RAD had been reduced to three months. This allowed for a faster turnover of replacements for the increasing number of soldiers being lost on all the fronts.

My RAD unit, which numbered about one hundred and twenty members, was located in a huge *Kaserne* (permanent military barracks) complex just outside the city of Hannover. These red brick barracks were sometimes three and four stories high. This garrison had just previously housed an infantry division that had been shipped out to the front. Was I next? I kept wondering. When I spotted a contingent of women Luftwaffe auxiliary trainees in their impressive military uniforms march by, those worrisome thoughts left my mind. My excitement soon evaporated, however, when I learned the women were being housed two long blocks from us RAD boys. We were given strict orders by our commander not to visit or fraternize with them, so I rarely saw them.

For the first week we were drilled in strict military fashion, shouldering a sparkling polished spade on the deserted parade grounds. Then followed instructions on how to properly use a shovel, spade and a pickax like "One, two, three, left, right, down, up."

After we mastered our formations and tools, we marched out to an area of wetlands just outside of the *Kaserne* for our first job assignment.

"Over there notice the number of foxholes and bomb shelters," my commander shouted. Of course I had a glimpse already and hoped they were not meant for us. "These have been dug by previous RAD units. You all should thank them for this," he continued. "Daylight air raids can happen fast, when your backs are turned and you're hunched over."

There was a drainage ditch that ran out through the high grassy field. It was our job to dig out the overgrowth so the water could drain better. I kept thinking, finally I will be out of harm's way, and doing a good service for Germany's army. And, indeed, a few quiet days passed without incident. Then, one chilly day after we had been digging for several hours, I happened to remember Fritz's words, "Herman, don't paint the devil in the sky," when, to my surprise, a hand operated air raid siren went off.

"What the heck is going on?" I asked my RAD buddy next to me. It was not the usual and familiar sound of an air raid siren. I looked around and discovered it had come from an anti-aircraft battery just to our right. Because of the tall grass, I hadn't noticed the installation.

"Over there, the gun barrels pointing in the sky," I exclaimed. What they are protecting? There's no factory or airfield for miles around, I wondered to myself. With little amount of anti-aircraft experience, I surmised the battery must be located on a frequently used approach route by U.S. bombers to attack targets in the city of Hannover. It also took the bombers right over our *Kasernes*! I started to worry.

Suddenly my theory proved correct. After all, it was a fine sunny day for an air raid. Just when we had marched out to the wetlands to dig I heard that all too proverbial noise of the heavy U.S. bombers approaching from the direction of our *Kaserne* behind us. By then the battery had opened fire.

"Hit the deck!" shouted my leader. Hadn't I heard that before? Instinctively, I ran as fast as I could and jumped into a one-man foxhole, putting on my steel helmet, pulling the chinstrap tight, and crouching down with my head between my trembling knees. I grabbed the thick dirt-straw cover that lay next to my hole and brought it down with all my might on top of my hole. I could hear the first bombs explode in the area of our *Kaserne* buildings. I took a peek through a small opening between the straws in time to see the explosives come rushing toward us. I already knew how fast a carpet bomb travels but before I could figure out where it would land a loud and violent explosion ripped the air. Despite the chinstrap, the suction of the blast lifted my helmet, almost tearing my head off!

I waited for the last clumps of dirt to rain down on top of the cover of my foxhole and listened for more explosions. There weren't any. So I pushed the cover aside, crawled out of my foxhole, and stared unbelievingly into a deep crater filled with smoke from where a five hundred pound bomb had exploded. It was so close to me; I couldn't believe how lucky I'd been. Still shaking and with my ears ringing, I looked for my comrades. Amazingly, they were all okay, just a little stunned. I could see my foxhole had been the closest to the carpet bomb.

"Get into formation and march back to the *Kasernes,* quickly," ordered my leader. We knew it had been hit. When we got there I saw that my building had suffered only a few broken windows and red clay roof tiles. Then I heard the news. The building where the Luftwaffe women were housed had been hit and there were a few casualties. In my mind I visualized this beautiful young woman lying on the ground, bleeding and sobbing. Only men are supposed to be wounded and perhaps die like that, I thought. Why was my barrack spared? With sadness I went about my task of cleaning up the debris in and around our building. We were not allowed to go and help the injured women. It would be bad for morale, our commanders said.

All us RAD men were seventeen and a few had just finished apprenticeships in the building trades, like carpenter and roofers. They would come in handy when the construction material arrives. But since we had to wait for window glass and red roof tiles to arrive before we could replace the broken ones, the next day we marched again out to our digging job in the wetlands.

This September day was a beauty, partly sunny with only a few clouds. My comrades and I, digging away in the ditch, were dripping with sweat when all of a sudden we heard the high pitched scream of aircraft engines. I looked up and saw in disbelief four enemy aircraft emerge from the white clouds and go into a straight dive toward my anti-aircraft battery. One after the other the pilots on the swarming P-38s opened fire from their four mounted machine guns and four canons. Boom, boom, boom, they came, in fast succession. No noise was coming from our guns. I was in shock.

"We're taken by surprise!" I screamed. Not one shot was being fired back. Our foxholes were too far away so all we could do was lie flat on the grass and witnesses the horror unfolding about four hundred yards from us. Dust and smoke started to plume upward from the location of our battery guns--and still, no response.

I saw the war planes circling what looked like a second strafing pass. None of us were speaking, motionless from shock and fear. I realized that all the guns must be so damaged as to be inoperable. The ammunition was probably stored deep inside the parapets, as there had been no explosions--even after the last vicious strafe attack. Soon the planes left. The American P38s known as "Lightnings" were the fearsome twin-engine twin-fuselages fighter bombers.

When the air cleared, my troop leader sternly said, "Stay put and continue to work. We cannot assist them. They have their own Luftwaffe personnel to take care of any casualties." I never found out about casualties among the gunners, and the battery never fired another shot during the remaining six weeks I stayed in the Kaserne. I wondered if any high school kids were among the gun crews as flak helpers, like I was. The anti-aircraft battery, only a mile away, had been decimated.

Replacing the glass in the broken window and the red clay tiles on the roof proved a welcome respite from the drudgery of muck digging out in the open. Especially since the Luftwaffe women were now housed in the undamaged building closer to ours. At times I could see them marching and hear them singing; their sweet melodious voices, like angels, sent my heartbeat racing. But we boys were constantly reminded of the strict rule: NO FRATERNIZATION!

One day, after a night time bombing raid on the city of Hannover, gathered on a green grassy area of a park waiting for lunch to arrive, my RAD unit was called upon to help remove the rubble from damaged residential buildings. We were told to look for any victims still trapped under caved in walls and ceilings. Luckily we didn't find any.

Just before noon our *Gulash* cannon arrived, smoke swirling out of the stovepipe and wisps of steam curling from under the edge of the kettle lid. Some one hundred and fifty years ago a unique "field kitchen" was built for the German Army to cook their soldiers' one hot meal per day. It consisted of a cast iron kettle that could hold between two hundred and three hundred servings. Underneath the kettle was a firebox with a five foot tall stovepipe. All of this was mounted on a single axle with two shells and a hitch for towing, originally by a team of horses, now, of course, by a vehicle. Because of the prominent stovepipe this contraption was nicknamed the "*Gulaschkanone*" (Gulash cannon).

It's customary for Germans to have a cooked dinner at noon for their main meal of the day, whether you are at home, at work in an office, business or factory. I lined up behind my RAD buddies, my mess kit in hand, ready to receive a generous portion of the delicious smelling pea soup with plenty of chunks of smoked bacon floating in it. It smelled like my parents warm living room at dinner time. I was starved.

"Mmm, does that taste good," I said to no one in particular. As I ate my soup I observed nearby a group of school children laughing and running home for dinner. The grownups walking them home, mostly women and elderly persons, had with their heads down, their faces grim. They had just survived another bombing raid and perhaps,

I thought, had lost a loved one or their home. The air still smelled of burnt smoldering wood and other materials, like after a house fire. The scene saddened me. I hadn't been in a city for months. I wondered if my father's factory had survived another air raid and how my mother, brother and sister were managing. Yet not for one moment did anything shake my belief that our Fuhrer, Adolf Hitler, would lead us and Germany to victory. That was what was being hammered into us by our RAD political leader at every weekly session. It was our duty to sacrifice our lives for the Fuhrer and the Fatherland.

After a day's hard work of cleanup in the city, we were trucked back to our quarters in the Kaserne. I barely made it through supper, cleaning the equipment and then my boots before I plopped dead tired onto my bunk and fell into a deep sleep.

A few weeks later our entire RAD company was transported to the town of Seesen at the western edge of the Harz Mountains about 40 miles southwest of Braunschweig. From a façade of emerald-like forested hills accentuated by the mountains in the background, I thought it to be one of the most beautiful areas I'd seen so far. I enjoyed the rare peace and quiet of the quaint town of Seesen. So far it was untouched by any allied air raids.

Our job was to erect several barracks for a camp to house refugees from the first German territories now occupied by the Russian Army. Shouldn't that have told me how the war going for Hitler and Germany? No. Even though the Volkswagen factory had been bombed, destroying the area where parts for the secret weapon, the V1 rocket, were made, I held steadfast to the belief we would gain back all the lost territory and with the help of those secret weapons still to come, Germany in the end would be victorious.

It was November and winter was fast approaching with the days becoming shorter. For weeks, cold rains were making work miserable for us young RAD men. Once the cold got into our barracks it seemed we never warmed up, our hands and feet constantly tingling or numb from the cold. It seemed like no daylight in sight for us. Finally, notification came that my time in the RAD was up and I would be sent home to wait for my orders to report for duty as a recruit in the Germany Army. Another new chapter in my life was about to begin.

Chapter 18

A Bittersweet Homecoming

The first days in November 1944 were gloomy and cold when I boarded the train in Seesen at the northwestern foothill of the Harz Mountain for my furlough back home to Wolfsburg. I had just been discharged from the RAD. I was, although briefly, a civilian again.

When I rang our doorbell, my mother, brother and sister greeted me with tears of joy and heartwarming embraces. But I immediately sensed that something was different.

"Where's Vati? I asked.

"Your father had been asked by Dr. Porsche to join him together with his co-worker, Joe Werner, and accompany him to his engineering offices in Austria," she replied.

I knew Joe Werner was one of the first German-American engineering specialists from Ford Motor Company to go to Germany in 1937 to help build the VW factory. Hitler had asked Dr. Porsche, then the director of the Volkswagen factory, to design a new tank that was to be bigger and more powerfully armed than the existing German Tiger *Panzer* (tank). My father and Joe Werner were to assist in the planning and design, my mother had explained. Having been gone for three months, my father's absence put a damper on my homecoming. My mother, brother, sister and I would not see or hear from my father for the next seven months.

Only home a few days, I became antsy not knowing what I would be doing next. So I called a classmate of mine who lived just two blocks from my home.

"Is that you, Hans?" I asked as a familiar voice answered.

"Yes, it is, and this must be Herman."

"Yes!" I replied happily.

After talking a little while we set a date to meet and chew the fat. Hans had also just returned home from serving in the RAD. We were both seventeen but Hans was one class above me. That's why he and his class served in a different anti-aircraft unit as flak helpers then I did.

During our time attending high school together, taking at first the bus and then the commuter train to and from Braunschweig, about fifteen miles each way, we became close friends. Hans was at the top of his class, smart, with a thirst for knowledge, a true intellectual, also a gifted musician. He took violin lessons. Since I craved knowledge, too, and Hans knew more and talked better, I would just listen to him. I remember when we passed a bank on the way to the train station from school. It listed the stock market standings and Hans would explain the workings of it to me. We didn't talk much about girls. Perhaps it was the fact that there was absolutely no contact between boys and girls during school hours. Boys and girls had their own high schools and the buildings were located far enough apart to discourage meetings. Another thing Hans and I had in common was that both our parents were from the northern city of Bremen. We had grandparents, aunts, uncles and cousins living there.

During one vacation time, in the late summer of 1941 when we were fourteen, Hans and I decided to ride our bikes on a one hundred mile tour to visit our relatives in Bremen. The route took us through the picturesque countryside of the North German heath, carpeted with tiny lavender colored flowers that grew in clusters in the sandy soil. Unbeknownst to us, we passed the Bergen-Belsen barrack complex, which shortly afterwards became a concentration camp. We ended up taking the train back home since, after visiting our relatives, it was getting dark. A stronger bond was created between us during that wonderful trip.

As Hans and I were sitting around one day, waiting for our induction papers to arrive and reaffirming our faith that Hitler would still win the war with more "wonder weapons" to come, Hans blurted out, "Herman, I can't wait any longer. I am going to Braunschweig and volunteer for officer candidate school. I would like you to come with me. Maybe you'll join, too!"

As patriotic as I felt, the thought never occurred to me to volunteer. So I replied, "Hans, I'll have to talk with my mother first. But I will accompany you regardless. I'll let you know tomorrow."

My mother was horrified when I told her what Hans had in mind and that he wanted me to join with him.

"Herman, don't you know officers have to lead their men into battle and are the first ones to get killed? We will certainly lose you!" she cried.

"Don't worry, Mother. I am fully aware of that, but I also have a duty to perform as a soldier to fight and sacrifice my life for our Fuhrer and Fatherland," I replied.

My mother fell still after that.

The next day Hans and I entered the orderly room of one of the brick-constructed military *Kasernes* in Braunschweig. We gave the "Heil Hitler" salute, our right arms stiffly outstretched. Hans stated our business to the sergeant sitting at one the desks. He promptly handed us the application forms to fill out.

As we were handing back our completed forms, the sergeant asked, "Who will go first?"

"Hans, you go first. Good luck," I promptly said.

Some time had elapsed when I got up and asked the sergeant, "*Herr Feldwebel* (Mister Sergeant), please, is the test difficult?"

The sergeant answered knowingly and with a stern voice, "Yes. Very hard. You must be one of the smartest, especially in the German language."

After seven years of schooling I never got a better grade than a C in German. In that instant I knew I wouldn't pass the test and I said to the sergeant, "*Herr Feldwebel*, I will think about the test, but I will not take it today."

"Okay, it doesn't' matter," he replied.

He probably noted I was born in the U.S.A from my application and drew his own conclusions.

Many hours later Hans came back into the orderly room with a big smile on his face and proudly announced, "I passed."

Several days later Hans got his marching orders; he reported to an officer's candidate school somewhere in the east, close to the Russian front. I would not see him again until the summer of 1971, while on a vacation trip to Germany.

Now I was left home to brood about what to do while I waited for my call-up orders to arrive. Hans, my young mentor and friend, left me feeling inspired by the patriotic and selfless actions he had taken.

Constant bombardment of "the end victory is ours" speeches and tirades from our propaganda minister, Dr. Joseph Goebbels, and his nationalist socialist party underlings came over our radio and in newspapers telling all able bodied men to join ranks now. With posters and newsreels the military urged us young boys to volunteer our services. I was swept up in this frenzied fervor to follow our Fuhrer, Adolf Hitler. I was willing to "sacrifice life and limb for the Fatherland so that future generations may live peacefully in the 'thousand year Reich' of a new Germany," words constantly drilled into us by the Nazi regime.

On one of my walks through Braunschweig, I passed the recruiting station for the Division Herman Goering. This was *Reichs marschal* Herman Goering's own little army. It was known for its heroic battles and was comprised primarily of volunteers. Their recruiting posters showed grim-faced confident-looking soldiers storming into battle. There were paratroopers, *panzer* crews, *panzer grenadiers* (infantry in armored tracking vehicles) pioneers, artillery, and signal corps.

As a volunteer, I thought, I get to choose my branch of service. Besides, the division's home garrison was located in Berlin and I would receive my basic training there, only about one hundred and sixty miles from home. So I decided to enlist.

I don't remember if I told my mother, but a few days before Christmas I received my orders to report for recruit training on December 28, 1944.

I didn't think about back home in Detroit much anymore, where holidays were about shopping at Hudson's with all the decorations, the bright lights, wreaths, and Christmas carolers. Or the days my mother took me shopping, trudging through the black slush the cars and trucks made in the snow. But this holiday would be different, the first without my father, who had vanished with Dr. Porsche.

"Herman, what does this mean?" Mother asked, surprised as she read my enlistment papers.

"Muttie, I thought I could be close to home since my training is in Berlin."

"It says here you are to report to Rypin," she exclaimed.

Chapter 19

A German Soldier

"He who lies once will not be believed again
even though he speaks the truth."
-- Anon.

To my dismay, my training was not to be in Berlin. I reached

for my high school atlas and found Rypin to be located in northern

Poland in the province called West Prussia, adjacent to the

southwestern border of East Prussia. The town was about eighty-five

miles north and west of Warsaw, or the Russian front. I knew in that

moment I would be fighting the Russians.

Next I planned the approximately three hundred and seventy

mile train trip out. My route would take a day and most of the

following night to reach Rypin. Allowing for delay due to bad winter

weather meant I would have to leave home early in the morning. I was

ordered to take along a suitcase or a sturdy carton in which my civilian

clothes could be shipped back home. My mother found a carton and

fashioned a rope handle to carry it with.

A bittersweet morning dawned with snow falling. I said a tearful goodbye to my mother and little sister Norma.

"Herman, please write when you can. I will be praying for you," my mother said with tears flowing down her cheeks. "I love you."

"Okay, Muttie. I'll write just as soon as I get there." I didn't tell a soul but her that I had enlisted. She saw my papers after all before I could hide them from her.

With my carton strapped on the back of my bike, my brother Ronald, now eleven, and I pushed our bicycles through ankle deep snow to the train station. My mother had sent Ronald to live with and help out at a farmer's house most of the time. As Ronald was at the eligible age for the Jungvolk, she hoped this would keep him from it. So it was brave for my mother to let him come along.

It was an exhausting two mile trek. When we arrived I was told my train would be up to an hour late. By now the wind had picked up, blowing the snow into small drifts, and making the temperature drop. Ronald started to shiver in the biting cold. Because our bikes were loaded with my personals, we could not go into the warm waiting room of the train station.

"Ronald," I said, "you better start back home before you get too cold. Who knows how much longer before the train arrives."

He nodded his head gratefully and, his eyes glistening from the cold with tears, blue as aqua, we said, "*Aufwiederschen*" simultaneously and hugged each other. I watched him trudge and shove our bikes along, disappearing into the blowing snow. Later my brother told me how he cried all the way home, he felt so guilty for not staying until I boarded the train. He was old enough to realize that I may not survive the war.

My train took me through bomb ravaged Berlin, yet the sight of destruction proved nothing to me; I still believed that the Germans would be victorious. We traversed on to Posen and Thorn in Poland. There I had to switch to a narrow gauge railroad for my final stop in Rypin, about an hour away. Thorn was a midsize town and an important railroad junction, with trains running north into East Prussia, southwest to Posen and Germany, and southeast to Warsaw where the Russians were, on the other side of the Vistula.

It was late at night when I arrived in Thorn; I was tired and hungry. During the last eighteen hours I had eaten all the sandwiches my mother had made and had munched on my last apple. The little food counter in the station's waiting room had closed for the night so I couldn't buy any food or anything hot to drink. The room was dimly lit and the coal-fired pot-bellied furnace barely kept us few passengers warm. It would be a long night, about six hours until my train was scheduled to arrive. I was afraid I would fall asleep and miss it.

"Excuse me, please," I asked the lone station attendant, "could you wake me if I fall asleep?"

He stared down at me and answered, "I'm too busy, but the departure announcement over the PA system will be loud enough and it will wake you up." He walked quickly away and I was alone listening for the next train.

It was a restless night. I kept waking up to the frequent, forlorn sound of a locomotive whistle that foretold an approaching train, which would then thunder pass the station with one last blast of its shrill whistle. I had time to observe trains going west were mainly occupied by German soldiers who were on leave, sick or wounded, and war materials in need of repair. The trains going east to the front were loaded with soldiers back from leave and replacements, provisions and new military equipment. The raunchy smell of burning coal and the steam from the locomotives made me almost gag after a while.

Short and timid whistle blows would be followed by the clang of freight cars being shunted into the railroad yard. As I watched and heard all this activity, it reassured my feeling that our military was in order and ready for the last onslaught to victory.

Finally I boarded the first train out to Rypin. When we arrived, it was still early in the morning and pitch dark. No way would I be able to find the way to the military camp. So I entered a church and luckily found the priest awake in his office. I told him I needed to report by ten in the morning and asked if he could show me the way.

He carefully looked me over. "Why, young man, no need to rush," he said. "You have plenty of time to catch some sleep. Lie down on one of the pews," he instructed and motioned me over to the nearest bench. He gave me a blanket.

"*Danke*," I said gratefully, as I'd had no sleep for the last twenty-four hours. I could get some rest and still be at the camp early enough to get breakfast and a hot cup of coffee.

The next morning the kind priest gave me directions and shortly afterward I stood at the camp gate in front of a sign that read: *Fallschirm Ersatz & Au.S.Bildungs Brigade Division Hermann Goering, Rypin/Westpruessen (*Parachute Replacement and Training Brigade of the Division Hermann Goering). I was startled. Are they going to make a paratrooper out of me?

I managed to get coffee and a piece of bread and butter for breakfast before I was sent to the quartermaster to receive my uniform, boots and all the equipment a soldier needs. My civilian clothes went into the carton my mother had tied the rope handle to, which made it twice as heavy.

Late that afternoon I was called into formation together with about one hundred thirty other recruits.

"Now you will be marching to a village about three miles away. Take all your belongings with you. All of you will be housed and trained there," commanded my new officer.

Just like that we started our march. It didn't take long before I realized how agonizing it would be for me, carrying my heavy carton of clothes while trudging through ankle deep snow. I moved it from one hand to the other; hoisted it on my shoulders; cradled it in my arms: I tried everything. Sweat was running down my back in spite of the cold. Because of the brand new lace-less ankle high boots, my feet started to ache. I was gradually falling behind. Nobody could help me. Everybody was struggling. I cursed that damned carton and wanted to abandon it. But my mother had so lovingly packed it with extra sets of underwear and socks; I just gritted my teeth and went on.

Night fell. After a long while I could hear the barking of large dogs, German Shepherds maybe from the deep, low sounds, in the pitched dark night. Someone had to house those dogs; perhaps we were near our destination. Exhausted by now I said, "The heck with it" out loud and I took the chance of dragging my carton the last few hundred yards through the heavy snow, praying that it would hold together. It did.

When I reached the others, twenty other men and I, from ages nineteen to forty, were immediately assigned to what were called huts.

These huts had two rows of wooden shelves seven feet deep and covered with a thick layer of straw. There we were shown to sleep one man head up, the next head down, so we wouldn't blow germs in each other's face. I didn't dare wear the pajamas my mother had packed. This was no four-star hotel.

This village had been used to train recruits before. The huts were made of logs cut in half with the rounded portions layered on the outside. The small window had shutters for protection against the bitter cold winds. We had to store our civilian clothes up in the attic. My hut included two or three officers, one of whom was my company commander (CO), and cadres of non-commissioned officers (NCO's). Sleep came instantly to me and the others.

Roll call was at six A.M. it was New Year's Day, January 1, 1945. Our training began with a close-order drill and then digging into snowdrifts, three to five feet high, for concealment. We had no weapons to train with except a few Danish World War I rifles.

"Your weapons are on the way," we were told. So we trained and stood guard with what we had, without ammunition and without firing a single practice shot.

The only villagers remaining in Rypin, our base camp, were mothers with young children, old women and old men. We had heard from our superiors that all able-bodied men and women had been sent away as forced laborers for the war.

Under these primitive and dismal conditions I began to think more about my family and Wolfsburg, stopping short of being homesick. My stoical belief that all would turn out well for Germany helped me to quickly adjust to the routine: I carried out everything I was asked to do to the best of my ability. Only once was I chewed out by my commander.

"*Actung*, Herman! This hole you dug is only big enough for a miniature hound. Do you want to get killed?" my command officer screamed. I had to dig into a snow bank but I didn't dare tell him I had a fear of being confined.

After my company and I had been in training a little over a week, I was ordered to report to the CO in his upscale hut. When I entered I marveled at how cozily and warm the "great" room was furnished.

"What a comfortable, large room you have with all these nice furniture pieces," I couldn't help remarking. Then I smartly saluted the lieutenant. He saluted back.

"Sit down there," he commanded.

He motioned for me to sit in a chair across from him

"So, I would like to know a little about you, Herman. How old are you?"

"I'm seventeen, sir."

"And where are you from?"

I dared not tell him I was born in the U.S.A and he didn't ask. So I simply said, "I live with my family in the new city KdF Stadt and I am a high school student. I first became a flak helper and I just finished my time in the RAD." I felt my stomach turn and the palms of my hands sweat.

"Okay, you are dismissed."

I left wondering what that was all about. Was my CO satisfied?

Our training continued routinely. Then suddenly one night we were jerked out of our sleep by the wailing sound of the camp's hand cranked siren. It was an alarm. But what about, I wondered? Shortly after the siren stopped our sergeant came rushing to us.

"The Russians have attacked. Be ready to march fully equipped in one hour!" he shouted.

Two weeks later, on the 14th of January 1945, we were commandeered into the woods for training a few miles away in below freezing temperatures. We recruits rolled up our blankets and strapped them to our backpacks with three leather straps for our trek back. Wearing our heavy, long wool greatcoats for warmth, we slogged through ice and snow and dreaded the march back to the base camp in Rypin. I wondered what was going to happen to my everyday clothes stored up in the attic there.

At base camp we ate our breakfast and then got our provisions and filled our canteens with hot coffee. Two more companies of recruits had arrived, making up a battalion of about four hundred troops. We still had no weapons other than a few ancient Danish rifles and little ammunition for them.

Shortly before we continued our march to the front my CO came over to me.

"Herman, you come with me and make it fast," he said.

He took me to the battalion commander and introduced me as his company runner. Together with the runners of the other two companies, I was attached to battalion headquarters. I still didn't know why I had been interviewed. I dared not ask why and my commanders were kept silent about it.

By nightfall we three runners, exhausted and tired, found ourselves huddled in a dark cellar at battalion headquarters. The sound of artillery fire had become stronger and there was a faint reddish glow hugging the horizon. Frightening rumors were going around that the new, raw German recruits would be rushing into the arms of Russian soldiers, thinking they were their own.

"Do you think this is true? How will we know what a Russian looks like?" asked one of the runners. We stared into each other's eyes and did not speak another word. The night soon became quiet and I fell into a deep sleep.

The next morning we runners marched ahead of the companies and continued towards the front lines while artillery fire resumed, ominously close. I was jarred out of my thoughts by a sudden command to get the soldiers into column and change direction.

"*Halt*! About face! Forward, march!"

The battalion staff and I stepped aside to let the three recruit companies pass. Then we three runners were told to go join our outfits. My duty as a runner was over.

The reason for this "about face" was an order that had come through from General Field Marshal Heinz Guderian, the famous "Panzer General" and Commander of the Central Eastern front, where we were.

"I will not sacrifice these young men as cannon fodder. They are all to march back to their garrison in Berlin!" yelled the General to my CO after he had just learned that the SS *Reichsfuhrer* Himmler, the commander of the entire Eastern Front, had ordered us recruits into battle without any weapons.

A big sigh of relief came over all of us. And perhaps for the first time I asked myself, will we win the race against the Russians?

My unit still had to cross the biggest river in Poland, the Vistula, which flowed into the Baltic Sea at Danzig, which was located just west of East Prussia. We were told that the only railroad and heavy vehicle bridge left standing by the previous German soldiers was in the large city of Grandenz, about fifty miles from our present position. That would be our immediate goal.

After we marched all day, and with darkness approaching, we passed through a small village and entered a wooded area. There at the edge of a ditch on the right side of the road I noticed two soldiers digging a foxhole. About half a mile through the woods was a house; my squad was assigned to stay there for the night.

I had just made myself comfortable and was ready to fall asleep when my sergeant nudged me and ordered me to report to our CO.

"Recruit Esfeld, I want you to find the two soldiers I left as outposts back at the road and tell them they are to leave and rejoin the company. Here is my written order. Take the shortest way through the woods until you reach the open field, then turn left to the road. Here, take this rifle just in case. That is all."

I repeated my order and saluted the lieutenant. He stiffly walked away and left me wondering why I was selected for this task.

My sergeant then told me to leave my aluminum mess kit, canteen and gas mask, stored in a cylindrical metal container, at the house.

"The sound of them clanging together might give you away," he warned.

It was a bitter cold night with a thin line of a half-moon etched through an overcast sky. The snow in the woods was deep and came over the top of my ankle boots. Soon my socks were soaking wet from trudging along as I consciously carved a visible path for my return trip. When I reached the path at the edge of the woods I could see ahead an open piece of land that stretched about five hundred yards toward the village we had previously passed through. I made a marker with some branches to show the spot where I needed to turn back into the woods. I then turned left and followed along the edge of the woods towards the road, where I expected to find the two men at the outpost.

Suddenly the sound of dogs barking from the village froze me in my tracks. Then I heard what sounded like goulashes crunching through the ice. Stiffened with fear that I had been discovered, I crouched down low and waited, trying to quiet my heavy breathing.

No lights went on in any of the houses and I didn't see any Russian soldiers. I crawled another hundred yards to the road to see if I could spot my comrades. They were nowhere to be seen! I came across a foxhole they had left behind so I jumped in, shivering with fear and the bitter cold. After a minute or two more of listening to the dogs barking and someone slogging on ice, I had to look and see what or who I needed to hide or run from. Holding my breath, I slowly looked up and saw a short, hefty woman holding something in her hand. Somewhat relieved I continued to watch her as she approached the area near the dogs.

As their barking grew louder and more persistent, I watched her shadow-like figure disappear. The dogs hushed. I hoped she was feeding those hounds. It was now or never!

Crouched low, careful not to step on any tree branches or make any sound that would alert others as to my presence, and knowing and feeling good that nobody from the village had seen me, I began to run back to my commander's housing.

When I got there I reported what had happened to my sergeant. I told him that nobody from the small village had seen me. I had barely gotten off my boots and wet socks when my sergeant told me that earlier that day another company leader had found the two men dead just a hundred yards from the foxhole I'd dived into.

Shocked, relieved, exhausted and distraught, I promptly fell asleep.

Chapter 20

The Wolf

The next morning we left the house and continued our march through the woods until nightfall when we stopped in a village where we found refuge in a hut that was already filled with a group of frightened village people. I had not been able to get my two pairs of socks dry so I decided to wear the foot cloths issued to us by the quartermaster. They were square pieces of cotton that had to be wrapped around the foot in a very precise way. I was beginning to develop blisters on my feet, which caused excruciating pain with every step. I felt like I was riding bare ass on top of an agitated porcupine. Also, personal hygiene was next to impossible to keep up. My suffering lasted a few days until we reached Grandenz, where I could wash with soap.

On our forced marched we met more and more groups of fleeing German civilians pushing horse-drawn wagons piled high with household goods and personal belongings.

At one point we heard shouting coming from a large farm we were passing.

"*Nein*! You cannot take away our food and clothes. Those belong to us. Please, we will starve. I beg you not to take the only salvation we have left. We will die of hunger!" screamed a German woman as she struggled to tug her cart away from a few German soldiers.

"It is better to give it to us than the Russians!" shouted back the German soldiers as they took the carts loaded with livestock and food and left the women standing alone. Other soldiers were rounding up pigs and letting cows out of their stalls to roam free into the fields. My comrades and I could not believe what was happening. The German soldiers' remarks let us know that the Russians were near and were commandeering supplies from our people.

As we preceded through the village our CO, caught up in this frenzy, commanded, "Take any horse-drawn wagon or cart."

Our sergeant caught sight of a horse sled loaded with a huge glass jar of honey, crates with live chickens and a goose, and other foodstuffs. "Recruits Esfeld and Meyer, you two take that sled," he hollered to us.

"*Nein, nein*! This is mine. You cannot take my sled!" protested the farmer vigorously.

We climbed on the seat. I had to shout to Meyer to drown out the farmer's screams, "Do you know how to drive this thing?"

"No." he said. "You take the reins".

From my early days in the Jungvolk and in high school on farms I remembered a little bit of handling a horse. I gave a command, "Yah!" and slapped the reins a little bit on the rump of the horse and off we went, the farmer cursing and shaking his fists behind us.

Our column snaked its way over a snow-covered field through open country with the battalion commander leading. Soon night fell. It was bitter cold in pitch black dark, only the snorting of the horse breaking the silence once in a while. Suddenly to the left of us we heard the sound of engines idling and voices. My commander immediately realized they were Russian T34 tanks. We heard their tank commanders shouting instructions at each other in Russian. Our CO quickly gave us an order to take full cover on the field to the right of us.

Not wanting to leave our horse sled with its precious cargo behind, I decided to take it through a ditch and up a slope to the field.

"Hold on tight, Meyer. Here we go!" With a few hard hits on its rump, the horse pulled us over the ditch and started up the slope where the sled promptly tipped over. All hell broke loose. Panicked, Meyer and I jumped off the seat just in time. The horse neighed loudly and struggled to get up. The chickens and goose, freed from their broken cages, made a terrible ruckus and scattered in all directions.

"Meyer, let's get this horse out of its harness and unhitch it from the till," I whispered intensely, determined not to give away our position. But that was easier said than done. The horse neighed and kicked. Meyer and I fumbled around, cursed and tried to avoid the horse's kicks. Our sergeant appeared and took charge. He knew what to do as we watched him free the horse and let it run off into the field. Luckily it was not injured. The three of us got down on our stomachs, hugging the snow-covered ground. We expected the searchlights from the Russian tanks to light up any second.

Through clenched teeth the sergeant hissed at me, "Recruit Esfeld, you *dummkopf*! How stupid of you to lead the horse diagonally up the slope. Just pray the Russian tankers didn't hear you, otherwise their tank tracks, 75mm cannons and heavy machine gunfire will make us into mincemeat!"

"Yes, Sergeant," I mumbled, feeling he was not taking in to account I was only seventeen.

Listening intently in the direction of the Russian tanks, we heard nothing except for the running of the tank engines and the loud shouting of the tank commanders among each other. After what seemed like eternity lying in that open field, holding our breath and listening, the Russians stopped talking. We heard the turret lids clank shut and, with a roar, the tanks rattled off, luckily away from us. All was still except for the faint sound of artillery fire to our right. Our battalion was nearly encircled. Soon we were ordered back onto the field path and resumed our march, leaving the sled with what remained of its precious cargo behind.

Shortly after, heading slowly toward the head of our column from the left was a truck. Immediately upon hearing the sound it was making I knew it was American made. It was exactly how the gears of the rear axle differential sounded on the trucks made back home at Ford Motor Company in Detroit. As a nine year old in the big city of Detroit I watched scores of them traveling the city streets. A slight touch of nostalgia brushed my heart, but I didn't have time to reminisce any further because my column was ordered to halt and crouch down low.

I watched as my battalion commander bent down and slowly approach the truck, which was bumping along a rough patch of road without its lights on. The driver must have been concentrating on keeping the truck under control because he seemed oblivious to the dark figure rising in front of him. I hunched there spellbound as I saw the major rise and fire the *Panzerfaust* (a hand-held hollow charged anti-tank weapon). With perfect aim the missile struck the cabin of the truck. There was an ear-splitting noise and the entire vehicle exploded into a ball of flame. Tons of black smoke billowed upward from the skeletal remains of the truck. It must have been loaded with diesel fuel destined for those tankers. I saw for the first time the devastating effects of a hit by a *Panzerfaustk*.

The major rushed back and shouted to our column, "Continue to march in double time!" He wanted us to get away as quickly as possible from that telltale sign of smoke and flame flickering in the night sky.

By now my wet foot cloths were bunched up in my boots, increasing the pain from rubbing against my raw flesh where the blisters had been. Between my feet and the "wolf," a nickname the German soldiers gave to a condition where hairs around the anus would freeze and dig into flesh like fish hooks, my walk turned into a limp. I was in sheer agony. But I gritted my teeth and kept up with the column.

What seemed like an endless night had turned into a glorious morning, with the snow-covered landscaped glistening in the bright sunshine. We had narrowly escaped encirclement by Russian T34 tanks and we were approaching a farm still some distance away when my major ordered us to halt and take a break. He called the three company commanders and their aids together for a meeting.

The beautiful clear skies had brought out what all of us feared: Russian fighter bombers--and in large numbers.

One, two, twenty, thirty, I counted to myself looking up into the sky and wondering how many aircraft this time. I could hear them in the far distance strafing anything that moved on the ground.

The CO meeting ended quickly. "We are going to split up into three companies and each company will strike out on its own to find cover and rest during the daylight hours. *Mach schnell!*"

Like trained ants, we scurried off into the three columns as instructed, the battalion CO and his staff electing to stay with my company.

"Young men, head for that farmhouse now!"

We trotted toward the farmhouse, hoping to reach it before the Russian fighter bombers discovered us. Fear taking over, I forgot about the pain in my feet and my ass. I just ran. We all did. Out of breath and completely exhausted, I collapsed inside the farmhouse. We had made it. Within seconds, I'd fallen fast asleep.

I woke up a short time later to hear instructions from my CO about detailing and forming guard duty. Shoot, was I going to have to do guard duty when I was so tired? Luckily I was not the first shift. I fell back asleep.

The farmhouse was spacious, cold and smelled of rot. The owners had fled and had taken most of the food and livestock with them. We hadn't had much to eat the last couple of days and found little food for ourselves here. We were not allowed to make a fire. So no let up from the biting cold and frost bite settled in fast. The farmhouse was located out in an open field, surrounded halfway by a dense forest three hundred yards away. A walking path led out of the woods directly to the farmhouse.

I awoke in the afternoon of the next day to the noise of a heavy engine and the clanking sounds of a tracked vehicle. I looked at my comrades and commander and we all froze. It was coming from the woods. Was it friend or foe? Was it a tank? We had no anti-tank weapons because the major used the only *Panzerfoust* we had to knock out the truck yesterday. My legs started to shake. Is this the end for us? The officers with binoculars kept peering to the spot where the path led out of the woods. Then the object appeared and stopped abruptly at the edge of the woods.

"Our German MK IV!" my CO shouted with relief.

It was a lone German tank with 75mm long barreled cannons pointed straight at our farmhouse. I figured the tanker's commander was probably watching for any sign of friendly life before proceeding. That very instant our major exposed himself to the tank and waved it on. It seemed to take forever to rumble up the slight hill, its commander standing erect in the cupola of the turret. I glimpsed up at the sky to see if any lingering Russian planes were near. The tank commander had his driver park the tank inside the barn a few hundred yards away, completely concealing it from the sky. We all let out a big sigh.

"Another close call," I mumbled to myself, sweat oozing on my forehead despite the cold.

My sergeant had become aware of my bloody feet when I asked for some bandages and disinfectant before we proceeded. One look at them and he said, "Recruit Esfeld, you have what we call trench foot and it will get worse if not treated properly. I will see what I can do for you to get a ride on the tank when we continue our night march."

Soon we caught up to another a tank going our way. A few other impaired fellow recruits clambered with me onto the back of the tank where the heavenly heated air came up from the engine below. For the first time in days I felt warm. I was so thankful to my sergeant for giving me this respite. The night soon turned bitter cold again and dark with the wind blowing snow into high drifts. Then the tank had to turn off and rejoin its old outfit. My free ride ended.

I tried to keep up as best as I could but I was still limping. I cursed the "wolf."

Columns of motorized German troops were passing us now. Then I recognized the VW *Kubelwagen* (Germany's military jeep) roll by. My father had described it to me when I was home on a short furloug.

I should be sitting in there, I muttered to myself with sarcasm. My father helped build the factory that is now producing the *Kubelwagen* you officers are riding in. I felt my feet swell, aching, and myself angry while I spat at the hard ground.

Eventually my company reached a main road where we were joined by hundreds of fleeing refugees as well as some injured German military soldiers. The all wanted to reach the city of Grandez to cross the last remaining intact bridge over the wide river Vistula before German engineers blew it up. As a military bake shop truck slowly passed us I noticed a long handlebar at the rear. I hobbled to my sergeant and asked, "Sergeant, I would like your permission to ride on the back of that bakery truck."

"Show me how you want to do that," he replied sternly.

I jumped up on the narrow bumper and slung both my arms through the handlebar and crossed them over in a tight grip.

"Alright," he said in a matter of fact way. "You ride along until we reach the outskirts of the city. Then I will take you off. The truck is moving along slow enough that I can keep up."

"Thank you, Sergeant."

Somehow, even slung over the handlebar of the truck, I managed to doze off a couple of times before we arrived at Grandenz in the middle of the night.

Accommodations in Grandenz weren't any better than the farmhouse. The MP's directed my company to a *Kaserin* where we were assigned to a building with rows of empty horse stables.

Exhausted and dead tired, my comrades and I sank down on the straw covered floors. I had something else to do first. I found a pail of water with soap and tried to tame that awful and painful wolf.

At the crack of dawn, right after a welcome hot cup of coffee, my company headed for the bridge. As soon as we got there we climbed aboard military trucks and slowly drove over the bridge, safely reaching the other side. Once again we all breathed freer. The sky had been too cloudy for the Russian fighter bombers to try and destroy the bridge. Fritz had warned me about painting the devil in the sky when we were anti-aircraft gunners together but I couldn't help but notice the weather anyway.

My company had had to dismount from the trucks for they were taking a different route. We had sixty miles to march to reach the German border. By now I limped so badly I could barely keep up with my column. In the early dawn we finally reached a small town where we discovered a creamery. We took a break and filled our stomachs and provision satchels with a firm white cheese that tasted delicious to us barrelful of hungry youngsters. It was during this brief rest when the sergeant walked up to me.

"Recruit Esfeld, take off your boots. I want to look at your feet," he said.

He shook his head when he saw them. "Recruit Esfeld, you now have advanced frostbite and may lose your toes. You cannot keep up with the company much longer and you will have to stay behind. That means the Russians will take you prisoner. I will report this to the lieutenant and see what he can do."

His stricken tone frightened me. I waited nervously for the sergeant to come back with bad news. But he returned with a smile on his face.

"Recruit Esfeld, the lieutenant just found out that the last train out of enemy encircled East Prussia is on its way to Germany and will stop here to take on a group of wounded soldiers. He got permission to include you and three other sick and walking impaired comrades."

Suddenly I had visions of lying on white sheets in a comfortable hospital with pretty nurses fussing around me.

"An NCO (non-commissioned officer) will be assigned to the four of you with written orders to lead you to the garrison Kasernes of the Division of Herman Goering in Berlin," he added.

As the train pulled into the station our group of four wounded and hurt managed to squeeze into a freight car already filled with refugee women, children and elderly men. The stench of urine and other bodily odors was overpowering. There was a bucket near the sliding door in which to relieve oneself. Two six-by-one inch openings on either side of the car were for light and fresh air. A wood burning stove in the center of the car gave us some warmth. By evening the train reached Frankfort, through which passed the peaceful river Oder. There we had to catch a passenger train for the last fifty miles to Berlin. Our NCO steered us to a Red Cross kitchen where we got a bowl of hot soup. A few times our NCO had to show our marching orders to the MPs. They were checking for the soldiers that got separated from their outfits--or deserters.

The coaches of the train were overcrowded, with people sitting on the floor and in the aisles. Most of them were German civilians trying to flee as far as they could from the approaching Russians. I wondered if my parents were doing the same as I huddled next to strangers. In the middle of the night, dead tired, my NCO managed to drop us off at the garrisons' headquarters of Herman Goering.

My three comrades and I were sent to the infirmary, a make-shift hospital or sick bay. We were given first aid. It was the first week in February 1945. I had been away from home since Christmas and only now was I able to write my mother:

"Dear Muttie,

I've been sent to Berlin to be treated for frostbite on my feet. But otherwise I am okay. I am grateful for my sergeant and lieutenant for getting me on the last train out of East Prussia and thus avoiding being made a prisoner of war by the Russians. I saw thousands of soldiers and civilians fleeing from the Russians. I hope you, Vati, Ronald and Norma are okay.

I love you all. See you real soon.

Herman

I did not know that rumors would soon spread to Wolfsburg about the Russians coming and taking Germans as prisoners.

Just then the sound of an air raid attack by the British air force launched me and my comrades into the air raid shelters of the *Kaserne.* These attacks continued nightly. Looking at the shocked and distressed looks on the fleeing soldiers and civilians while we took cover, I wondered, where are the Fuhrer's promised secret weapons?

During my healing process at the *Kaserne* I was excused from marching, order drills, and KP (kitchen duty). This somehow irked my top sergeant, who thought I was feigning the pain. "Recruit Esfeld," he said sarcastically, "why don't you do drills with the rest?" He was clearly hinting that I was a slacker. Was this a ploy of his?

One day at chow there was a stirring in the ranks. A group of recruits from my original company had made it back. As I approached a few of them I couldn't help but notice the exhaustion and the agonizing experience of their forced marches imprinted on their faces. I dared to ask, "How was it? Are there more of you coming back?"

"*Schrecklich* (terrible)," they answered with just a slight shaking of their heads.

Feeling somewhat ashamed about having left my company, I turned away before finding out what happened to the lieutenant and my sergeant.

After about eight days of recovery in the *Kasernes* the infirmary doctor declared me fit to travel. I was ordered to be ready to join my new company by two o'clock A.M. Together with three other new recruits, I climbed aboard a truck that appeared to me to be loaded with army provisions.

Four hours earlier there had been another bombing attack in the next town. The truck drove us through the streets where I saw row after row of six-story apartment buildings burning, the flames shooting from the ground floor all the way up through the roof. It made a roar that sounded louder than a blast from a furnace. For the first time I had witnessed the devastation caused by a new type of incendiary bomb the British started using in 1944. It consisted of a steel canister, about six inches in diameter and twelve inches long, filled with highly compressed gasoline. It would crash through the roof of a building and immediately ignite from a detonator, spewing out burning gasoline onto every floor. It caused all floors to burn simultaneously, trapping anyone that stayed behind.

There was not a soul to be seen in these hellish streets. The fire department merely let the fires burn themselves out. Our truck slowly drove on, avoiding the newly made bomb craters, accelerating only after it neared the countryside. We reached our destination late in the morning and were led to a barn where we were told to bed down on the straw for a short rest.

I sighed with relief as I lay on my back. At last my wolf condition was healed.

Chapter 21

Training as an Infantry Man

"In the name of a spirit brought upon by premature and
inapprehensible death,
In honor of the essence of one's short life,
Any life is worthy of living beyond doubt"
--Edna Esfeld

Before I knew it I was hearing instructions from my CO

detailing and forming guard duty. Shoot, was I to do guard duty after

being so tired? I woke up, realizing it was a dream, but then I heard a

loud voice scream for real: "Up and out, now! You are assigned to a

newly formed battalion called *Wachtbattalion*, a security battalion.

You will be moved into new company quarters within a week. You

will be dispersed around the perimeters of Hermann Goering's

personal *Jagdschloss*."

Such was the greeting we received from a sergeant-major after

we four recruits were led out to the glass enclosed veranda of the

Gasthouse, close to the barn. Herman Goering was known for his extravagances. This was part of his elaborate hunting lodge located about thirty miles north of Berlin.

My duty as a German runner ended with my training as an infantry man thus began.

It was now the 8th of February 1945. After the introduction to my new battalion the sergeant-major left us with another sergeant who had one MG42 (model 42 machinegun) and two Karabiner 98 *Gewehre* (model 98 carbine rifles) brought in and spread out on a tarp. He showed us how to disassemble and assemble the weapons, naming each part and explaining its function. By the end of the day the four of us had become quite proficient. I sure could have used this rifle earlier.

The next day was a repeat of the same demonstration but this time, toward the end, we were blindfolded. I learned that the MG42 was made out of several metal stampings, making it a little lighter to carry than its predecessor, the MG34. Also its rate of fire was twice as fast, about fifteen hundred rounds per minute. But the sergeant warned us that the sustained rate of fire should not exceed more than two hundred rounds per minute, at which point the hot barrel should be exchanged for one that had cooled down. That was accomplished ingeniously and quickly by the gunner with a push of his right palm

against a locking lever: he would grab the spare barrel handed to him

by his assistant gunner, shove it into the breach, and slam the locking

lever shut.

The sergeant went on to explain that the need for a new

machine gun with a faster rate of fire became apparent shortly after the

German invasion of Russia in 1941. As in WWI, the Russian forces,

regardless of casualties, would overwhelm the Germans by

counterattacking in waves of tightly packed infantry soldiers. After

going into action on the Russian Front the new MG42 was quickly

nicknamed "Hitler's Buzz Saw"; it proved highly successful.

Of the four of us recruits, two were already buddies who got to

know each other back at the garrison in Berlin. Therefore I was paired

up with a lanky, six foot tall eighteen year old named Franz. He was

the quiet type, methodical, a fellow who used his head. He was very

likeable and we hit it off from the start.

"Recruit Franz, you will be the machine gunner and Recruit

Esfeld, you will be his assistant machine gunner from here on in," the

sergeant decided since we had both showed that we had the same skill at taking the MG42 apart and putting it back together, and our know-how was better than the two other buddies. So Franz and I worked as a machine gunner team until the end of the war.

The four of us were to move with a newly formed company of recruits who had just started basic training while we were in weapons training. On the day of our departure we had to help in the kitchen to prepare a hot meal before leaving. When the boiled potatoes that cooked in the *Gulashkanone* were done, the cook ordered us to drain the fifty gallon kettle by opening the petcock located on the bottom. Wearing a pair of heavy kitchen gloves, each of us tried to turn the petcock. It wouldn't budge and we didn't have a wrench.

Joseph, being bigger than I, spoke up and said, "I know what to do. Back home I used to siphon the remnants of wine out of the barrels at my dad's bar."

"This isn't cool wine," we retorted. "This is boiling hot water. It's too dangerous.

"Nah, I can do it," Joseph exclaimed, and off he went to seek the innkeeper of the place where we were staying. He came back with a length of the rubber hose similar to that which he used back home.

"But it's too dangerous!" we screamed.

But before we had time to stop him, Joseph stuck the tube into the kettle and took a deep suck. Only a trickle came out the end. Without hesitating, he tried again. This time a stream of boiling hot water gushed out and before he could pull the hose out of his mouth it ran down his throat. Sputtering and screaming in pain the young boy clutched his throat as the three of us stood frozen in shock. Then his buddy grabbed him and ran to the office of our sergeant-major. In the meantime, with an ashen face, our cook grabbed a wrench from his workbench and opened the petcock as if to prevent us from making the same deadly mistake.

It took an ambulance several hours to reach our location and transport Joseph to a hospital. By then it was too late and our comrade died of suffocation. Poor fella. He was the first casualty in our company--without a shot being fired.

Soon my company was transported to a town about ten miles further north, closer to our assignment. We were housed in a large dance hall of a *Gasthof* (hotel). Together with recruits from two other newly formed companies we comprised the security battalion for

Herman Goering, *Reichsmarschall* of the Luftwaffe, and his elaborate hunting lodge.

Despite having to sleep on a straw covered parquet floor, we were given all the amenities of the hotel, such as sufficient toilets, hot showers, and hot meals from the kitchen. Surprisingly there was even an in-house post office. I welcomed the respite. I could write home and deposit my accumulated soldier's pay into a post bank savings account. My battalion was to stay at the hotel only until the barracks being built for each security company were completed. We were to be dispersed in and around Karin Hall. In the meantime our training had begun without weapons.

One morning I awoke furiously scratching my head and body. Embarrassed, I glanced over at Franz; he was doing the same thing.

"Oh my God! Are you itching like I am"? I asked in dismay.

Beside me I could see another comrade scratching, and then another. In fact, everyone, right down the line, was scratching and rubbing and tugging at their scalp and skin. We had head lice.

My battalion commander took immediate action to get us deloused. While we waited for the battalion to be taken to a city called

Oranienburg, just north of Berlin, where the delousing facility was located, we scratched and itched, catching the lice and squashed them with our bare hands. The facility was in a barracks camp that housed forced laborers. Unbeknownst to us, next to it was an early concentration camp established by the Nazis. Of course nothing about it was mentioned to us soldiers at the time. It was after the war ended that I read in the German papers of these concentration camps.

We had to take off all our clothes for delousing. Zyklon-B, also known as hydrocyanic acid (gas) was used on our clothes and ourselves and the wood floors of our barracks. We were huddled naked inside a small chamber during the process, which lasted nearly two hours. Our commanders told us this process had been used for people with typhus and had saved millions of lives. It was tortuous to have to stand amidst the arid and gaseous conditions of a cold chamber. When at last we were able to return to our barracks the old straw had been replaced with fresh straw. It felt and smelled like sleeping on freshly laundered bed sheets like at home.

One day our field training exercises led us to a maze of earthworks consisting of heavily fortified bunkers and emplacements for machine guns. They were all connected to each other via deep trenches that zigzagged for about a mile. The orientation faced east, toward where the Russian troops had dug in near the River Oder after their advance out of Poland. When I realized that the Russians were only, as the crow flies thirty miles from the village of *Friederichswald* where my company would be encamped, a cold shiver ran down my back.

"Franz, do you realize how close the Russians are?" I asked.

"I sure do," he answered. "And within a day after a determined attack they could be right on top of us," he growled.

Right then it occurred to me that our company might be called upon to occupy these earthworks for the defense of Berlin. For the first time a brief feeling of doubt gnawed at my steadfast belief that Germany would win the war. Where were the secret weapons Hitler had promised? Not once did I discuss the war situation with my comrades. Over the years Nazi propaganda had hammered into the minds of the young not to question any orders of the hierarchy. We followed them blindly.

In late February our company moved into new barracks just outside the village of the *Friedrichswalde* and about five miles from Hermann Goering's hunting lodge, where he established his headquarters. He had a company of personal bodyguards to protect him. Our job, along with two other companies, was to protect the perimeter of his headquarters.

Shortly after our arrival we received our weapons. I got a carbine 98 with a bayonet, a knife with a six inch fixed blade for close combat, and a gas mask inside a cylindrical metal container. As an assistant machine gunner I had to carry three full ammunition boxes and two spare machine gun barrels. My aluminum mess kit and canteen were strapped to a canvas pouch for carrying food; this was attached to the back of my belt. Next to it, on my left side, I carried the entrenching tool. That was a lot of equipment for a seventeen- and-a-half-year-old five-foot-six-inch youngster with a small build. To top it off, I carried a rolled up wool blanket slung over one shoulder.

Franz, my machine gunner, was issued a brand new MG42 and a P38 Walther pistol. He also carried one full ammunition box. My comrades and I were now being trained as infantry soldiers. We frequently went on forced marches, fully equipped to toughen us up.

Several times we went to the firing range to practice how to fire our weapons or the grenade range to learn how to throw both the stick grenade and the egg shaped hand grenade. I was taught how to use primer cord to blowup railway tracks and to wrap around trees to fell them across roads as barricades. I was amazed at how clean the exploding primer cord would cut through a tree with a diameter of at least forty-five inches.

After several weeks of intensive training I felt like a veteran, confident to face the enemy on the battlefield. By nightfall, I was too tired to dwell on the worsening situation of the war for Germany. Constant gun fire and explosions nearby didn't faze me. I was now addressed as *Schutze* Esfeld (marksman).

During free time we were allowed to walk into the village of *Friedrichswalde* and I became acquainted with the merchants. I could not buy anything, since everything was rationed and the army issued ration cards only to those who went on furlough. After I had been at the bakery a few times I got to know the lady behind the counter by engaging in some small talk. She was around forty, about the age of my mother. I had been eying a few delicious-looking leftover hard-crusted rolls when she looked at me and said smiling, "Here, you can have this one before I feed it to the pigs. Nobody will know the difference."

"*Danka Schon*," I said, beaming with joy. I quickly left the store. Our company cook didn't bake hard rolls and the only cake I got was sent in packages from home which I shared. Then one day, after our company had returned from training exercises in the field to get ready for the evening meal, a flurry of rumors went through the barracks and got us all excited.

"A stranger tried to steal some bread. There was a shooting and an arrest was made," yelled one of my comrades. I swallowed hard.

Later that day as we were assembled in the mess hall our top sergeant entered the hall.

"At ease," he commanded. He told us what happened in the village that afternoon. "At this very moment," he began, "there is a deserter locked up in the brig located in the headquarters' barracks. I challenged this man, who was dressed in a military winter long-coat, in front of the bakery shop with my pistol drawn on the street. He raised his arms and surrendered meekly without me having to fire a shot. After interrogation by the company commander, our captain found out the man was a soldier who left his post without authorization on the front just east of us. The captain relayed the information to headquarters in Berlin and was told to keep the prisoner under guard and await further instructions."

With that the sergeant left the hall with a warning not to talk to the prisoner. "And by the way," he added, "the village is off limits until further notice."

I turned to Franz and said, "This prisoner's life is sealed. When I was retreating out of Poland I heard rumors that deserters were hanged on the spot for everyone to see."

The next morning a detail of high SS officers arrived from Berlin. They interrogated the soldier again and went to the village to talk with eyewitnesses. The next day our captain received his instructions.

He called our company together and announced, "The prisoner will be shot to death as a deserter of the German army. The execution will take place tomorrow morning at seven a.m. on the company

parade grounds. An eight man firing squad will be selected by lottery

from this company."

My knee shook a little and I looked a Franz to see his solemn

face turn a bit pale.

The commander continued, "The two other companies of the

security battalion will also be present."

That meant us. Franz and I did not draw a ticket for the firing

squad; I couldn't have been more relieved. Franz and I chuckled while

we gave each other a hard hug.

The next morning the battalion formed a U-shape with the

open side towards the execution site. My company was in the middle

behind the firing squad. Shortly before seven o'clock the so-called

prisoner was led out and tied to the post. I noticed he was not wearing

the great coat nor did he have a cap on. Judging by the sparse hair on

his head he looked to be around the same age as my father, about

forty. My battalion commander then stepped up and faced the

condemned man while he read the indictment and execution order.

"This prisoner has been found guilty of committing desertion from the *Weinmarcht* (German Army) and will therefore be executed by firing squad. Please put the blindfold on," he commanded.

My top sergeant secured the blindfold and stepped aside. Our captain positioned himself at the end of the firing squad and to give the command.

"Ready." The soldiers brought their rifles up and loaded them. Then they raised them up to fire, pressing their cheeks up against the rifle stock, fingers on the triggers, aiming down the barrel at the prisoner. Within seconds the sergeant screamed, "Aim, fire!"

I cringed from the noise of the eight rifles as the fingers pulled the triggers simultaneously. I noticed the soldier being hit, jerking slight to his left and slowly gliding down onto the ground. My top sergeant drew his pistol, walked over to the lifeless figure, and aimed for his head. He fired another three shots for the final coupe de grace. For a moment I had a sickening feeling in the pit of my stomach. I had to keep from heaving. In fact, one of my comrades in the row in front of me had to be propped up by his buddies. Our captain then dismissed us all and we went for breakfast. None of us were hungry. For me witnessing the execution was a sobering experience. That day had been a somber lesson meant for all us soldiers present: If you desert, you die.

Chapter 22

I, the Translator

"The unknown can be mind boggling."
-- Edna Esfeld

By the end of March of 1945 boys and men from the ages of thirteen to sixty were ordered to the front lines by the Nazi party. Many, barely trained, were given just hunting rifles for combat. We heard about this member club called *Volksstum*, which included working men in their forties, boys as young as thirteen, and even women and girls, all of whom were trained to guard sites. This helped our morale since we weren't' receiving much news about the war anymore.

It was spring and the skies were starting to clear, which meant open season for frequent bombing raids on Berlin by the U.S. 8th Air Force. After a raid the bombers would fly over our area on their return to England. On occasion we saw planes damaged by German flak struggling to keep up with their flight formation. One day a heavy bomber was actually shot down over our area. I saw several parachutes emerge from the falling plane. They drifted down to where we were conducting our exercises.

"Now we must split into two groups so we may intercept the crewmembers when they land," yelled my captain.

Sure enough one of the parachutists drifted into a heavily wooded area nearby. When my squad found the airman, his parachute was caught in the crown of a thirty foot pine tree. He was dangling by the nylon ropes and I could hear him moaning.

"*Schutze* Esfeld, ask him if he is hurt," ordered my captain.

I was surprised that my captain chose me. Instinctively I called up to the man and said in English, "Are you hurt?"

"I think I have a broken leg," he replied.

One leg did look askew. It would be a challenge for my squad to get him down. This particular pine tree, like so many in Germany, was completely devoid of any branches right up until you got to the top. One could slide down but not climb up. My squad leader suggested we throw our knives up to him so he could cut himself loose, then grab the trunk of the tree and slide down.

I explained to the airman in English what we intended to do. One by one we threw our knives up to him, he wasn't able to catch any of them. Then Franz, my machine gunner, turned to our squad leader and said, "I have an idea. I will rest my machine gun on Schutze Esfeld's shoulder and shoot at the nylon cords to try and sever them right above his head."

Thinking this over a moment, our squad leader replied, "Okay. Let's give it a try."

Before I had a chance to let the airman know our intent, Franz hoisted the MG42 on my right shoulder, loaded through and started firing. Bark chips and split pieces of silk from the parachute were flying all over. I heard the airman scream, "Don't kill me!"

Franz fired a few more bursts but not a single cord had been cut.

"*Halt!*" ordered our leader, realizing the futility of our efforts.

I was nearly deaf in my right ear for being so close to Franz's firing chamber. After running out of ideas, my leader decided to move on. He instructed me to tell the stricken airman that we would leave the rescue to the fire department. I started to translate but I could not remember the English word for fire department. I knew the word *feuer* meant fire but what was the English word for *wehr*? I remembered all those times back in the U.S. when my mother took me downtown to Detroit; it was always bustling with fire *wehrs*; but still I could not come up with the word. So, in desperation, I yelled up to the airman, "The fire *wehr* is on its way." My comrades looked at me curiously as our squad trudged off in search of another downed crewmember. I know my face was beet red.

When we reached the edge of the forest my squad leader ordered to us to stop. Across the clearing, about one-hundred fifty yards on the other side, we saw a lifeless figure on its back draped over a large boulder. Just his luck, I thought to myself. But where was his parachute?

"You fellows stay here while I run over and check this out," our captain said.

Upon his return he told us the individual was another crew member who had crashed on the boulder and probably broken his back. He was unconscious and barely alive.

"One of our other squads had already found him. They took his parachute and went for help. There is nothing we can do, so let's turn back and go home," he ordered.

Later that evening while Franz and I were cleaning the machine gun and reloading the empty ammunition belts, the sergeant of the guards entered our barracks and ordered me to follow him to the orderly room.

"*Schutze* Esfeld, our company commander wants to see you," he said.

On the short walk over to the orderly room all kinds of nervous thoughts ran through my head. Why does he want to see me? What did I do wrong? I did not know the captain too well. He was a young blond, about twenty-eight years of age and rumored to have some combat experience. To me he appeared aloof, a typical demeanor between officers and enlisted men in the German army; this I had observed from the beginning of my service. During training he was stern and dedicated to transforming us raw recruits into fighting men. To him orders were orders and they had to be followed. Perhaps because of his short combat experience he wanted us tougher and stronger. But I do not recall him ever giving us political pep talks, such as those I was given during my years in the Hitler youth corps. He was a pragmatic officer and soldier sworn by oath to defend the Fatherland.

Upon entering the orderly room I saluted the captain, stated my name and purpose of being there. I remained at attention. With a faint smile on his face the no nonsense captain acknowledged my salute.

"*Schutze* Esfeld. I had you brought here so that you can translate our conversation with the American pilot whose bomber was shot down over our area and captured by our soldiers. Sit down at this table."

The pilot was led in and seated opposite me. The captain's assistant and top sergeant sat at another table. The captain remained standing at my table and faced the pilot.

"*Schutze* Esfeld," the captain began, "ask the prisoner his name, rank and the outfit he was flying with."

I had no time to formulate the English words, but I proceeded carefully. "My captain would like to know your name and rank as a soldier."

"My name is Walsh and I am a major." He then added his serial number. Whatever question my captain had me translate, Walsh gave the same answer. Frustrated, and realizing he was not going to get any other information from the major, my captain wanted to know one more thing.

"*Schutze* Esfeld, ask the major how he felt killing innocent women and children by bombing our German cities, towns, and villages?"

Now, I thought, here in front of me sits a genuine American. I had not seen one since I came to Germany almost eight years ago at the age of nine. During the questioning, for the first time in over seven years, flashbacks entered my mind of the happy, carefree life I had enjoyed back home in Detroit. My teachers, the parents of my friends, the soda fountain clerk who made me a delicious tuna fish sandwich on toast before my guitar lessons, and the conductor on the streetcar I took to and from the lessons--they were all friendly, helpful and caring toward me. Now, across from me, was one of those "countrymen." I began to like the major.

"*Schutze* Esfeld, ask the major how he felt killing innocent women and children by bombing our German cities, towns, and villages?" my captain repeated.

After I translated the question the American major leaned over to me and said, "Soldier, you tell your captain that he already has lost the war and Germany is finished."

"What did he say?"

Instinctively, as if a voice inside of me was saying "you cannot translate that word for word. It might cause the American harm," I modified my translation by saying, "Yes. The major feels bad, but it is his duty and the duty of his fellow airmen to keep bombing until the war is over." I held my breath for the captain to react but he just nodded his head and ordered the guard to take the prisoner back to his cell.

Turning to me he said, "*Schutze* Esfeld. You are dismissed and you may go back to your barracks."

I saluted and left the orderly room with my knees shaking. I let out a deep breath. Suppose there was someone present during the questioning who knew enough English to interpret my false translation? I knew the crime of aiding and abetting the enemy.

However, nothing more was said to me and our training continued.

Chapter 23

Herman Goering's Guard

"We shall defend our Island, whatever the cost may be,
We shall fight on the beaches, we shall fight on the landing
grounds,
We shall fight in the fields and in the streets, we shall fight in
the hills;
We shall never surrender."
-- Winston Churchill

A few weeks later, right about the first of April, the top

sergeant asked anyone who had any anti-aircraft gunnery experience to

report to him. In my early days as a Hitler Youth flak helper I was

trained as a gunner on an 88mm anti-aircraft gun. So I reported to the

top sergeant. He explained that the flak tower guarding Herman

Goering's hunting lodge headquarters needed a temporary replacement

recruit on their 20mm four-barrel anti-aircraft gun. Flak towers were

re-enforced concrete, round or square, with a bunker for civilians to

hide in along with beds for the guards to sleep in. At the end of the war

the massive towers were built twenty to fifty stories high and were sometimes the only structure left standing among ghostly demolished edifices. Anti-aircraft guns were placed on the roofs and hidden from view.

"Do you have any experience with that type of gun?" he asked me.

"*Nein*, only on an 88mm gun," I answered. Since I was the only one in the company who answered the sergeant's call, he figured he better send me--and sure enough I found myself on a truck transporting me to the flak tower the next day.

When I arrived I reiterated to the sergeant in charge of the gun crew that I had no experience with the 20mm gun.

"That's alright. I'll use you as an ammunition handler and for guard duty. It will only be for ten days while one of my crew is on furlough," he said.

He showed me the bunk I would sleep in and introduced me to a crew member. The other was on top of the tower on guard duty.

I thought this duty would be a nice respite for me from those strenuous field exercises my company goes through daily. I could write home more often too.

"*Schutze* Esfeld, come with me now," my new sergeant ordered.

We climbed the stone inlay steps up to the gun platform toward the tower.

"*Schutze* Esfeld is the new replacement for now," he said to the second crew member who had a pair of binoculars hanging around his neck.

The gunnery sergeant showed me where the 20mm cartridges were stored and how to load them into the magazine and then into the gun breaches.

"Since my crew and I have occupied the tower for two months not a single Russian or allied warplane has attacked this place. Take a few minutes to get familiar with the surroundings. Look at the landscape and the four directions in the sky," the sergeant said.

I noticed the gun platform was even with the tops of the tall fir trees, about fifty feet high. Looking down I spotted a terrace on the backside of the lodge. To my amazement I was over-looking Herman Goering's hunting lodge; I remembered the name as Karin Hall through stories told at meetings when I was a member of Hitler Youth.

It was practically right below the tower! The story was told to us youths about how Hitler's right hand-man, Herman Goering, the Reichsmarschal and commander of the Luftwaffe, had acquired the *Jagdshoss* or hunting lodge, and named it after his Swedish wife Karin: hence, Karin Hall. I never dreamed I would get this close.

A few days later when I was on guard duty on top of the tower, I glanced down at the lodge. There in plain sight I spotted Hermann Goering himself stepping out onto the terrace. There he was in full view, dressed in his white puffed out uniform with his arms crossed behind his back, his black sparse hair combed across his balding head. He didn't wear a hat. I was mesmerized but quickly stepped away from the tower wall; I didn't dare raise my binoculars for a look out of fear a hidden security guard would be watching the tower. Suddenly a second person emerged from the edge of the terrace and walked up to Goering. Greeted only with a handshake, this person was dressed in a black uniform and wore a visor-like officer's hat.

My gosh, I exclaimed silently. That is Heinrich Himmler! I had to contain my astonishment when I recognized him. The shorter and thinner *Herr Reichsfuhrer* Himmler was all too familiar with his rounded spectacles; he was head of all the SS formations and just recently had been put in charge of the entire German Army on the Eastern Front. These two powerful men were, in what appeared to be a secret meeting, right before my eyes.

The meeting lasted about a half hour. They quickly shook hands; Himmler hurriedly left the terrace and Goering disappeared into the lodge. By now sweat was dripping from my forehead. Later, in the middle of the night, my fellow crew members and I were aroused out of or sleep by the noise of trucks moving in and out of the hunting lodge compound. This went on for hours. By daybreak all was quiet and we were left wondering what had gone on.

A day later the man whose place I had taken suddenly walked into our quarters. He was had been called back, his furlough cut short. I in turn was ordered to pack my belongings and get ready to be transported back to my company.

Chapter 24

My Eternal Faith Subsiding

Rumors were rife in my company upon my return. Everyone wanted to know what was going on.

"I watched Himmler and Goering having a secret meeting alone together when I had guard duty at the tower," I exclaimed. "On my watch! Then in the middle of the night trucks were moving in and out."

"Did Goering move his headquarters or is he still at Karin Hall?" someone asked.

"Those rumbling trucks kept us up most of the night…," and before I said another word the Russians attacked. It was April 16, 1945, Hitler's birthday. Fortunately for my company the main thrust of the attack was directed at Berlin, bypassing our location. Little did we know the amount of destruction that occurred that day to Germany's capital city.

The next day my company and I loaded onto trucks and were transported to the south in the direction of Berlin. Thirty miles later we were ordered to get out of the trucks and continue on foot. Civilians, their belonging piled high on carts and wagons, were passing us in droves, fleeing to escape the fighting.

"Go chase the Russians out of our country!" a few women screamed at us.

The following day my company took a lunch break in the woods, out of sight of the roaming Russian fighter bombers. Suddenly loud shouting and barking of orders could be heard about one hundred yards from where I was sitting with my squad. Then I saw a group of men with their arms stretched up above their heads being herded toward us by our soldiers, who were pointing rifles at their backs. The men were dressed in torn civilian clothes and wearing caps.

"Halt!" ordered the sergeant accompanying the group near the spot where I was sitting with my squad.

A lieutenant from the other platoon explained. "These men were captured by us as they ran across the field into the woods."

After my company commander briefly questioned the prisoners, he declared, "These men are either saboteurs or spies who parachuted out of a plane. They have to be shot on the spot. But first they must dig their own graves!"

And with that the lieutenant ordered Franz, me, and three others on our squad to give the prisoners our entrenching tools.

"Now dig," the Lieutenant commanded the prisoners.

As the solemn looking men starting digging, I could not help but study each one at close range. The first man looked to be about fifty years old; the next three, in their late twenties to mid-thirties. The last one couldn't have been more than a teenager. I turned to Franz and remarked, "Franz, they seem more like family to me rather than trained saboteurs!"

"Herman," Franz replied with a shifty look, "just be still and keep your thoughts to yourself."

After the lieutenant deemed the pit deep enough, he ordered the five men to kneel at the edge, facing into the pit; the younger one was at one end. He turned to us and asked, "Who is going to volunteer to shoot these prisoners?"

Only the sounds of the restless forest answered him.

"If none of you wants to do it," the lieutenant bellowed, "then I'll have the sergeant here do it." His anger was so intense, I wanted to run and hide behind a tree.

The sergeant walked up and stepped behind the first man. He pulled his pistol out of its holster, loaded it and pressed the muzzle against the base of the man's skull. A shot rang out. I tried not to jerk but I felt my muscles tighten into a knot. The man tumbled into the pit. I could hear whimpering coming from the young man at the other end. Bang. Bang. Bang. The shots echoed loudly through the trees as the sergeant methodically moved down the line. By the time he reached the end, the kid was sobbing uncontrollably. Bang! The last shot rang out. It was all over pretty quickly. My heart was pounding so hard and fast I thought someone would notice for sure.

My squad was instructed to fill up the grave. For the first time I could remember, my mind was empty of thoughts; I was numb from the sight of it all.

That night we were told to bed down in the woods. As I lay quiet and stiff, I could still see one of the victim's shocked face and the perfect round hole in his forehead where the bullet exited. There was no blood. Then more thoughts came rushing into my head. "The war for your captain is over. Germany is finished!" Those words from Major Walsh, the American bomber pilot, started to crack my mental armor as I tried in vain to block out the day's events. But I couldn't stop the doubts from creeping in. Is Germany really losing the war? Where are those secret weapons? Isn't it too late for them now? Suddenly my father's words came flooding back to me; the words he spoke when Hitler declared war on America in December 1941. Because Vati knew the awesome production capacity the American industry was capable of, he said with the utmost confidence, "Germany has now lost the war." I wanted to be with him now at the factory.

I could not shake my thoughts that night. What kind of behavior was it where "honorable" members of the glorious German Wehrmacht resort to the killing of innocent civilians just because they were running free?

Later on I learned that in Oranienburg, just a few miles south of where we caught those five men, there was a forced labor and concentration camp. With Russian troops rapidly advancing on the camps and the German guards fleeing, these five men not only saw an opportunity to free themselves from their German captors but also from the Russian troops who, as it turned out, would have forcibly send them back to their home country under a communist regime. Or, they could have been forced laborers for German farmers.

The killing of those five men haunted me--and still does to this day. I have been fighting for the enemy all along.

By the next morning the murdering of these five men somehow convinced me that Germany was finished. I thought about asking to be transferred to the Western Front, running over the lines, and surrendering to the Americans. But my company was told that we would not continue our march to Berlin. The Russian troops had closed a circle around the city. Instead we were to take up a defensive position along the Ruppiner Kanal, about seven miles west of Oranienburg and fifteen miles northwest of Berlin.

Chapter 25

Ten Days in a Foxhole at Ruppiner Kanal

After a four hour march we arrived and were ordered to dig in. I noticed across the canal from our spot a thickly grown forest of trees with arm-sized trunks standing in shallow pools of water.

After Franz and I dug our foxhole, I whispered, "Franz, we better not sleep tonight. The Russians could sneak through that dense forest undetected right up to the edge of the canal and overwhelm us with a surprise attack."

Franz nodded his head and zeroed in on his MG42. I laid out a belt of ammunition for him to feed into the breach. But nothing happened that sleepless night.

The next morning artillery fire started up again in the direction of Berlin. It sounded much closer this time. The order came down the line for us to abandon our foxholes, form up and follow the canal westward. After a few miles my squad reached a road that led out of a village called *Kremmen*, crossed a bridge that led over the *Ruppiner Kanal*, and headed straight north.

"Halt!" my sergeant ordered. Then, turning to Franz and me, he said, "Dig your foxhole at the bridge on the left side of the road."

After we had finished and Franz positioned the MG42, we each took a look around to familiarize ourselves with the surrounding area and landmarks. On the other side of the bridge, on the right side of the road, there were three houses. The first house I estimated to be one hundred yards away. On the left side of the road, directly across from our foxhole, was a square shaped piece of land with its front side running along the canal, the right side along the road. A cottage bordered with a three foot high hedge was on the back and left side of the land with a large garden, about one hundred yards square.

Thirty feet behind our foxhole and a few feet below the surface of the road was a small three-room farmhouse. On the other side of the road from us, about two hundred yards away, there was a single-spur railroad bridge. That section and the bridge were covered by three platoons of our company. The left flank of our platoon was covered by the remaining platoon for a distance of two hundred yards.

Each squad had two MG42 machine guns. There were three squads per platoon and three platoons per company, making it eighteen MG42 machine guns facing the enemy on a line of about four hundred yards. I thought this was an awesome amount of fire power.

Suddenly, while most of us in the platoons were still digging our foxholes, a hail of mortar shells bombarded my platoon, exploding all around us. Since this was our first shelling by mortars most of us green soldiers, like me and Franz, didn't recognize the typical sound of shells being fired out of their mortar tubes. It happened so fast, we had only seconds to take cover before the noiseless shells came plunging straight down to earth.

As these one-foot rocket-looking shells hit, they made a distinctive "plump, plump" sound.

"Get down, get down!" yelled our commander. "Stay down until I say it's all clear. Do not move. Do not make any noise."

I froze until I could not breathe. I looked over at Franz to see both his hands, white-knuckled, clenched tightly on our machine gun. Then—the noise stopped. I breathed a sigh of relief.

"Help. Help. Help me, please!" I heard the cries coming from our platoon the instant we were being attacked.

One of my comrades who had been walking on top of the canal embankment had been hit. I could see where the blast of hot shrapnel had hit his lower torso, tearing up his private parts. He screamed and writhed in pain as he lay there on the ground while the rest of us, helpless under fire and frightened, were unable to do anything to help. I could hear the cries become weaker and weaker. By the time the medics could get to him he had bled to death. He was our first casualty that day. It was clear: the Russians knew where we were.

After the mortar attack ended, all of us in my platoon stayed in our foxholes, peering intently across the canal to the Russian side, only few hundred yards away. The canal was twenty feet wide and about five feet below ground level with a slight embankment on both sides. As I looked out over our foxhole towards the hedge at the back of the garden plot, I spotted a Russian soldier crawling behind the hedge to my left.

I turned to Fritz and whispered, "That Russian is heading for the canal. I'm going to try and stop him"

"Go ahead," Franz whispered. "But make sure the gun sight is set right."

So I aimed my rifle and tracked the guy briefly until he reached a small opening in the hedge. Now he was a better target. He looked bareheaded and appeared old for a soldier. But he's enemy!" I screamed silently to myself and quickly squeezed and pulled the trigger. Instinctively I pulled back the bolt to eject the spent cartridge and reload for the next round.

"Herman, I think you hit him. I don't see his head and there is no movement," Franz said softly.

To my dismay the spent cartridge casing would not eject. It was, however, the first shot any of us made from this location. Just then my squad leader crawled up to us.

"What the hell happened?" he asked out of breath.

"I saw the enemy coming towards us! I didn't want happen to us what happened to our dead comrade," I pleaded. We told him about the crawling Russian and then I showed him the breach bolt I had pulled out. One of the two ejector claws had broken off and both are needed to pull the cartridge casing out of the firing chamber to be able to reload.

"*Schutze* Esfeld, you did the right thing to shoot at the Russian," our squad leader said, "but I will have to report this to the captain before I can give you another rifle. In the meantime, use the rifle bore cleaning rod to push the cartridge out of the chamber."

"Franz, I'm at a disadvantage with this rifle anyway. How can I defend my life with a broken one? It's a good thing I have you next to me with your MG42."

He nodded in agreement and for the first time I felt some relief. We both strained our eyes to try and detect any further movement of enemy soldiers. Dusk was settling in. The first day's events had been scary. Franz and I were sweaty, tired and hungry. Loud shouting suddenly brought us back to life.

"*Ivan* is in the canal. Hurry, get up here and shoot!" our platoon leader, a master sergeant with frontline experience, yelled.

"Cover me!" shouted our sergeant as he suddenly jumped up on the embankment and began to fire into the canal with his *Schmeisser* machine pistol.

A few of our men began to spray the opposite side of the embankment with bullets from their rifles. I got out of Franz's way by crouching against the back dirt wall so he could yank his MG42 to the left side of our foxhole. But he dared not fire. It was too dark and he was afraid he might hit our own men. In a few minutes it was over and all was quiet. The sergeant had killed the few Russians who had made it into the canal and tried to wade across, possibly to test the strength of our position.

What a waste of men, I thought.

"Franz, that was too close. You sure showed some patience."

He nodded again.

In order to get a warm meal of potatoes, bread and butter, later on we had to hunch down crawl, one at a time, one hundred fifty yards into to forest where our company's cook prepared our meals in an abandoned farmhouse. Soon afterwards Franz and I agreed on the time of our guard duty as we both turned in for a fitful night in our foxhole. We almost skipped dinner.

The next morning our platoon leader came to Franz and me and said he wanted to relocate our position.

"Follow me," he ordered.

Our new position was dangerously closer, about fifty yards from the bridge and about thirty feet from the canal. Ten feet to our left and slightly ahead was the foxhole of the second machine duo in our squad. Both guns had an open field of fire on the enemy side; being so close together this strategy would be more effective in case of an attack. Our leadership didn't think *Ivan* would attack across the bridge for fear we would blow it up in their faces.

After Franz and I had dug the foxhole our squad leader came around to tell us about our mission. He explained that after Herman Goering's overnight departure from his headquarters in Karin Hall and the final push of the Russian Army to Berlin on April 16, our battalion had been ordered to march straight for Berlin and link up with SS General Felix Steiner's divisional combat team to help defend Berlin.

So that's what all the moving trucks were up to at the lodge, I realized.

The squad leader told us that the Russians were faster than us and had completed the encirclement of Berlin by cutting off the link-up with our battalion. General Steiner defied orders and took it upon himself to break through the encirclement and fight his way through to the German city of Flensburg in northern Germany, near the Danish border. There Gross-admiral Donitz, who was admiral of the fleet and also known as father of the German U-boats, was gathering a force for Germany's last stand.

Somberly I realized that my conclusions of a few days ago were correct: Germany is losing this war.

"And after *Der Fuhrer's* birthday on the 20th of April, he has declared Donitz his successor," explained our leader. "General Steiner's breakthrough is planned at the village of *Kremmen*, just a mile south of us. It leads across the bridge on the road north."

Our Fuhrer's successor? Now I know why the bridge is still intact. The breakthrough could happen any day now! My thoughts and doubts were coming at me like bullets now, but the difference was, I no longer dodged them.

The *Zeithan* Castle was located in *Kremmen*. It was there that Heinrich Himmler had been plotting peace negotiations with the western allies behind Hitler's back.

"*Schutze* Esfeld, clean your rifle and be at the small farmhouse tomorrow afternoon for an exchange," the squad leader ordered.

He finally left us to finish digging our foxhole; by now we felt starved.

Franz and I managed to get a few eggs from the farmhouse which we ate raw. Shortly afterward I got the call of nature. I climbed out of the foxhole and had my pants in ready position, halfway down, when I heard that distinct plump, plump sound of mortar shells being fired and echoing like clashing thunder. I jerked my pants up and, like an oiled streak of lightning, ran and jumped back into the foxhole.

What the hell am I doing this place? I mumbled in English.

Franz looked at me with half a grin on his face. By then the mortar shells were exploding all around us, dirt and debris spitting at us like a wind storm. One shell blew up dangerously close. I looked up into the sky, for a second thinking *Ivan* must have an observer somewhere who saw me climb out of the foxhole.

The bombardment continued off and on for hours, until dusk. All movement on our side came to a halt. Nobody dared get out of their foxholes. Luckily my platoon did not suffer any casualties. After it ended, I managed to clean my broken rifle and bore, covered the muzzle with a piece of rag and place it against the wall of the foxhole. Tomorrow could not come soon enough.

Franz and I agreed on our guard duty: two hours on and two hours off. We tried to make ourselves as comfortable as we could by curling up to get some sleep.

In the middle of the night Franz woke me up for my turn, saying, in a low voice, "Herman, keep a sharp look-out. I heard noises on *Ivan's* side, like digging into the ground."

"That's what the long-lasting, harassing mortar fire was all about yesterday. To keep us from seeing the Russians moving up to the canal into position," I said.

Towards the end of my two hour guard shift I began to get a little drowsy when a dark shadow popped up in front of me. I waited a few seconds and there it was again. I grabbed the MG42, pushed the butt into my shoulder, and started firing a long burst of ammo until I noticed how the tracer bullets were slowly creeping up into the dark sky in a graceful arc. But I couldn't stop. My finger was frozen on the trigger until the fifty rounds on the cartridge belt were spent. I hadn't taken the time to lean forward and dig my feet into the ground. The recoil force of the machine gun pushed my back against the dirt wall of the foxhole knocking my rifle into it. I paid no attention to this since my back felt good. Chalk that up for inexperience.

Now everything was quiet again except my heavy breathing. No more shadows. Amazingly, Franz had slept through it all. I woke him up for his turn.

"What was all that noise about?" he asked sleepily. Aha. He heard it and didn't *want* to wake up.

The third day began with more harassing mortar fire. I was confounded as to how I was going to get through this and get over to the farmhouse in the afternoon. I observed that the mortar shells had not been coming closer than about thirty yards behind our foxhole. So that must be the range. I figured if I ran like hell for that distance and then cut left to the tree lined road and head back to the farm house and take cover in its ditch, I could make it.

During a break from the shelling barrage I took a glance at the foxhole on my left. To my horror I saw the machine gunner with his head sticking out of the foxhole, looking backward into the distance.

Before I had a chance to shout a warning a shot rang out from across the canal. The sound of "ping, ping" came from inside his helmet and I gasped as I saw his head flip forward. Then he disappeared down into the foxhole.

His assistant gunner screamed, "Medic, Medic. My machine gunner has been hit!"

I had wanted to warn him to keep his head down. I knew *Ivan* had moved up steadily during the night and they were dug in only ninety feet from us across the canal. Sleep deprivation can cause lack of judgment. Later the victim's assistant told Franz and me that the bullet had entered the back of his head just below the protective rim of the steel helmet. The Russian who shot him must have been an excellent marksman. The machine gunner was looking over toward the direction of the village of Sommerfeld, only two miles behind us over open country. He was born there. Now he would be buried there.

For long days and endless nights Franz and I sat cramped in our foxhole, bored and stressed. During the day we had to be constantly on the alert yet not able to stick our heads out too far, let alone leave the foxhole. My neck and back were in constant pain. We could only relieve ourselves between dusk and dawn. The only warm meal was delivered to us after dark.

The fourth day, as Franz and I were dozing in our foxhole around noon, noise from an artillery gun being fired startled us. The noise was immediately followed by a "whoosh" sound and a projectile flying close over our heads crashed into the roof of the first house at the right side of the road and across the bridge from us, exploding inside the attic. Smashed red clay roof tiles combined with splintered wood hurled through the air. A black plume of smoke rose lazily into the sky. Before I could say anything to Franz, another shell hit, completing the destruction of the attic. Several more shells followed in rapid secession. They slammed into the second floor and upper half of the ground floor, as if following someone running down the stairs. Then the shelling stopped. The house was destroyed.

"Franz, that looked to me like an 88mm anti-aircraft gun firing those shells. Firstly, because of the straight trajectory the shells came in on from behind us from about one and half miles. Secondly, because of the rapid speed the shells hit after being fired. These are the characteristics of the German 88mm anti-aircraft guns attributed to its high muzzle velocity."

Later we found out that one of our squad leaders had been watching the house from our small farmhouse. He spotted someone slowly removing a roof tile and then a pair of binoculars appeared in the opening.

"That's him. That's the Russian observer for their mortar crews," the squad leader had reported to our platoon sergeant. The sighting went up the chain of command. A flak battery officer had arrived that morning to be briefed at the small farmhouse and it was he who set up the firing coordination of that house. We didn't see the Russian observer leave the house either during or after the shelling. Nor did the mortar shelling continue with precision aim at us. We took care of his vision alright. Now it was time to crawl my way to the farmhouse.

No longer had I to fear being chased by aimed mortar fire, but the deadly sniper fire still threatened. So I scrambled out of the foxhole, grabbed my rifle which Franz handed to me, hunched over, ran like hell all the back way to the farmhouse. No mortar or sniper fire followed me.

I knocked and entered through the side door--the front door faced the enemy and was too dangerous. Our platoon leader, the *Hauptfeldwebel* (master sergeant), had made the house his quarters. He told me that an SS officer would hear my case for a new rifle.

An SS officer? I was beside myself.

Shortly a black shiny staff car drove up. I watched in a state of shock as the SS officer, wearing a long black leather trench coat, knee high black boots and black cap, got out of the car. He did not wear a smile. He came up to me and, in a flat voice, asked me directly, *"Was hat sie tun?"*

In a shaky voice I told him what had happened and added that it was the first time I had fired the rifle since about four weeks before on the rifle range.

"Remove the bolt and give me the broken off claw," he commanded. In silence, he proceeded to examine the fit. The quiet made my nerves tight. Then he lifted my rifle up in the air with the open breach against the light, looking through the bore. He lowered the rifle and thrust it back to me. With outrage in his voice he glared at me and asked, "Schutze Esfeld, how dare you show me your rifle with dirt in the bore." He grew more agitated and, red-faced, screamed, "This is sabotage on the battlefield. I could have you shot on this spot as a saboteur!"

I was mortified and horrified at the same time. With my voice shaking I barely managed to explain that when I fired the machine gun the force pushed me back against the soft dirt wall of the foxhole and knocked over my rifle.

"Schutze Esfeld is a good soldier. This was an accident in the heat of battle," interrupted my platoon sergeant.

The SS officer listened to him and then turned to me and said, "There is still evidence of negligence and you need to be punished. Therefore I will not replace your rifle. You will have to get along with it the best you can. Dismissed!"

I felt relieved—at least I was not going to be shot--but still shaken, wondering what might have happened if my sergeant hadn't stood up for me. When I got back to my foxhole I told Franz what had happened. He calmly said, "You were lucky getting off so easy because of the good word the master sergeant put in."

It took all day before I felt somewhat normal again.

Later that day Franz and I once again agreed on our guard shifts. I tried to make myself comfortable and readied myself for another night of high anxiety. I reflected on the day's events and how that bitter SS officer had treated me. I remembered my comrade's talk that Hitler's birthday was on the 20th of April, which had come and gone. So was my enthusiasm and blind faith to follow our "beloved" Fuhrer and my willingness to give life and limb for future generations to enjoy a glorious thousand year Third Reich. That will never happen now, I told myself. Like the captured American bomber pilot had said, "Germany is finished." Determinedly, I resolved to try and get out of this war unscathed and avoid being captured by the feared Russians. I wanted to be back with my family in Wolfsburg.

It was in the middle of that night, as Franz and I were changing shifts, that we were startled by a strange rattling noise up in the dark clear sky. It was approaching us from the right and following the canal. Then we saw what was: a double-decker airplane flying slowly at a height of about six hundred feet. Just then an order was shouted down the line from foxhole to foxhole.

"Don't shoot at the plane!"

"The sewing machine you mean?" I said to Franz.

This enemy reconnaissance and artillery observer plane was nicknamed "sewing machine" by German soldiers on the Russian Front because the small engine sounded like a sewing machine. And if the pilot spotted a lucrative target he would lean over the side and drop a small bomb--like needling it down.

As I watched its path, the plane flew all the way down our line, turned around and made one more pass, as if teasing us to shoot at it. We all had to hold our breath and not be tempted to shoot at it. A long burst from one of our machine guns would have brought it down. But orders were orders.

"Any moment we can expect a well-aimed barrage of mortars," I said to Franz. He nodded in agreement. But nothing happened and the remainder of night fell quiet.

Four days after we dug in our foxholes along the *Ruppiner Kanal* there still was no word of a breakthrough by SS General Felix

Steiner's group. Franz and I alternately peered over the edge of our foxhole toward *Ivan's* side, being careful not to be spotted by the Russian soldiers only thirty yards in front of us. We barely saw the water.

Suddenly we heard shouting. It came from the direction of the farmhouse where our officers were. Only a few seconds later we figured out why.

"Hans, get down you fool!" yelled a comrade a few foxholes down.

Franz and I looked up and saw Hans, a tall and slender young soldier, striding purposefully on top of the canal embankment and heading in our direction. We saw him holding a stick grenade (also called a potato-masher) in his right hand with two more stuck in his belt. When he neared the first Russian foxhole he pulled the cord and lobbed the grenade in a perfect arc into the foxhole. They exploded with dull thuds. I could not believe no shots were being fired.

Hans repeated and threw another grenade into the second foxhole. We watched in shock as Hans came toward the third Russian foxhole, located right across from ours. His third grenade sailed into the foxhole. Milliseconds before it exploded, a Russian soldier reared up halfway out of his foxhole and then slumped back down at the point of explosion. By then a spray of Russian bullets came down in a line; they struck and killed Hans. Franz and I were petrified and stunned by this feat of self-sacrifice. Nevertheless we griped our weapons as hard as we could to prepare for a harsher retaliation by *Ivan*. But nothing happened. The sounds we heard from the other side of the canal were silenced.

The medics had to wait many hours later before they could carry Hans away. I tried not to look at his body, though it was lying just a few yards away. When evening came, two medics quickly dragged his lifeless body back to into the woods. Eventually the story spread through our ranks that Hans had received word that American troops had taken his hometown, *Aachen,* and destroyed the house where he lived with his parents. He had no word on the whereabouts or welfare of his parents. In despair, he allegedly muttered to his comrade in his foxhole, "I have no longer anything to live for."

I wish I could have reassured Hans that the Americans were not bad people. Thinking about the fate of those three unlucky Russian soldiers in their foxhole, a twinge of sadness overcame me that night. I imagined them agonizing over their split-second decision to run, risk being shot, or stay and hope that the crazy German kraut would miss his foxhole.

As night after night wore on, we held our position. We took turns climbing out for food and water back at the farmhouse. We'd crawl only a few feet behind to a tree to relieve ourselves, which, for me, became farther and fewer between.

The ninth and last night Franz and I heard that familiar engine noise up in the sky again. It was the "Sewing Machine." This time someone from the farmhouse took a pot shot at it. I could see the tracer bullet slowly arch it way up to the dark outline of the plane. I knew that Franz, like me, held his breath. I was afraid it was going to hit. But no--at the last second it narrowly missed the tail. The plane flew on and, unlike before, did not circle back.

"Something is going on," I said to Franz.

We didn't have long to wait. Around midnight we heard rifle and machine gun fire, joined by the explosions of artillery and mortar shells erupt. It was coming from the village of *Kremmen* about one and a half miles in front of us. The ripsaw sounds came from the German

MG42s, intermingled with the slower taps of Russian water-cooled

machine guns. Buildings in the village started burning, their flames

lighting up the horizon. The fighting grew more intense. I could see

dark figures perfectly silhouetted against the inferno, running towards

the village, their long great coats flapping around their legs.

I cried out to Franz, "Look, what a perfect target and they are

within range of our machine guns. Why are you not shooting?"

"Because no orders have come down the line to open fire," he

screamed.

So in silence and filled with angst, we watched the Russian

soldiers disappear into the village one by one to join their comrades in

the fierce fighting. Unnoticed by us, they crawled out of their

foxholes. We were, so to speak, asleep at the wheel.

Several hours later, shortly before daybreak, the firing and

shelling finally stopped. We tried to catch up on some sleep, with one

of us alternately keeping a watchful lookout for a Russian

counterattack. Instead we were aroused by shouts.

"Here they come. It's General Steiner and his men!"

"So that's what the fierce battle was all about last night," I said to Franz. Steiner had broken through the Russian lines at *Kremmen* and now he and his exhausted, battle-weary survivors were crossing the bridge at the farmhouse.

He stopped his staff car at the bridge and we could see that a brief conversation between our company commander, our captain and General Steiner was taking place. Then the SS General drove on, followed by several tanks, armored vehicles, and trucks. We could see long columns of bedraggled SS infantry soldiers trailing behind like a rundown caboose. A detail of their men had been assigned to collect any ammunition and spare barrels for their machine guns that we felt we could spare. I was too glad to hand over one full ammunition box and one spare barrel to a nice looking young soldier.

"Say, how is it going?" we asked him.

"*Es war schlimm* (Very bad)," he replied.

We shook hands and, half lazily, said, "Good luck."

There was no indication of Hitler's suicide after his birthday. All propaganda from the Nazi's was still working. And, I had no knowledge that Wolfsburg and the factory laborers had just been liberated by the British.

Besides my broken rifle, the bayonet, the entrenching tool, and the gas mask, I still had three ammunition boxes and one spare barrel to carry on my five foot-six inch, one-hundred, forty-five pound, and slightly undernourished frame.

Shortly after the SS column disappeared over the horizon, the order came through for us to prepare for an evacuation of our foxholes at three o'clock the next morning. Finally, after ten days in a fox hole at *Ruppiner Kanal,* our assignment came to an end. Our mission was accomplished. Or was it?

Chapter 26

One Step Ahead of Ivan

Three o'clock that morning under a dark moonless sky, impatiently waiting, Franz was first to get out of our foxhole. He reached down to help me lift the three ammunition boxes out of the hole. Then he grabbed one and, with his machine gun in the other hand, took off running in a crouched position to the rear. We had agreed to leave behind the gas masks which were stored in a bulky metal container. All of us did the same thing, we found out later, and nobody said a word about it. With my blanket roll, rifle and spare barrel slung over my shoulder, it took me a while to climb out and pick-up the other two ammo boxes and scamper after Franz. I looked around to see if anybody was behind me. I made a mental picture of *Ruppiner Kanal* so I could tell my parents back in Wolfsburg about my survival on the Russian front. I was the last one to hightail it out of the foxholes.

During the whole way to better cover, all I could think was that if Ivan (the Russians) had heard us their bullets would be pelting into our backs or they'd be chasing after us. But all remained quiet. Like frightened deer, my platoon kept running over an open muddy field until we reached the road where the trees shielded us from view.

Our sergeant ordered us to halt. Out of breath and wheezing I sank to my knees. The other two platoons of our company caught up to ours. We had a quick five minutes to compose ourselves, then we continued our march in double file along the single spur railroad tracks. The spring thaw had softened the soil of the field so much that we could not make good headway.

At the first light of dawn, having covered just a little over four miles, we reached the edge of a forest. The three platoons were assigned a sector along the edge of the woods: two platoons on the left side and ours on the right side of the railroad, facing the enemy. We were all dead tired but before we could think of getting any kind of rest the platoon sergeant gave us another order.

"Dig out four-man shallow shelters for protection against any shell fragments. Then cover yourselves with the thickest tree branches and post your guard. Then find some sleep," he snapped.

Once done the quiet didn't last long. As the sun slowly rose up over the horizon under a slight cloud cover, Franz and I were aroused out of our slumber by explosions of artillery shells landing in the tree tops above us.

Our sentry came running to us and, out of breath, blurted, "Those are Russian T-34 tanks firing at us!"

I peered through the foliage that covered us and I could barely make out the 76mm gun barrels of a few T-34 tanks peeking over the top of a slight hill, about fifteen hundred yards ahead and across the meadow.

"Franz," I said, my voice filled with fear, "if they should attack us we are done for. We have no anti-tank weapons."

"Don't worry," he assured me, "the minute those tanks start to roll the captain will pull us back. We have the woods to give us cover. Remember, he wants to come out of this war alive too."

I started to calm down but the trees bursting around us with the shrapnel and broken tree limbs raining down on us were unnerving. All at once the shelling stopped. It was once again quiet. Amazingly nobody in our platoon was wounded, thanks to our combat experienced platoon leader who had us dig those shallow pits. It didn't take long to find out why the tanks had pulled back so quickly. On our left about one hundred yards down the tracks stood silently an armored freight train pulling out of a clump of trees, biggest I'd ever seen, black and shiny. I couldn't believe my eyes.

Our backup iron horse had rolled stealthily out of the woods and poked its nose out far enough for anyone to recognize the 105mm Howitzer cannon surrounded by armor plating mounted on the first car. Right behind it, mounted on a flatcar, was a 4-barrel 20mm anti-aircraft gun. A 105mm Howitzer shell hitting anywhere on top of a T-34 tank spells disaster! A quad 20mm anti-aircraft gun used against infantry, lightly armored vehicles and trucks causes sheer devastation. Shortly after the T-34s disappeared, so did our armored train—and without firing a shot. Neither the tank crews nor the Howitzer or anti-aircraft gunner were spoiling for a fight. Like the rest of us, they all just wanted to survive this war and go back home to their loved ones.

Franz and I were flabbergasted and deeply grateful at the sight of this heap of cannon.

The company commander and my platoon sergeant walked into the area we were to defend. "Here you must dig your holes. And hurry up," they commanded to each rifleman and 2-man machine gunner.

My platoon was on the company's right flank, on the right side of the railroad embankment, which was approximately one-hundred yards away and raised just enough to keep us from seeing the positions of our other two platoons. Our foxholes would stretch roughly one hundred yards to the right for our first machine gunner. Next to it the two-man crew was already busily attaching their MG-42 on a gun mount or tripod, making it into a 25 pound machine gun capable of firing accurately at a distance of 2,000 meters. Each assistant machine gunner had a pair of binoculars to help his gunner find the target and zero in on it. The gunner would kneel or sit behind the gun. Next to that heavy 21 inch long barrel was our position with the fourth MG fifteen feet on our left.

Franz and I started digging our foxholes. "With the Russian T-34 tanks knowing where our company is, their infantry cannot be far behind," I exclaimed. Knowing this, we dug quickly into the light brown sandy soil that we piled up in front of us at the edge of the hole.

Suddenly our lookout yelled out, "Ivan is coming!"

There they were, cresting the top of the hill over where the tanks had poked their gun barrels at us earlier that morning. Wearing their long grey coats, the Russian soldiers were steadily advancing across the meadow pulling water-cooled machine guns mounted on 2-wheeled carriages.

We dived into the foxholes and got our weapons ready to fire. There was no time to camouflage the freshly dug soil. A knot started to form in my stomach as I surveyed our position. In front of the foxhole, about one hundred fifty yards away across a patch of grass, was a thick hedgerow that ran from the railroad to near the edge of the lake on our right. There was a gate for access to the grass patch.

The hedge reminded me of the hedgerows I saw in newsreels in Normandy, France. It might as well be barbed wire, I thought; it could serve as a natural barrier. The tension inside me began to ease somewhat. Glancing to my left across the railroad embankment I spotted the roof of a barn. I estimated the barn to be about two hundred yards from where our other two platoons were bunkered down. The rest of the terrain was meadowland--ideal fields of fire for riflemen like me and the machine gunners.

My attention went back to the advancing Russian infantry. They had formed a skirmish line and were well within range of the heavy M-42 machine guns next to us.

Knowing Franz was a bit older and perhaps a little wiser, I asked him, "Wonder why they haven't opened fire?"

"Because they don't have orders to fire. Besides, our captain is smart. He doesn't want to provoke the T-34 tanks into joining the attack in spite of the armored train hiding in the woods," he replied.

We saw the Russian infantry break into a trot. Soon they would be at the hedge. The crew next to us had received orders to remove their machine gun from its mounting and use it as a light machine gun. Because of the height of the hedge, for a brief moment Franz and I lost sight of the oncoming Russians.

Then Franz hissed under his breath. "I see Ivan lurking behind the hedge. Give me your rifle, Herman. I want to take a potshot at them."

Without protesting I handed him my rifle. He rested it on the piled up sand, took aim and fired. Then he quickly ducked back into the foxhole. I took the rifle from him to knock the spent shell out of the chamber with the cleaning rod.

"Did you hit him?"

"I don't know. I couldn't tell."

A moment later we heard a shot ring out from the hedge and at the same instant sand peppered our faces. The bullet zipped between our heads and buried itself in the back wall of the foxhole. A little shocked we looked at each other in silence. How lucky can you get, I thought. Ivan knows where our foxholes are because of the fresh soil piled around us. Now they know somebody in our foxhole shot at them.

"Franz, no more snipping," I urged.

He muttered, "Listen. There is some shooting going on right over there on the other side of the railroad embankment."

Suddenly my platoon sergeant shouted from behind us, "Schutze Esfeld! Run over to the machine gun crew on the right flank with my order to immediately report to me with their weapons and equipment."

For a split second I hesitated. Then the admonishment came: "Schutze Esfeld, *mach schnell!*"

Blind obedience replaced mortal fear. Without batting an eyelid, I scrambled out of the foxhole with bullets buzzing around me like hungry hornets; I ran as low to the ground as I could and faster than a scared rabbit over to the gun crew. After I repeated the sergeant's order, I hugged the edge of the woods where there was more cover and made it safely back to our foxhole.

With a grin on his face, Franz said, "Good job. You ought to get a medal for that."

I just nodded my head and tried to catch my breath.

We continued to keep a lookout as best as we could without getting shot in the head. Out of the corner of my eye I noticed that the machine gun crew that I delivered the message to had moved to the railroad embankment. Our captain was expecting Ivan to attack his two platoons on the other side of the railroad from ours. He figured the Russian commander wouldn't want to sacrifice his troops by funneling them through the ten foot high gate in the otherwise impenetrable hedgerow. The newly placed machine gun on the embankment would pour flanking fire into the ranks of the attacking Russian infantry. Should any of their troops try and rush the machine gun or fire upon us from the embankment, they would come under flanking fire from the machine gun located to the left of our foxhole.

All had been too quiet for far too long. The calm before the storm, I kept thinking.

"Ivan must be gathered inside and behind that barn waiting for the order to attack," Franz remarked with a matter–of-fact tone.

Before I could give a reply our MG-42 machine guns from two platoons unleashed a volley of fire into the barn. Tracer bullets and perhaps a star shell caused the barn to go up in flames in no time.

Now Ivan had no choice but to attack.

"*Hurraa, Hurraa, Hurraa!* For the first time I heard the war cries of the Russian infantry. Simultaneously our MG-42s made their ripsaw sound, the machine pistols their popping noise, along with the echo shots of rifle fire. It was bone chilling. All hell had broken loose. But my sector was quiet. The captain had been right. Then I heard our platoon sergeant's voice.

"Men, get your weapons and equipment ready. We are moving out in ten minutes," he yelled.

The Russian '*hurraa*' cries had stopped and the sounds of gunfire had ebbed.

"Do you suppose that the Russian attack has been driven away?" I asked Franz.

"Look," he replied, pointing, "our two platoons are abandoning their positions."

Just then our sergeant hollered, "Let's go, men!"

Stiff with anxiety and fear, we climbed out of our foxhole and, running, headed to the nearby woods behind us. We were not fired upon from the hedge where Ivan had been spotted earlier. We scampered like scared deer again, zigzagging around the trees through the growing darkness. About half an hour later we emerged upon a road that led us across a bridge into a stand of tall pine trees. Our squad leader led us to the edge of a hill.

"Now dig your foxholes about here," he ordered.

Our foxhole would be about four feet behind a large pine tree. The bridge we had crossed was a short distance to our right. I looked down the steep and tree-thicketed hill and saw, at the bottom, a creek about a hundred fifty yards away. With all the tree roots, the digging was backbreaking. Franz and I were becoming exhausted.

Two riflemen from our squad appeared. "Give us your canteens and mess kits. Our captain has managed to scrounge up a *Gulaschkanone* (mobile field kitchen). We are having meat stew and hot coffee."

Our first hot meal in ten days, it was a welcome relief, especially after digging that foxhole. We were dead tired. We divided up our watch, then slumped down in our hole. Franz fell into a deep sleep and still on my watch, I soon followed.

In the early hours of the next morning before dawn, we were awakened by the growling noise of diesel engines and the clanking sound of tank tracks. The noise stopped so we fell asleep again. When the first rays of sunshine made their way through the canopy of treetops we awoke to the call of nature. I went first. When I finished I thought I would just step to the edge of the hill we were on for a peek. I looked down right into the menacing gun barrels of three Russian T-34 tanks. They were standing side by side on the other side of the running creek. I rushed back to Franz.

I tried to stay calm but the urgency in my voice said it all. "Franz, you better hurry. We got company. T-34s staring at us from below."

"So that's what we heard last night," he said, quickly running off to take care of business.

Moments later we heard small arms fire erupt from the woods across the bridge. I guess we weren't the only ones awake now. The Russian T-34s simultaneously opened fire with their 76mm gun cannons. Their shells burst into the trees right above us and as whole tops of trees came crashing down. The shells that made it through the trees exploded harmlessly on the ground behind us.

Franz and I crouched low in our foxhole, our weapons at the ready. Just then a shell hit the trunk of the tree in front of us at eye level and exploded with a deafening bang. For awhile my ears rang like church bells. Luckily the shell hit dead on and did not ricochet off, which would have showered us with deadly splinters.

The sounds crackled like thunder and lightning coming from overhead.

As the rifle and machine gun fire grew louder, I held my breath as the first men of our other two platoons sprinted across the bridge to our side to safety. A self-propelled four barreled 20mm anti-aircraft gun began bellowing out salvo after salvo of deadly fire. Under cover from that tremendous defense of fire the remainder of our platoons rushed by us on the road to the small village of *Wustrau,* situated at the edge of the woods, roughly three hundred yards behind our position. Among the last stragglers were two soldiers dragging a wounded comrade between them. By now Franz and I were getting nervous waiting for the order for us to retreat. Then the anti-aircraft gun stopped firing. We watched as the crew raced across the bridge and along the road to the village. Finally, after several hours of endless worry, our platoon got the order to withdraw.

All the Russian tanks had now stopped firing. Unscathed, we reached the village at a half trot, holding ourselves low to the ground, and thankfully, there was an 88mm anti-aircraft gun that stood in the road mounted on its four-wheeled carriage with its barrel pointing in the direction of the Russians. The crew took off but managed to destroy the breach block in the hedge with an incendiary device. The captain had my company together again.

"Now, go into these houses to rest. Do not destroy anything. You can look for food only," he ordered.

We occupied several houses on a side street off the main road. They were all empty.

"Franz, everyone has fled."

"Or they are hiding somewhere," he replied.

"They must have feared the footsteps of the Russian soldiers," I muttered out loud as I looked in cupboards and pantries for food. All we could find were preserved pickles and fruits in glass jars, typical of every German farmer. I was grateful for the custom and we dug into the jars like hungry wolves.

No more than half an hour had gone by when our platoon sergeant yelled, "Ivan is in the village. Everybody out!"

As I rushed out of the door and glanced to the right I could see Russian soldiers running down the main road towards us. I ran like a soldier, the ammo boxes clanging against my body, weighing me down. I was breathless. Being the last one I followed our captain, who led us to a dirt path heading out into the fields. We were parallel with the Russians but hidden from view by the hilly landscape. Franz and I got permission to bury two of three ammo boxes and the last spare machine gun barrel. While I was relieved of the burden of weight, I felt uneasy without our defenses.

To my startled but great joy, our captain announced, "Our Company will no longer deliberately engage any Russian troops. The mission to cover SS General Steiner's withdrawal from Berlin is accomplished," he explained from the middle of the field. I didn't know to laugh or cry in that moment.

My worn-out scrappy body was thankful for the lighter load I carried now. My company fell into a trot and after a little less than an hour we reached the top of a barren hill. Without any trees or bushes to take cover we were completely exposed. We were ordered to lay down for a rest.

It was Franz and I that discovered the road down below.

"Franz, that's the road from the village we just left."

"Look over there! A Russian cavalry on the other side up on the hill!" he blurted out.

I followed his eyes and sure enough to my astonishment I saw a mass of cavalrymen galloping on beautiful horses along the crest about a mile away also heading west. They were holding shiny sabers high above their heads.

I quickly explained confidently to Franz, "Those are the skillful but fierce Mongolian horsemen Stalin brought in from the Far East to help stem the devastating losses his army is suffering, according to our army communiqués. These horsemen are descendants of Attila, King of the Huns, a nomadic tribe of horseback herdsmen from back in the fifth century. He created a huge empire and ravaged large areas of Europe including northern Italy."

But before I could finish my history lesson Franz pointed down to the road below us. "Look, I see a column of civilians coming out from a strand of trees over there to our right."

We watched the German evacuees some walking briskly with their heads down, carrying suitcases, some riding horse drawn carts, all pulling wagons piled high with belongings. They were fleeing from the Russian troops and were almost abreast of us when I heard cannon fire. Shells exploded on the road immediately in front the column. Panic broke out with men, women and children screaming, trying to find cover, diving into the ditches and running toward the trees. A few German military vehicles drove into the field and managed to get around the head of the column and back onto the road. A few of the shells had fallen short.

I could barely hear our captain yell, "Everybody up, double time!"

I couldn't take my eyes off the scene below us. Those pesky T-34 tanks must have caught up with the column and tried to cut it off, I realized. I wondered if the tow vehicle of the 88mm gun had made it ahead of the column. It would have the wounded and perhaps the dead of our other two platoons on board.

No sooner had we left when a group of quarter-ton trucks pulling 5-barrel 6-inch diameter rocket launchers mounted on a single two-wheel axle joined us. They wanted to get on the road but we told them it was under fire.

Franz and I and most of the platoon managed to hitch a ride on the rocket launchers. We had to hang on for dear life as we bumped along the pocketed, bomb shelled roads. Always staying one step ahead of Ivan, at last we were putting some distance between the T-34s. When we reached a railroad running north and south on the side of a hill, we got off the rocket launchers. It was too dangerous to ride them down the hill. Besides, there were numerous Russian fighter bombers roaming the skies. German military vehicles of all types were their favorite target.

The captain ordered us to disperse along the railroad on the hillside and lay low while he went down to check with the MPs on how best to proceed. As we waited I observed endless streams of German military vehicles on the highway going north, away from the Berlin and the advancing Russians. Suddenly a group of Russian fighter planes appeared on the horizon flying low and in line over the retreating troops. I felt my body tense up, expecting a strafing attack any minute, but they flew over us without a fight. I figured they probably had more lucrative targets in mind. Our captain returned and said, "We will continue our march northwest toward the town of *Perleberg*, nine miles from the river Elbe."

After a tedious forty-five mile march with thousands of other troops we arrived, twelve hours later, in the middle of the night. I was relieved to have left the Russian tanks at a safe distance behind. But to my dismay I found out that the bridge across the river Elbe at the small city of *Wittenberg,* another nine miles away, had been blown up in the face of the advancing American troops. *Wolfsburg*, my hometown and home of the Volkswagen factory was only eighty-five miles from us.

Chapter 27

I'm an American

"Franz, I'm a good swimmer. I could swim across the Elbe River and give myself up to the Americans," I confided.

"I think it would be too dangerous because of the swift current and the cold water," he replied. "It's only April 30th."

Franz's judgment was confirmed when we talked to a few soldiers who had just returned from *Wittenberge*. They also reported that the Americans were shooting at anybody trying to get across the river. That changed my mind. I hadn't come this far only to be killed by my own countrymen. By now, there was no trace left of the brainwashing I received as an impressionable youth over the last eight years under Hitler's regime.

We'd spent many days retreating from Ivan. Hitler had committed suicide, though we didn't know it still. If our commanders knew they were not talking, which was typical for all ranks because of the Nazi propaganda, which had a hold on all of us, and their strict discipline. My unit was supposed to report to Hitler's successor, Admiral Doenitz. Our only thoughts each day were that we were lucky to be alive: we were in survival mode.

Our field captain had located a field kitchen that was handing out warm food for the thousands of withdrawing troops. After the meal, he ordered us to help locate gasoline for the army trucks that would transport us. That turned out to be futile. So, tired, beaten, and still hungry, our company started on foot again in search of an intact bridge to cross the Elbe River where we would make our last stand.

After marching twenty-seven miles my company reached the town of *Ludwigslust*. Knowing we were exhausted, the captain ordered us to find a place to sleep for the night. In the early morning we would continue to march to a bridge twenty miles away.

"One more day and we will reach our destination," our captain said.

Oh my gosh, I thought, this isn't going to end.

Early the next day my company was called into formation. As we stood there our captain climbed up on a crate and announced,

"Men, I have received a change of orders. We will not cross the Elbe River here but instead continue our march north and attempt to join up with…"

All of a sudden his voice was drowned out from the squeaking of wheels and the clanking sound of motors running. We looked down the road about 500 yards and saw a convoy of military vehicles go by. The noise of halftracks, a vehicle with only front wheels for steering and the tank treads in the back racing into town, carrying personnel roared. I looked down the street at the intersection about three hundred yards away and, as the vehicles rushed by, I immediately recognized the white star painted on the sides. They were Americans!

It was an unbelievable moment for me. American troops this far north in Germany! It was May 2, 1945. As shocked as I was to see my American countrymen in uniform, I knew right then war was finally over for me! I was happy.

Our captain took a quick look at the American troops. Over the din of racing engines he loudly and sternly announced, "We are now prisoners of war. Remove your paratrooper knives and throw them down the drains in the street. Discard all ammunition but keep your weapons. Remain here until I get instructions from the Americans."

I watched with anticipation and as the captain and his second in command lieutenant walked to the intersection holding a broomstick with a piece of white cloth attached to it.

Shortly the lieutenant came back alone. "The American paratroopers of the 101st Airborne Division have taken our captain in a jeep, probably for interrogation," he told us.

A few American soldiers at the intersection took over our column and directed us down the road where we had to throw our weapons into a pile. Then they frisked us. I marveled at how nonchalant the paratroopers went about their business, their helmets askew, chewing gum and smoking. There was no shoving or kicking. They were good to us. For them the fighting in Germany was over too.

Thousands of us POWs were now gathered and marched into a field within sight of the River *Elbe*. It was a temporary collection point for resting and getting our canteens filled with water. We received our first taste of American food rations, the letter "C" marked on the cartons.

Franz and I were curious about our surroundings so we took a short walk around an hour later. I noticed three of the American paratroopers standing on a small rise, lackadaisically guarding us, their rifles and carbines hanging carelessly from their shoulders. They were talking and laughing. One was constantly chewing gum.

"Franz, I'm going to go up to those three and try to talk to them. Nobody told us we couldn't talk to the guards. Stay here and wait for me." Before Franz could say anything I turned and left.

I approached them slowly while pulling my *soldbuch* (a German soldier's pay book) out of the breast pocket of my tunic. Holding it up, I called out to them, "Pardon me. I speak English. Can I talk to you?" I put on my biggest smile.

They looked at each other and said a few words. Then one of them waved me up. I showed them my pay book and opened it up to the first page. "I am an American and I was born in Detroit Michigan."

The soldier bearing a couple of white stripes on his sleeve took my book and read: "Born in Detroit, Michigan on June 24, 1927. "You're still a kid! Tell me the name of the Detroit baseball team?"

"The Detroit Tigers," I said without hesitation.

With a faint smile on his face he handed back my pay book. "Yup, you got that right."

Then the soldier who was chomping his gum so furiously stepped in front, looked me over top to bottom, and growled, "Then what the hell are you doing in that goddamned German uniform?"

I was stunned. I had expected a hand shake. I couldn't' find the words to answer him. I became speechless. Silently I put my pay book back into my breast pocket and turned and slowly went down the embankment to where Franz was waiting, my head hung low from the American troop's rejection.

"Herman, what happened up there?"

During all the time Franz and I had been together in training, in our foxholes and marching, I never told him how I got to be in Germany as a boy from America. Now I told him and when I finished Franz patted me on the back and said, "That is an amazing story, Herman. If you would have just found those words in English, I am sure those guys would have understood your situation."

"Thanks, Franz." But there was something else that kept me from finding the words in English. I was ashamed. How could brainwashing instill in me such a blind faith in Hitler's cause to make me enlist in the German Army before my inevitable call-up? I could still hear my mother's exasperated voice, "You are only boys! Too young to fight. And for whom?" My parents had not heard from me for several months. I wondered if they were still alive.

The next day a group of us POWs were marched to a larger compound eastward, away from the River *Elbe*. Frightening rumors were circulating among us, like, "The Americans are going to hand us over to the Russians. The Russians are demanding that the Allies give them all the German troops that fought against them." This prompted the American Commandant of the new camp where we were now housed to throw up a barbed wire fence around the command post, separate from the quarters for the guards and the kitchen facilities. The American guards patrolled us from inside the fence to better defend against a feared uprising. It put in my mind the circled wagon trains in the cowboy and Indian movies I saw as a kid in Detroit--although most of the time the white settlers didn't make it out alive. However, using the PA system, the American commandant assured us numerous times, that we would not be turned over to the Russians.

Gradually we settled into a daily routine. We slept on the hard outdoor grounds, creating makeshift beds with leaves we gathered and covering ourselves with our blankets. Every day we were able to walk around in an open farmer's meadow. Kitchen helpers were selected and rotated daily. Food was brought up to gates of the fence where assigned POWS would pick it up and distribute it among us. "Toilets" consisted of five foot deep trenches, two feet wide and five feet long; they were out in the open with no privacy. A four inch diameter log was laid out so you could sit on it, your behind sticking out just at the right distance to keep from losing your balance and falling into the trench--or pinch your jewels. They were called *Der Donnerbalben* (The Thunderbeam). Each soldier regularly sprinkled lime into the pit and cleaned the beam with disinfectant.

After a few weeks of imprisonment an announcement came over the PA system: "Starting tomorrow morning at 9 A.M., all non-German citizens are to report to the commandant's office in alphabetical order starting with the letters A to D."

I tried to figure out what the meaning behind this could be. I decided to report when the letter 'E' got called out.

Shortly after the PA announcement had been made, my now former top sergeant approached me. "Schutze Esfeld, after hearing the PA announcement just now, I was reminded that you can speak English. You had interpreted for our captain in questioning the American bomber pilot back in training camp. I would like to ask a favor of you."

I didn't know what to say so I just listened. Even though my German pay book had me listed as born in the United States, neither he nor any German commander had ever said one word to me about it. Of course he knew I was born in the United States.

"Ask one of the American guards for a few cigarettes. Would you do that for me? Just for old time's sake. In return, I'll give you a boiled potato that one of my soldiers smuggled out while on KP duty."

I looked at my former sergeant-major and hesitated, thinking, oh, now you want me to be your friend? You didn't like me right from the beginning when I was assigned to your company. You thought I was shirking my duties because my frostbitten toes were still healing and I was excused from the first few weeks of training in the field. Or, because I volunteered temporarily for that posh duty on the flak tower overlooking Herman Goring, or getting off so easily from that broken rifle affair. And now you want me to do you a favor. Hmm. Nonetheless, when the sergeant smiled and held his hand out for me to shake, I reluctantly said, "Okay, I'll try."

So I walked up to the fence and waited for the guard to come by. I didn't dare tell him I was born in Detroit, Michigan, so I spoke in broken English. "Say, sir, a few cigarettes—have you, maybe?"

"Oh sure, but at the moment I don't have any on me. Meet me here after I get off duty in about two hours," he replied.

Dusk was settling in when the American trooper approached the fence. Without saying a word he slipped a small package wrapped in a piece of newspaper through the fence. I was happy everything went so smoothly.

I immediately went up to the sergeant-major and, without checking it out first, handed him the package. "Thank you. You will get your potato tomorrow," he said.

The next morning the sergeant-major rushed up to me red-faced and agitated. He showed me an opened pack of Lucky Strike cigarettes. Through his clenched teeth he said, "What is this, a joke?"

Then I saw the mess: an ugly mixture of wet tobacco and dissolved cigarette paper inside the pack.

"I can't smoke this," he said, his face getting even redder. "And you won't get the potato!" he shouted as he left. I was happy I didn't smoke.

Later on a few buddies of the German sergeant-major's walked up and started taunting me. "Look, how awkwardly Esfeld is shaking out his blanket. He can't even fold it right." After a few more insults they left and I wondered what would follow next.

What did happen next came from the American compound: loud hooting and hollering. Shouts of joy sprang out. "Germany has surrendered. The war is over!"

It was V- day, May 9, 1945.

The mood among us POWs was a mixture of subdued disappointment and anticipation of going home soon. I never reported to the commandant's office. The letter 'E' was never called. Instead about a week later all of us POWs were ordered into formation and marched out of the camp.

When we reached the highway British soldiers with rifles clutched at their sides were waiting for us. They were to take over guarding us. I was now a POW of the British Army. Their animosity against us Germans was palpable. They swore at us in the worst way and kicked us in the behind. One British officer hit a man next to me squarely in the shoulder blades with the butt of his rifle. I saw his next swing aimed at me but since I was on the inside row and saw it coming I managed to duck, receiving only a glancing blow to my right shoulder. It still stung, though. This continued on all the way down the line until we reached a railroad siding and were ordered to climb into the waiting boxcars. I wondered why these British soldiers were treating us this way. It wasn't until later that I discovered that most of them were easy to get along with.

The train took us in a north-westerly direction, meaning further and further away from the Russians. It was a relief to think there was no chance of being handed over to them anymore. We passed through the heavily bombed port city of *Lubeck* and finally reached our destination near *Eutin* in Germany's Northern Province of *Schleswig Holstein*. As my column marched into a heavily wooded area we passed a military truck parked on the side. There two British soldiers were handing out cans of Spam to us POWs. We were then marched into the woods and told to disperse and find shelter among the huge beech trees.

There was a farm a half a mile away where we could get drinking water and wash ourselves. There I found a pile of rock salt and I took a piece with me. The farmer used it for his cows to lick on. Our food consisted of a half loaf of dark rye bread per man per day: that was it. It didn't take long for my hunger pains to set in. With about one-hundred thousand POWs in our immediate area, it was difficult for the British to feed us properly.

While in high school in Braunschweig, during my days of collecting herbal plants for medicinal teas, I learned about an obnoxious weed called stinging nettle: when you touched it, it left a reddish burning rash. But it was edible when boiled and quite tasty and healthy when properly seasoned. There was plenty of it here in the woods and I had salt. I wrapped my hand in a handkerchief my mother had thoughtfully packed and collected a whole bunch of stinging nettle in my blanket. After I told the farmer's wife what I wanted to do, she gave me an empty can and some matches. *"Viel Gluck,"* she wished me.

Franz just looked on and shook his head as I made a fire and started boiling the nettle, adding a little rock salt. I said, *"Hunger trebt es rein,"* a German expression meaning "hunger forces it into you." After I figured the nettle leaves had cooked long enough I drained the water and mashed them with my spoon. Then I tried the first spoonful. I winced and almost spit it out. But with a piece of rye bread I managed to choke it down. At least it stopped the hunger pains for a little while. But I didn't try it again.

I started looking for other sources of food. Every morning I noticed on the dew laden ground these fat, plump snails crawling around. This kind of snail I knew was edible, like the escargot the French cooked with wine and considered a delicacy. My mother taught me that, too. I didn't t have any wine but I had some rock salt. So one morning I gathered up about fifty slimy creatures and dropped them into boiling water. Immediately the meaty part of the snails separated from the shells and bobbed around on the surface. I couldn't wait. I fished out the empty shells, added salt and cooked the meat a little longer. Then I tasted the first piece of snail meat. It was as tough as shoe leather. No flavor except the salt! I chewed and chewed until my jaw ached. I managed to swallow all of them. I won't do that again, either.

I gave up. It wasn't worth the effort. Besides it was June and the British started to serve us soup along with the bread once a day. Eight weeks of near starvation.

As the weather got sunny and warmer, I started to daydream about going home. Was the factory bombed out? Did my family survive? I didn't reflect much on the answers. I just wanted to go home.

Then we received this news: All farmers, farmhands, and anybody connected with farming were to be sent home first and ordered to turn in their "sold book", or pay book. Every German soldier always carried his personal and military data with him, which was contained in this booklet and was about the size of a U.S. passport. The pay books were sturdy and came in a clear plastic jacket made to fit a breast pocket on a tunic or uniform jacket. It listed the name, the birth date, the place of birth and, among others, your occupation. In my pay book the word *Schuler* (student) was clearly typewritten. As I gazed at that for a while it occurred to me that if I hand wrote the word "agriculture" in front of student I would be classified as being connected to the farming industry and eligible for early discharge.

I shared my idea with Franz. "Do you think I could get away with it?" I asked half-jokingly

He mulled it over for a moment, then said, "Herman, go for it. The worst that can happen is they will shoot you for document falsification."

I laughed. "You sure have a morbid sense of humor, Franz." What the heck. I decided to take the risk.

The next day I asked the farmer for a sharp pencil and paper. After practicing a few times I carefully printed the word *Landwirtschaftlicher* (agriculture) in front of the word *schuler*. At the appointed time I turned over my pay book to the British commandant's office. For the next few days I anxiously waited for my name to be called. Sure enough, I was notified that I had been cleared for discharge. I was overcome with joy. I tearfully said goodbye to my number one machine gunner and pal, Franz.

"Franz, I will give you my address. When you get home look me up. Okay?"

"Okay, Herman. I don't know where my family fled, now that the Russians have occupied my town. Take good care."

But I never heard from Franz again.

Showered, sprayed with DDT powder, and wearing a sagging but freshly laundered German uniform, I stood in front of a desk where a friendly British officer was filling out my discharge papers. He looked up at me and smiled, "Congratulations. I see today's your birthday." It was June 24, 1945; I was now eighteen years old. I thanked the officer in English. He wished me well. We shook hands and I left.

No doubt my speaking English to the British commander during our conversation helped in my discharge, although the papers were not signed by the British Commandant until three days later. So on June 27, 1945, eight years after my family arrived on German soil to fulfill my father's dream to build a new grand automobile for the people, I was officially discharged as a POW.

While I waited for a British military truck to pick me up, I learned that Germany as well as its former capital, Berlin, had been divided into four occupation zones. The north went to the British, the east to the Russians, the south to the Americans, and the southwest to the French. That meant Wolfsburg and the Volkswagen factory were now in the British zone. Though it was only five miles west of the Russian zone, I nonetheless felt some relief.

Finally, with several hundred of us POWs, the British convoy left on a journey south, leaving each of us off at or close to our destinations. After about one hundred and twenty miles I was dropped off. I hitchhiked the last fifteen miles to my home in Wolfsburg.

At last, my eight weeks as a POW in American and British hands had come to an end. As I slowly dragged my scrawny body the last few hundred yards I felt my heart start to pound. Through tears welling up in my eyes I noticed no mortar damage to any of the houses. Even the oak trees that lined both sides of my street were in place. I had to take a moment to contain myself before I pushed our

doorbell for the first time in six months.

Chapter 28

Welcome Home

"Mutti! Mutti! Herman is back!" shouted Norma, my now eight year old kid sister who opened the door. As I entered the foyer my mother came rushing down the stairs with my younger brother Ronald and flew into my bony arms. We were all crying and hugging each other.

"Herman, you have returned home safe and sound!" exclaimed my mother.

Then my sister said, "Wait, we have something for you." She ran into the living room and handed me a birthday card. It was a five-and-a-half inch by seven inch open face piece of cardboard with a red and blue border of hand painted flowers. On the top, printed in black letters, was a written: "To Our Dear Herman. The best wishes for an eighteenth birthday." Below that, framed in a colorfully painted floral wreath, was stapled a photo of me at sixteen in the uniform of a flak-helper with a shirt and tie. Though deeply touched, I noticed my father

was missing.

"Where's Vati?" I asked.

"We don't know. He has not returned yet from southern

Austria," my mother answered.

"What is he doing in southern Austria?"

"He and his colleague Mr. Joe Werner were asked to meet with

Dr. Ferdinand Porsche at his engineering works. They left last

November." She went on to explain that their task was to study the

feasibility of designing and building another one of Dr. Porsche's

heavy tanks, only bigger. She said nothing further about my father's

disappearance.

1945. My 18th Birthday card from my brother Ronald and sister
Norma. "Our Beloved Herman the best wishes on your 18th birthday."

The next day after I returned home I had to report to City Hall to register as a legally released German POW and to receive food and clothing ration cards. By then the city was bustling with smartly dressed marching British troops and the traffic of their stub-nosed Bedford trucks, which looked like part Jeep. On the side of the trucks penciled in white paint were the words "No fraternization." I didn't know what that meant until I looked it up in our American dictionary at home.

When I reached City Hall I was informed that I would be assigned to one of the farmers in the area to help out, as per the conditions of my early release as a POW.

"Sir, as soon as the American Consulate in Hamburg opens up again, I would like to apply for a new U.S. passport and return to America," I eagerly stated. I showed him my passport from our voyage over in 1937.

The official looked it over and said, "I'll have to get permission from the *Burgermeister* (mayor)."

Soon the mayor came into the office and greeted me warmly, welcoming me back home with a long hand shake. "I know about you

American families living in KdF Stadt" he said. He then told me a story about the eruption of the town that occurred back in April and the disturbing events from the freed forced laborers as well as the threat of becoming the Russian zone.

"Twenty American-born children saved the city," he exclaimed. "A riot broke out. Forced laborers from the VW factory escaped and started breaking into shops and burning buildings for several days. All hell broke loose. Thank God for our local priest who knew a little English. He had heard about an American military convoy in a town fifteen miles away. So he went by bicycle as fast as he could to alert them. He told the Americans that there were children born in the US living here that needed to be saved. Sure enough the Americans came that day and they brought a bus."

Both my sister Norma and brother Ronald were two of the twenty children left in the town who were put on the bus.

"And our city was restored to calm," the Mayor said with a broad smile. After the mayor finished his story he handed me my ration cards and wished me luck on my return trip to America.

Our Wolfsburg house was a duplex. Next to us lived the Martini family, with a daughter and son. Mr. Martini had been a captain in the artillery and had not yet returned home. Their son Hans was sixteen years and had been a schoolmate of mine. My mother told me how anxious Hans had been to help defend the Fatherland. He would take his father's old WWI pistol and practice firing it in the backyard. "Then in April, just three weeks before the war ended, he was sent with the *Volkssturm* of Wolfsburg to the east to fight the Russians around Berlin," my mother said, shaking her head. "He was killed with a bullet through his head."

The *Volkssturm,* made up of German boys and men from ages sixteen to sixty, was a last minute disparate army organized by the Nazis by orders from Hitler in 1944. I thought of the young boy and remembered the old bald man who I witnessed getting shot point blank. That image I had to erase. I dared not tell Hans's mother.

I paid my respects to Hans's parent's next door the next day. Two blocks away I stopped at my classmate Hans-Herman Bokelmann's home. I knocked on the door and his mother tearfully told me the only thing they knew was that Hans-Herman was missing in action on the Russian Front. They never found out what happened to him and he remains missing to this day. Two houses down from Hans-Herman lived a dear friend and schoolmate, Hans Evers. Hans Evers had wanted me to join him in applying for officer training school in November of 1944. When I rung his doorbell his mother opened the door holding a baby in her arms. Holding back tears she said, "I received word Hans has been captured by Russian troops and is now a POW somewhere in Russia."

I did not see Hans Evers again until a 1971 vacation trip to Germany. He had returned home in the fall of 1948, went to the University and earned a doctorate in economics. (As of this writing Hans is suffering from a debilitating stroke he suffered in 2000; he is being cared for by his wife at home in Germany.)

"I will be going back to the U.S. soon. I will stop by again before I leave," I told his mother.

I continued my search for schoolmates, going door to door on both sides and across the street. Siegfried Rechenbach was a year older than me and one class ahead. His father was another of the original six German-American engineers Dr. Porsche recruited and hired in 1937.

I knocked on the door and his mother answered. "Welcome home Herman! Siegfried is not here. He was a paratrooper and broke his thighbone on a training jump. He is now recuperating in a hospital in southern Germany. The severe injury left him with a limp."

When Siegfried returned to the U.S. we were reunited.

The next day I walked into town to look up my schoolmate Ernst Koeppe. I could not believe the live oak trees that lined each side of the streets had not been felled or harmed by shelling or bombing. Wolfsburg had been missed somehow.

Ernst was born in Munich and his father was an electrician at the VW factory. I found him sitting in an easy chair, despondent and looking dejected. "A piece of shrapnel from a Russian artillery shell tore into my leg," he said with a tone of bitterness. "I almost bled to death. The doctors had to amputate it."

It was hard for me to find the right words to console him. Ernst was a tall, handsome looking young man with dark wavy hair. With his outgoing personality he would have no trouble finding the prettiest girl. So I let him continue without saying a word.

"Herman, who would want me now, an invalid with a wooden leg?" His voice was filled with despair.

I left his house reflecting on all the heartbreak I had encountered in the last couple of days. I felt so grateful for having survived this terrible war unscathed. A few weeks later I sent a letter to my classmate Fritz, with whom I had shared my first foxhole in the early weeks of serving as a flak helper with the anti-aircraft battery in Braunschweig. I received a reply from his mother informing me that Fritz had been taken prisoner by British forces and sent to England to work the coal mines.

"Fritz wrote and said he typed the word 'student' in his pay book as an occupation," she explained in her letter. So I was not the only one of us boys that was dishonest for a minute during the war. Coal shoveling or placement in another country would have been my fate too if I had not been bold and hand printed the word agriculture in front of "student." I felt lucky.

In late July of '45 we still had no word from my father or from the U.S. Consulate in Hamburg about my U.S. passport and when I would be reinstated so we could leave for the States. Since over sixty percent of the Volkswagen plant was destroyed, in spring of 1944 clean-up operation and repair work were under way by the remaining forced laborers and volunteers.

Even after the British arrived in May 1945 and the war had ended, the Nazi *KDF-Wagon* or *Kubelwagen* and the *Schwimmwagen* (the German Jeep and amphibian military vehicles) were still in production. British Major W. Hurst was put in charge of operations. He discontinued the production of the *Kubelwagen* and *Schwimmwagen* and instead married the body of a Volkswagen "Beetle" to the high-riding chassis of the *Kubelwagen*. This hybrid became popular and practical for the British and French occupation forces, with the first shipments going to France. Thus the Germans of Volkswagen's labor forces were provided with continued jobs.

My mother meanwhile had written to my father's parents that there was no word about my father. Food was rationed to the point that the VW workers would exchange parts for fruit. All we had to eat everyday was potatoes and bread, like everyone else.

These two versions of a jeep type VW were produced at the "Wolfsburg plant during WW II"

Produced 1938. L- *Kubelwagen*, R-*Schwimmwagen*

"I would like to send Herman and Ronald over to get fattened up," she wrote. My father grew up in a large house his father had built located in a small town just outside the city of Bremen in Northern Germany. As a hobby my grandfather raised hogs and kept a cow for milk, butter and cheese. My grandmother raised chickens and rabbits and tended to a fruit and vegetable garden. There was always an abundance of fresh meats and delicious tasting sausages, or *wurst*. I remembered how on one of our vacations in the '30s, after I tasted these sausages, I wanted to come back just for them.

"They should come," my grandmother wrote back. "We were restricted to the number of animals we could slaughter for ourselves. We had to give away so much of our food to the government these past two years."

Chapter 29

Grandparents' Home Cooking

My brother Ronald and I boarded one of the few passenger trains that were in service and headed for the city of Hannover where we would have to change trains. On the way I thought back to 1936 when I first met my grandparents. I walked into my grandfather's pigpens just before feeding time. The pungent aroma of the sty made it hard for me to envision eating the meat. I remembered my grandfather would mix in chocolate powder that came in one hundred- fifty pound drums from Holland with the fodder to fatten up the pigs--and maybe to sweeten the flavor of the meat. I had stuck my wetted finger into the barrel to try it. It was bitter, not sweet. Sitting on the train I thought how hogs eat everything, even chunks of soft red bricks.

Once heavily traveled, the railroad to Hannover linked the Ruhr industrial area in the west with Berlin in the east. Because the city of Ruhr had been mostly destroyed during a five month bombing campaign by the British Air Force, the tracks stopped ten miles east of Wolfsburg at the border between the Russian occupied East zone and the British occupied West zone, making Wolfsburg the forlorn station at the end of the line.

When we entered the Hannover station Ronald and I were aghast at the destruction: it was one of the most heavily bombed cities in Germany. Eighty-eight air raids destroyed over ninety percent of the city; six thousand citizens perished. Thankfully, many of the ancient surrounding castles and medieval churches were spared. My grandparents lived in the country nearby.

Huddled close together, my brother and I stayed most of the night in a musty former air raid shelter. Ronald had a bigger and more rounded head than I, with shorter cropped dark hair. He had the attractive full red lips, like my younger sister. He stood next to me at shoulder height. All of us, including our father, had large piercing light blue eyes. Mine were hidden behind my round wire spectacles. We looked at the frightful sight of the townspeople sitting around us. Most were unwashed and dressed in shabby looking clothes, especially the men who were unshaved and hollowed looking. Occasionally we caught one or two folks looking at us. The blank stares scared my

brother, who was only eleven. I put the small suitcase my mother gave

us between us.

"Ronald, put your head on it and try to get some sleep. I'll stay

awake. I'm used to guard duty," I told him. Reassured, he fell asleep

and the night passed uneventfully, which I was glad for.

We arrived in Bremen early the next morning.

"Excuse me sir," I inquired in German to the station master,

"we need to catch the next train to *Kirchwiehe*. Which one is it?"

"There is no train going to that town," he said starkly. "The

railroad bridge across the River Weser has been blown apart. It is still

under repair. But the bridge at the road a few miles downstream in the

city is intact," he generously explained to us.

"Come on Ronald. Let's go," I said.

"You can take the streetcar across the bridge, but be sure to get

out at the end of the line," he hollered out to us as we hurried as fast as

we could through the big dreaded city. I couldn't help but think how

generous the station master had been, considering all the chaos from the cleaning up and dealing with the starved misplaced people. But we still had ten miles to go.

The city of Bremen with its Bremerhaven port on the North Sea was an enclave in the British sector occupied and governed by the American military forces. At the end of the streetcar line was a checkpoint manned by U.S. soldiers.

"Where are you two headed for and where do you live?" one of them asked.

I handed him the two U.S. passports my mother had saved from 1937 when the Nazi's told us to give them up or face the Nazi's high court, which meant going to a camp. My brave mother refused and got away with it. The registration cards showed that we lived in Wolfsburg, now located in the British occupation zone.

The soldier looked at the passports and chuckled. "Boy, are these old! But I see you are a couple of American boys born in Detroit, Michigan."

"Yes, we are. We want to visit our grandparents in the countryside to get few good meals. But now we are stuck here and will have to walk the rest of the ten miles," I explained in English.

He looked us over from head to toe, both of us bedraggled and skinny, and exclaimed, "It's your lucky day. I can help you. Every day about this time a postal truck comes through here to deliver and pick up mail around here. Wait here in the guard shack." With that the friendly GI (by now I had learned American soldiers were called GIs) gave Ronald and me each a stick of gum.

"Thank you so much," I said.

"You're welcome, kid," he answered.

The lingo sounded familiar to me and chewing the gum made me feel like a true American again. Shortly the postal truck arrived. Low and behold it was a converted Volkswagen *Kubelwagen,* like those the factory started to build towards the end of the war for the *Reichspost* (government postal service).

After the guard checked the cargo he turned to the driver and said, "Anton, I want you to take these two boys and drop them off as close as you can get to their grandparents' home!"

Indignantly, Anton protested. "I can't do that. It's against regulations." Typical response for a Prussian disciplined government employee.

"These are tired and hungry American boys and you can do that for me," the GI ordered, offering Anton an American cigarette.

"Alright," Anton muttered, "I'll do it this time." He motioned for us to climb into the back of the little truck among the mailbags.

"Thanks again, Corporal," I called out, recognizing his rank.

"Good luck, fellows," the GI replied and waved the driver on.

The roads were bumpy from allied shelling. Wreckage was strewn where once an apartment building or store stood. Burned out homes held up only with blackened frames and the smell of ash overcame me and my brother. We had to cover our noses to keep from getting nauseous. The further out in the country we went, the less there were any signs of a war zone. Distant farm houses were still erect with chickens, hens, cows, goats and pigs squealing about.

In the summer of 1945 Germany looked like a conglomeration of giant ant hills with people moving all over, many in slow motion. Hundreds of thousands of forced laborers were trying to get back to their home countries.

VW wagon *Reichspost* or Postal Delivery Truck, Post WWII.

The highways and roads were clogged with millions of German refugees uprooted from their homelands, trying to find shelter and a new home in their shattered country. The food supply was scarcer now than it was during the war. Containers filled with agriculture products the farmers were trying to get to the markets were stuck in warehouses. The last minute destruction of railroad junctions and bridges by allied bombing or by Hitler's "Scorched Earth" orders hampered the movement of goods.

When at last we reached our grandparents' farm I hugged my brother with watery eyes and exclaimed, "Ronald, we made it! *Oma* (grandma), here we come! Get the bacon and eggs ready!"

When Ronald and I finally stepped through the wide door into our Uncle Fritz's saddle, harness, and upholstery shop, in no time the rest of the clan had gathered to give us a tearful and warmhearted welcome. There were Oma and Opa Esfeld, Aunt Greta, my father's sister, her husband Uncle Fritz and their two children, my cousins Hermann and Anita. Hermann was one month shy of sixteen and already as tall as and bigger than me. His younger age had spared him any combat war experience. His sister, at fourteen, was short and stout.

When I was in the Hitler Youth and before I was sent to the Russian front by the *Wehrmact* (Germany army), my father took us by train to visit his relatives in *Kirchwiehe* for a few days. I first met my younger cousins back in 1937, the year my mother put me into a German class, since there was nothing else for me to do on our vacation. That's where the taunts became embedded in me. My two cousins, only two and six at the time, attended a different school. School vacations in Germany were at shorter intervals than in the U.S.; just a nine-and-a-half year old's luck.

All the initial excitement could not have calmed down fast enough for me and Ronald. We needed to freshen up for supper. As long as my Oma was alive she did all the cooking. This time she was frying potatoes left over from the main meal at lunchtime with smoked bacon bits and fresh vegetables. We each got a glass of fresh milk. For my brother and me it was a meal sent from heaven.

During the course of the evening dinner I briefly related to them what had happened in Wolfsburg during the five years since we last visited and about the bombed out factory.

"Have you heard from your father?" Oma asked quietly.

"No. Nothing yet," I answered.

No one else said a word.

Soon sleepiness overcame me and Ronald. We blissfully fell into bed with everyone else sleeping in the large and roomy house my grandfather had built and my father grew up in until he was twenty-five and immigrated to America as a journeyman machine builder with a degree in mechanical engineering.

The next day my brother and I quickly fell into a routine, helping out with various chores. We felt obligated to earn our keep for the abundance of food we were receiving. Ronald helped keep Uncle Fritz's workshop clean by sweeping the floor and putting away tools. I helped my Opa (grandfather) rake up the fresh grass that he had skillfully cut with gracefully executed swings of his scythe. Every so often he would stop and pull out a sharpening stone from his overalls' pocket and hone the blade. It made me think of how often we boys had to clean our skinny long rifles for battle and before inspection. He cut the grass as fodder for the cows from a large meadow he owned nearly every day; twice on Saturdays so he could have the day off on Sunday. I cleaned the pigpen and cow stalls, not minding the smells after having to dig ditches and foxholes under heavy attack by fighter planes and army tanks.

After a week of good and plentiful hot home cooked meals my brother and I had noticeably gained a few pounds.

One morning our cousin Herman took us into the shed to show us how to get a rabbit ready for the cooking pot. Oma was going to make rabbit stew for dinner. Herman picked out a nice plump rabbit from its cage and grabbed it by its ears. Then he held it up by its hind legs, took a steel rod and with a swift well aimed blow struck the animal just behind the ears, breaking its neck. It died instantly. He tied the legs of the lifeless rabbit to a hook, cut its throat to bleed it, the blood dripping into a pail, and began to skin it.

He laughed as he looked at my kid brother's snow white face. "I've done this many times. You get used to it." All my brother and I could do was look on amazed at our cousin who, unlike us, grew up in the country.

Shortly after the war ended horrible stories and photographs were published in newspapers and magazines showing allied troops liberating numerous concentration camps in Germany. The most notorious ones were the mass extermination camps of Jews in Auschwitz and Birkenan, Poland. I had never heard of them during the war. I remember from our last visit with our grandparents there was a Jewish family named Jacobson and their young son Otto that lived next door to them. That was it.

After about ten days and ten pounds heavier, it was time for Ronald and me to return home. Trains were running again, although there was still one spur of track being repaired on the bridge across the River Weser to Bremen.

"Herman, do you think we will have to stay in that air raid shelter in Hannover again? "Ronald asked.

"Uh, I don't think so, Ronald. The train is running over the repaired bridge now and traffic has improved," I said as calmly as I could, remembering how horrible that night was in the shelter and praying we would not have to repeat it.

Tante Greta, my father's sister, and her husband Uncle Fritz had come by to see us and to find out what happened to her brother. Even though we had nothing to tell her, she handed us a piece of goat meat tightly wrapped in newspaper "to keep the red juices from spilling" she commented, and to take home.

We said our goodbyes. "*Vielen Dank, Tante* Greta, and Uncle Fritz. I know our mother will appreciate this."

"*Ja*, Herman, and please inform us as soon as you hear about your dad," my Oma said.

Chapter 30

Damaged Goods

"We sail to see, not fail to be."
--Edna Esfeld

We walked the three quarters of a mile back to the train station, this time with a hop in our step. We felt renewed and invigorated. But as the train slowly approached the platform I saw to my horror that passengers were sitting on top of the carriages, clinging to the sides like bunches of grapes.

"Are we going to get on?" Ronald asked as the train came to a stop.

"Yes! Hurry up and hang on the outside," I yelled. We jumped and squeezed onto the running board. I managed to clutch our suitcase tightly under one arm which held the delicate meat my Oma and Opa had given us. With my complete strength back, we managed to hang on for dear life the rest of the way home.

We arrived home late in the day. When I presented my mother with the gift, she exclaimed, "What is this? Why on Gods' earth goat meat?" She seemed disappointed. "Why not a nice ham?"

"Oma said that even among the farmers the number of hogs and cattle they are allowed to slaughter is rationed. The rest is sold to the government for the millions of refugees and displaced people who lost their homesteads and farms," I explained. I looked around, hoping to see my father. "Where is Vati?"

"Herman, I have good news and bad news. Your father and Joe Werner returned home safe. But the authorities promptly came and took them into custody by the Belgian Secret Service. They are being held at the county jail in *Gifhorn.*"

"*Giforn* is thirteen miles away and in the country!" I exclaimed. I was shocked; my father, in jail! For what?

"I've made arrangements for us to go there," she asserted. "We will talk to the British military government about the charges."

After the war ended it took my father and Joe Werner weeks instead of days to reach Wolfsburg from Austria; they had to hitch rides on coal trucks and supply trains.

When Mutti and I arrived at the jail the next day, after having the breath squeezed out of us on another crowded train ride, we were told that since my father had supervised a group of engineers from occupied Holland to work in his tool engineering department at the Wolfsburg VW factory, he was being investigated for charges of mistreatment. The British government had asked the Belgian Secret Service to conduct investigations of all such charges.

My mother and I got a pass and went to see my father. The mere sight of him in his jail cell nearly broke my heart. Tears welled up in my eyes. Hardly recovered from the long and arduous trip back home from Austria, he looked frail, his dress suit hanging loosely on his thin frame. His eyes, peering from dark circles, looked bewildered.

"Why, why? For what am I here?"

We did not say much. It was a sad reunion.

My mother went back a few times with a fresh change of clothes and extra home cooked food she managed to spare from our meager rationings. After being incarcerated for about two weeks the British determined that my father could serve on a work detail until the investigation concluded. He was assigned to help unload barges that brought in supplies on the *Mittleland Kanal* to the docks at

Fallensleben, which were just four miles west of Wolfsburg. The work

detail consisted of a dozen other Germans held for investigations and

they all were guarded by a handful of British soldiers; a sergeant was

in command.

One day the sergeant spoke to my father. "I hear you speak

English," he said.

"Yes, my wife and I took English courses back in the United

States," my father told him.

"You lived in America?" asked the sergeant.

"Yes. I worked as an engineer for the Ford Motor Company for

a few years,"

"Ahh, I could use your help."

So the sergeant befriended my father, making him an

interpreter. Before long he gave my father an additional daily

assignment to organize the work each morning and supervise. It was

an arrangement made in heaven for my father. He was back in his

element.

When my mother and I saw him back in good shape and in good spirits with a smile on his face, we were happy. Now on my mother's weekly trips to the *Kanal,* instead of her bringing him food, she was the one who brought back food. My father called it "damaged goods."

In time the investigations ended with no charges of mistreatment brought against my father. He was released from custody and returned to work at the Volkswagen factory, but not in his former position as head of the Tool and Process Engineering Department. Because of the uncertainly of the outcome of the charges, father's former assistant was put in charge of his old department; the new British management deemed it necessary. So my father continued in the same job he had started with back home at Ford Motor.

Even though my father was happy with his new position, he had no financial gain to show for the eight years he worked for Volkswagen; nor was the VW he had worked and paid for sitting in our driveway.

During the war Hitler did not allow the German people to buy property or homes or even build them. He did not allow anyone to send money abroad for investment. Besides keeping any income in cash at home, one could only deposit money in banks in Germany. Any withdrawal my father made went for living expenses and other basic needs. The feeling of being penniless weighed heavily on my father's mind.

Finally, in the late summer of 1945, I received word that the American Consulate had opened in Hamburg. I was going to be traveling alone once again to Hamburg.

Circa late 1940s. VW Factory Post WWII. Courtesy of my late sister Yachana (a.k.a. Norma).

Chapter 31

My Apprenticeship at the VW Factory

Knowing it would be difficult to find lodgings in the heavily bombed city of Hamburg, I planned for a two-night trip. I walked between blocks and blocks of ruined apartment buildings that stood like skeletons-no windows, doors, walls or roofs. Mountainous piles of bricks and the smell of burnt corpses clung to the foul air. Hamburg was reduced to ruins. Finally, I found the bed and breakfast that I saw posted on the bulletin board back at the train station. There was a room for me. It was already too late in the day to walk the three miles to the consulate, which was located in the center of the city, so I rested a little on the nicely made up single bed and then gathered with the other guests in the dining room for supper. Each of us had to give the hostess enough ration stamps to cover the meal.

The next morning, when I set out for the U.S. Consulate, I discovered I could take the streetcar part of the way. Using mine carts, the Germans had worked quickly to remove all the rubble from the debris-strewn streets. The stench of death could not escape me though. I tried to close my eyes at the remaining burned bodies left to be attended to.

When I arrived and saw the US Stars and Stripes waving in the breeze on top of the building, shivers ran down my spine. Full of anticipation I entered the building and got into a long line of other expectant people.

"And why are you here, young man?" asked the clerk seated at the small wooden desk when at last my turn came.

"I've come to get my passport papers renewed so I can go back home to the U.S.," I proudly stated. My English, a bit broken now, nonetheless passed the test.

The desk clerk handed me a colored card with a number on it. "Please be seated and your number will be called soon."

"Thank you," I politely replied. I sat for what seemed an eternity. Finally my number was called. I had all my documents ready. My birth certificate from Detroit, the U.S. passport I came over to

Germany with in 1937, my Hitler Youth membership card, and my British discharge papers from service in the German Army.

Before I was led into an office I read the nameplate on the door: it read consul-General. I immediately became alarmed and a light sweat broke out on my forehead. Why, I wondered, would the consul-General see an American citizen born in the United States if all he wanted was to have his passport renewed? As I entered the consul-General's office I hesitated momentarily. There in front of me, behind a large and shiny mahogany desk, sat a man dressed in a business suit. His salt and pepper hair told me he was in his mid-fifties.

"Have a seat," he said, motioning me forward with his arm. With a straight face, he introduced himself in a husky voice. "I am consul-General Ed McKenzie and I understand you would like to have your passport renewed and return to the United States."

"Yes, Sir, consul-General. That is correct," I answered in a firm and clear tone. That seemed to please him because a faint smile crossed his face.

"Let's see what we can do for you, Herman," he answered and proceeded to ask me a barrage of questions. Then he shocked me. "Why did you and your family come to Germany in 1937?"

"My father was offered a position by Dr. Ferdinand Porsche with the building of the Volkswagen factory in KdF Stadt."

"I see. Are your parents U.S. citizens?"

"Yes, sir." I kept my answers brief.

"Uh-huh. Do you have any siblings?"

"Yes, sir. A younger brother and sister."

"Where were they born?"

"We all were born in Detroit, Michigan, sir." I noticed his grey eyebrows move upward.

"Why didn't you and your family return to the States shortly before the war in 1939, when there was still time?" Before I could answer, he quickly added, "We could have helped you. Our embassies in Germany were still operating because the U.S. was not yet at war with Germany. And why aren't your parents and siblings here with you now?"

I started to get warm under the collar and felt my face gushing with color. The questions were getting tough to answer. I tried to answer them as truthfully as I could.

"Were you in the Jungvolk? Were you a member of the Hitler *Jugend* and the *RAD*?"

"Yes," I replied. Then I was asked the last ominous sounding question.

"Did you serve in the German Army?"

"Yes, sir." I hesitated.

"Then show me your discharge papers," he ordered.

I handed over my discharge papers which he studied carefully, turning it over. Then he looked me straight in the eye and said, "Sorry, young man, you have lost your American citizenship."

It felt like a ton of bricks had just hit me. A lump formed in my throat. In utter disbelief I meekly asked, "But why?"

Slumping back into his leather chair the Consul General explained. "Even though your discharge papers from the German Army were made out on your birthday, June 24th, they were not signed until three days after your eighteenth birthday. Our immigration law states that American citizens living abroad must report to the nearest American Consulate to reaffirm their citizenship before the age of eighteen. You missed that deadline by three days."

"What do I do now?" I asked, totally dejected.

"There have been several cases like yours that have come to the attention of our Congress in Washington, prompting it to draft an amendment to the immigration law suspending the age limit for those of you who were unable to reach an American Consulate because of the war."

Seeing that the Consul-General was trying to sound encouraging I asked, "How long will it take Congress to pass that law?"

He rose up from his chair and walked around the desk. Looking down at me with half a grin he answered, "You know how slowly our Congress moves." I nodded my head slightly, as if I knew what he was talking about. "About two years. The Consulate here in Hamburg will notify you." He extended his arm and we shook hands to say goodbye. "Good luck, young man," were his final words as he cordially dismissed me.

On the long train ride home I had plenty of time to ponder about what to do next. We all discussed it when I got home and came up with a plan. Even though my mother, eleven-year-old brother and eight-year-old sister could return at any time because they still had their valid U.S. passports, which my mother had kept hidden from the German authorities, we did not want to split up the family in this manner. We instead decided to wait until I received my U.S. citizenship and the four of us would return together. Once back in the U.S., as soon as we established permanent residence, my mother could apply for my father to join us: this fell under the Dependent's Quota Act, which significantly reduced the normal waiting time for immigrants.

When Hitler declared war on the United States in December 1941, the Nazis told my father he had two choices: "Give up your American citizenship and continue with your job at the Volkswagen factory or you and your entire family will be place in an internment camp." Just like the U.S. did to many Japanese and Germans in the United States too. Rather than risk having his family incarcerated at the hands of the Nazis, my father forfeited his American citizenship. Thus my father had to re-immigrate to the U.S.

Now the question was: what should I do while I wait for my citizenship? The thought of commuting back and forth to bombed-out Braunschweig to finish high school did not seem feasible since I would fall back yet another grade and not graduate until I turned twenty. "What good would that do for a new start in America?" I asked my mother.

"Herman, your father has to stay here in Germany. Until he can join us in America, you will be the head of the household." By this she meant that I had to find a fairly good paying job--and quickly. "Why not enter into a tool-and-die making apprenticeship with the Volkswagen factory?" my prudent-thinking father suggested. I thought about it.

Considering my father's excellent connections as a respected tool-and-die designer and process engineer for Ford Motor Company for ten years in the early '30s, I figured I could always finish my apprenticeship in the Detroit area. "That is a good idea, Vati," I agreed.

So, on the 11th of September 1945, ironically, I started work as a tool-and-die maker apprentice at the Volkswagen factory. The British by now had seized control of the plant and the VW organization, which it would hold for the next two years: it no longer belonged to Germans during that time. The town was renamed Wolfsburg in May of '45. The British had German factory workers cleaning up at a fast pace. I would finish as a journeyman in four years. By that time I expected to be back in the United States.

Towards the end of the war my mother got to know a family that owned a farm in a village thirty minutes away by bicycle. The farmer's wife and my mother, about the same age, became friends. My mother, who had always dressed stylishly, soon bartered with some of her clothing with her new friend for fresh eggs, butter, milk and bacon to supplement the meager portions of food she got with ration stamps. With the war over, food had become even scarcer as distribution from farmers was tightly controlled. While my mother received less and less, she found ways with money and clothes to stock her kitchen. Soon a joke went around our small town that the farmers were carpeting their stalls with expensive Persian rugs. In addition, my mother used all of her ingenuity in cooking to stretch our meals and keep the hunger pains down.

As the winter of 1946 approached it became obvious to the Volkswagen management that the amount of coal allotted them to burn was not enough to sufficiently steam heat the plant and the city of Wolfsburg. The same was true with electricity, which was generated by steam turbines and distributed to the city by means of underground cables. There wasn't a single overhead electrical wire in the entire city. Together with the plant management, the city fathers devised a plan whereby each household would be furnished with a so called *Bunkerofen* (bunker stove) by the plant at no cost; they would then be assigned a number of trees to cut down and sawed into three foot lengths to be used in the stove. The Volkswagen plant had produced thousands of these trapezoidal shaped sheet metal stoves for the German army; now production would start up again.

The wood cutting began with forest rangers taking groups of households into the forest on designated days. The VW management would tag the trees with the family names. Then my mother, brother, sister and I would go to work cutting, sawing and stacking the logs in a neat pile. It was backbreaking work, hauling the logs home, especially

through the ankle deep snow. But we managed to keep our home warm

throughout the next couple of cold and snowy winters.

All of those employed at the plant received a warm meal at

lunch, for which we had to turn in food stamps. In spite of the severe

post-war food shortages in Germany, it was an adequate and

nourishing meal consisting of butter, chicken, pork, potatoes and soup.

At home my mother only had to cook for herself and my brother and

sister, except on the days my father and I didn't work.

During the first six months of my apprenticeship I worked as a

pipe fitter. I helped restore the delivery of gas and water to the heavily

bombed section of the production facilities in the factory. In March of

1946 I witnessed first-hand the 1000th Volkswagen roll off the restored

assembly line. Most of these cars were sent to the French and British

occupation forces for their own use.

The following letter makes note of my three and a half year

apprenticeship, which began on September 11, 1945, shortly after I

returned from the American and British POW camps. It notes how I

started out as a volunteer, then became an apprentice in mechanics, maintenance of tools, factory plumbing, stamping press for VW, training in the tool and die making facility, as well as some training in automotive repair. The letter continues by saying that my work ethic is very good and I always had a positive attitude and that I attended trade school. Finally, it states that my apprenticeship has been discontinued only due to my interest to emigrate.

VOLKSWAGENWERK GMBH
CCG (BE)
WOLFSBURG

Sehr geehrter Herr   E m f e l d !

Ihre zehnjährige Zugehörigkeit zum Volkswagenwerk nehme
ich mit Genugtuung zum Anlass, Ihnen die Anerkennung der
Werksleitung und der Werksangehörigen auszusprechen.

Über ein sehr bewegtes Jahrzehnt hinaus, das nach dem groß-
zügigen Aufbau des Werkes die Umstellung von der Friedens-
zur Kriegsproduktion und von der Kriegs- wiederum zur Frie-
densfertigung mit sich brachte und in einer Zeit, da zwangs-
läufig auch moralische Werte wie Arbeitsdisziplin und Be-
triebstreue starken Erschütterungen ausgesetzt sind, haben
Sie von den ersten Anfängen an dem Werk die Treue gehalten
und einsatzfreudig und zuverlässig mit den besten Kräften
gedient.

Mit dem Dank für Ihre vorbildliche Berufsleistung verbinde
ich die besten Wünsche für Ihr persönliches Wohlergehen und
für eine weitere langjährige und erfolgreiche Zusammenarbeit
zum Nutzen des Werkes und seiner Belegschaft.

Wolfsburg, den 15.10.47

Mit vorzüglicher Hochachtung

Generaldirektor

Chapter 32

The Face of Liberty

"Give me your tired, your poor,
Your huddled masses yearning to breathe free,
The wretched refuse of your teeming shore.
Send these, the homeless, tempest-tossed, to me:
I lift my lamp beside the golden door."
-Emma Lazarus

Later in the summer of 1946 I watched a new wave of refugees roll into Germany as hundreds of thousands of Germans were forced to leave their homes, farms, businesses and factories that were located in centuries old German territories located along the eastern border with Poland. These lands were awarded to the Poles by the Allies. A number of these displaced Germans had only the belongings they could carry with them when they arrived in our small city, now officially called Wolfsburg. They were in sore need of housing and other services.

A local housing commissioner came to my family one day and said, "We have a widowed mother and her teenage daughter who need a temporary place to stay. Do you have a room for them, please?"

"Yes, of course," my mother replied. "Our two-story duplex has a maid's room in the attic where they can stay. We have three bedrooms on the first floor. We can all move in to those to accommodate them." That meant my brother Ronald would have to give up his "secret bedroom" in the attic. He did so grudgingly and moved in with my sister. I, however, looked forward with anticipation to the arrival of this teenage girl. I had just turned nineteen and my limited experience with girls was when I lived in Detroit and carried their books home from school, and the time I gave a peck on the cheek of a seven year old girl named Helga.

When the day arrived for them to move into our home we were introduced. I looked her over. She was slender with dark pretty eyes and a face framed by black hair tied neatly in a ponytail. A faint smile briefly formed around her mouth.

"Hello, my name is Herman."

Shyly she stretched her hand out for me to shake. "My name is Gretchen." Her mother took her by the hand and, together with their few belongings, went with my mother to the attic.

Later my mother reported back to me and said, "Herman, she is only sixteen."

When I found that out I kept wondering how best to ask her if she would like to go to the movies with my friend Walter and another girl. But I started to see how protective her mother was. They would always go out together, no matter what time of day. I never saw Gretchen in the house by herself; her mother was always there. That nipped the bud of any kind of romantic notions I had and I was left to my fantasies. After a few months the mother and daughter moved away to live with relatives in another part of Germany.

It was around that time that I read a notice in our local newspaper: *Americans Can Now Join the U.S. Army in Germany,* it stated briefly: *All those interested report to the recruiting officer located in the former headquarters of the I.G. Farben Industries in Frankfurt.*

I looked closely for a telephone number. There was none given. "Muttie, Vati, I would like to go see about this," I said to them. "Maybe I could get back to the U.S. more quickly."

After a brief discussion they both agreed it would be worth the roughly six hour railroad trip to Frankfurt for me to get more information and possibly join up. So the next morning, which was on a Saturday when I didn't have to work, I packed an overnight bag and left with a great feeling of excitement.

It was a long and tedious train journey south that got me into Frankfort late in the evening. I managed to find a small room at a hotel near the train station. The next morning I had no difficulty in finding out how to get to the I.G. Farben complex. Almost everybody who grew up in Frankfurt knew about I.G. Farben. The original company started out by making paint (*farben*). By 1925, through acquisitions, it had grown into the largest chemical company in Germany and, by war's end, employed 200,000 scientists, laboratory technicians and chemist. Later on I found out that Hitler used the I.G. Farben Company to produce the poisonous gas used in the gas chambers of several concentration camps, like Auschwitz. For now it was being used as the military headquarters and administration building for the American occupation forces.

As I stepped off the streetcar on a tree-lined boulevard, I could hear the faint sound of music. As I got closer I recognized the sound as American big band music, like the dance music I heard when I was a German POW. Then I saw the source of the music: the guard office, with the large I.G. Farben structure looming in the background. When I reached the guard the music streamed full blast out of the open entrance door. The guards had their feet propped up on desks, some smoking, others lazily chewing gum and tapping their fingers to the beat of the music. I stood there for a moment, shocked and stunned at their laidback behavior of these men who were supposed to be on guard duty.

Hesitantly I took a few steps inside when one of the soldiers spotted me. He motioned with his hand and yelled in a brusque tone of voice, "Come on in. What do you want?" On instinct I blurted out, "I want to join the army!" I said this in German.

The soldier turned to his buddy sitting near the radio and shouted, "Hey, Charley, turn the damned volume down and listen to what this Kraut has to say." His voice was loud and sarcastic and his use of the term 'Kraut' was meant to be offensive to Germans.

From the stripes on his sleeve I recognized that he was the sergeant in charge of the guard detail. But why was he so unfriendly to me? Maybe because I barged in on him and disturbed his dreamy and lazy world of leisure.

"You what?" the sergeant asked again.

"I want to join the army," I repeated. This time I spoke in my broken English.

The soldiers looked me up and down and then burst out laughing. When their laughter died down, the sergeant chuckled, "Here we all can hardly wait to get back home and get discharged out of this godforsaken army and you want in?"

I told him in rambling bits and pieces where I was born and why I wanted to join. I wasn't sure I was making sense but it seemed to have satisfied the sergeant. He picked up the phone and I heard him say, "Major Wilson, I have an American boy here who wants to join the army. What should I do with him?"

"Uh-huh... Uh-huh," he repeated. After a few more minutes on the phone he said, "Yes, sir. Will do, sir," and he hung up.

"Major Wilson will see you now," he said in a friendlier tone.

"Thank you," I replied, and said goodbye.

"Good luck," the soldiers said.

I then set off for the office of Major Wilson accompanied by one of the American guards.

The major greeted me quite warmly from behind a huge mahogany executive desk that looked like it had belonged to one of the I.G. Farben executives. It sat in a rather small and sparsely furnished office with stale cigarette smoke hanging in the air against the rays of the bright sunshine, shone through a large window behind the major's back.

"Let me see your papers," he ordered.

After I showed the major my I.D. card from the British occupation zone, my passport from 1937, and my birth certificate from Detroit, Michigan, as well as my German Army discharge papers, the major asked, "What brought you to Germany and why did you not return to the States sooner?"

I told him about my father and the Volkswagen factory contract. The major listened intently and with great interest. He didn't interrupt. When I finished he said, "That is an amazing story. And all these documents are fine and dandy. But in order for me to enlist you into the United States Army, I need proof of your American citizenship in the form of a valid U.S. passport. Do you have that?"

I couldn't believe my ears. I felt the same disappointment that I experienced the year before in Hamburg when the Consul General told me I had lost my American citizenship. I desperately tried to tell the major the reason why I had lost my citizenship. He just shook his head and said, "I'm sorry, kid. But let me try this for you. I have a direct connection with the American Consulate in Hamburg. I'll call the Consul-General and see what your status is."

I stepped out for minute while he phoned Hamburg so I could gather myself. When I was called back in, the major said, "Your case, along with several others, is still moving through Congress and it will take about another year for your citizenship to be reinstated." With that Major Wilson rose up from his chair, stretched out his hand to say goodbye, and said, "Come and see me after you get your citizenship back and if you still want to join the Army."

Yeah, right, I thought.

I thanked the major for seeing me and for trying to help me. Numerous such gestures by Americans I came in contact with would continue well into the following years. It made me feel proud to be American. So many tried to help me.

Back in Wolfsburg I settled into the routine of going to work, pursuing my apprenticeship, and attending the trade school, all in hopes of going back to Detroit with my family as soon as possible.

Two and a half years later, in January of 1948, I received a letter from the American Consulate in Hamburg informing me that my American citizenship had been reinstated and that I could apply for my passport and return to the United States. My family and I jumped up and down in jubilation until I suddenly wondered, "But how do we pay for the ship's passage and meals for of us?"

"No problem," my father said as he continued to read the letter. "The U.S. government will lend you the money! Uncle Sam said so!"

It was a tearful goodbye we all gave to my father but also a moment of elation for the four of us as we boarded an American troop ship at Bremerhafen, the same port where we had arrived in 1937, for the two week ocean voyage back to New York City.

The women and mothers with small children were assigned quarters on the decks. My brother and I, together with the other men and boys, were led down bulky iron stairs into the dimly lit hold where the only daylight came through twelve inch portholes. My brother and I picked our bunks, which were stacked four beds high. Shortly after we settled we were called to supper. As I entered the galley and walked toward the long tables with benches on either side, my eyes grew bigger and bigger and my mouth dropped. Spaced along the center of the table was the most beautiful sight I had ever seen: stacks of gleaming white bread flanked with bottles of Heinz Ketchup and mustard, large jars of peanut butter and jelly, mayonnaise and tubs of butter.

I stood at the table transfixed by the sight of it all until one of the stewards said, "Go ahead, sit down and help yourself."

I'd been so constantly hungry during the last few years since the war ended, with food still in such scarce supply and so carefully rationed, it didn't take me long to shake myself from my daydreams of better food. Hastily I picked up two slices of the delicious looking soft bread from packages labeled Wonder Bread and lathered them with creamy mayonnaise for a sandwich made in heaven. It brought back memories of my first tuna fish sandwich which I had in Detroit as a free and happy eight year old on my way to my guitar lessons.

A week later with a bigger belly, I saw a large statue holding a torch in the near distance, about a few miles out. "Muttie! Muttie!" I cried out, "America! I can see the face of Liberty!"

Landing on U.S. soil in 1948 was an experience that will be with me for the rest of my life. As we slowly sailed past the Statue of Liberty and into the New York harbor, chills went up my spine and tears filled our eyes.

When I stepped off the ship at one of the many bustling piers, strangers waved at us. I could feel my heart pounding. I was at home again after eleven years. It felt good.

One year later, at the same port, the first VW, or Beetle, in the US rolled off the MS *Westerdam* freighter, sputtering to bad publicity.

1948, February. Back row: L-R; Ronald, Norma, me, Muttie (Frieda) on the ocean liner returning to the U.S. Front row: L-R; Muttie befriended the woman next to her who was traveling alone: name unknown.

PART II

1949-1953

Redemption in Germany

Chapter 33

Two Bits

"Land is the only thing in the world that amounts to anything, for 'tis the only thing in the world that lasts.... 'tis the only thing worth working for, worth fighting for-worth dying for."
--Margaret Mitchell
Pt .1, Ch., 2, Gone With the Wind 1936

The unfamiliar smell of factory smokestacks and hot greasy kitchen fryers that filled the streets of New York City put hunger pangs in my stomach. I welcomed it. When we heard the bitter cold winter had already taken a few lives, we knew we needed to get on the train to Detroit quickly. When we arrived, I got off and waved goodbye to my mother, brother and sister as they continued their journey on to Chicago where they would stay with friends of my mother. These people, who emigrated from her hometown in Germany, could accommodate only three people, so I stayed with family friends in Detroit.

Twelve German-American friends and relatives of my father had stayed behind in Detroit when we left for Germany in early 1937.

The Weidle family was the first I got to see again since I was to room with them. When I reached the front door it opened before I could knock. There stood a stunning young woman around my height, 5'feet 6" tall, dressed in a beautiful long gown. She was eighteen and about to graduate from high school.

"Hi, Herman. It's Hannelore. Don't you recognize me?" she said giggling.

She must have seen the surprised look on my face. I instantly thought back to a visit we had with the Weidles when I was seven and their daughter Hannelore was four. She had shown me her Christmas present, a baby doll cradle. She took the doll out of the cradle to show me how it could cry. I leaned over the cradle, reached down with my right hand and pushed the bottom out.

Hannelore ran crying to her mother, screaming, "He broke my cradle!" All I had wanted to do was test the tiny mattress.

"Hello, Hannelore," I said back. But before I could get another word out she ran out the door to meet her date, who had just arrived to pick her up for the high school prom. She was happy and laughing when she skipped out the door while her parents waved proudly after her. I looked on as she climbed into the car, her long arms waving back. A twinge of sadness tugged briefly at my heart. Here I was, standing off to the side, alone, penniless, in debt, and without a high school diploma. I had missed all those wonderful and seemingly carefree moments of teenage life. But I didn't have time to dwell on those thoughts. I was grateful to be alive and aware that I had the responsibility of temporarily being the head of the family. I became determined to forge ahead until my father could join us and take the helm again.

Mr. Weidle was an engineer who had worked with my father in the same department at Ford Motor Company in the 30s. The Weidles had been close friends to both my parents. The house they built right after the war was a bright white colonial style house, located in an upper middle class neighborhood of northwest Detroit. There was a foyer, a spacious living room, formal dining room and a large kitchen with a breakfast nook. Upstairs were four bedrooms and two full baths. One of the bedrooms was used as a study. The full basement had a laundry room and half a bath. A separate two-car garage with room for a tool bench and storage for lawn and gardening equipment was behind the house. When I arrived I was awestruck. I had not seen such luxury before.

Since the fourth bedroom in the Weidles home was being used as a study and sewing room, a roll-a-way bed was put into Gunter's room, Hannelore's younger brother, for me to use. I took it as a subtle sign that my stay would be temporary.

Mrs. Weidle was a gracious and warmhearted woman. She had breakfast ready every morning and made sure my coffee was hot when I came down. Mr. Weidle clearly had the upper hand in all family matters and kept his household firmly together. At times direct, he was nonetheless friendly and helpful. He had risen up the ladder at Ford Motor Company to a position of influence and was later able to help my father get re-employed as a tool design engineer in the Ford's rear axle manufacturing plant.

Little by little, during evening discussions in the living room, I told them of our life in Germany and what my father, together with the five other original German -American engineers, had accomplished. Mr. Weidle knew a few of them, since he had also been asked to join Dr. Ferdinand Porsche to build his dream car and factory.

During one of our discussions Mr. Weidle expressed his anger over Germany. "Under Hitler's regime the lives of loyal and honest U.S. citizens of German descent were affected!" he yelled. "What happened to you could have happened to us, too, had we gone. Instead, we were interrogated and our houses were searched for short wave radios and weapons by the FBI. We were humiliated and scared for many years!"

As he ranted and raged in that moment a memory came back to me. I could hear the sounds of a classical music piece being played by the Nazis just before an announcement came over the short wave radio we had taken to Germany about a German victory. In silence, I acknowledged Mr. Weidle's remarks.

Just a few days after I moved in with the Weidles I was hired as a bench hand in a tool and die shop owned by a German-American named Mr. Lehmann, also a former colleague of my fathers'. My first job in the United States was a challenge. I only knew the metric system and had to switch to the inch system. But I dug in my heels and kept my nose to the grindstone. My English needed work, too. I still had a German accent.

When it was time to have my white shop apron cleaned, I asked the deliveryman, "How much"?

"Two bits."

Two bits? What is two bits? I asked myself. I had never heard that expression before. I got red in the face when I asked again, "How much?"

With a half-assed grin on his face the apron man replied, "Its a quarter young man, twenty-five cents."

"Oh, thank you," I stammered. I fished a quarter out of my pocket and handed it to him along with my soiled apron.

He handed me a fresh one, laughingly slapped me on my back and upon leaving said, "Learned something new, eh greenhorn?"

I knew the expression "greenhorn" from the factory workers at the tool and die company where I worked as an apprentice. They teased me with that remark from time to time. But I never got it before. I vowed from that moment on I would double my efforts to lose my German accent.

Chapter 34

The Beetle is Still Alive

I had been working a few weeks when the owner, Mr. Lehman, asked me to see him in his office. He said to bring an oil can with me. After greeting me he asked me to lubricate the wheels on his desk chair. As I did so, he engaged me in a conversation about my family in Germany.

"So, Herman, I hear you and your family were living in Germany during the entire war. That must have been hard on Henry. How is your father doing?" he asked.

I told how my father could not come back because he had given up his citizenship to keep us out of the internment camps as had Joe Werner. The two of them had been held for months for interrogation about the inside workings of the VW factory. When I started to leave Mr. Lehman's office, he said, "Herman, I have no tool and die apprenticeship program. You should look for a shop that has one so you can finish your apprenticeship and get a journeyman card. I will make a phone call and refer you to the Drettmann brothers, Henry and Alfred, who own the Active Tool and Die shop. They have an apprenticeship program."

The shop, however, was located at the opposite side of Detroit from where I was staying. I called my mother in Chicago and asked her if any of her friends lived on the east side and if they could put me up.

"Yes, Herman," she said. "There are the Pauluses. Mr. Walter Paulus is from my home town. We went to school together."

"Well, Mr. Lehman referred me to a Mr. Henry Drettmann who owns a tool and die shop that has an apprentice program."

"Oh, what a coincidence," she said excitedly. "I went to school with the wife of the third Drettmann brother, who stayed home in Bremen to run the family business when his two brothers immigrated to America. Mention this to Henry when you talk to him and look up the Paulus's telephone number. Walter should be able to remember our schoolmate, too. She married the Drettmann brother in Bremen. Give my regards to the Pauluses and let me know how things work out."

I hung up, amazed how my mother could be so thrilled and at how small the world was.

I called Henry Drettmann at his shop and told him what my mother said and what had happen to us.

When I finished, he said, "Herman, come in and see me next Saturday morning. I think I can help you."

Two weeks later I started at Active Tool & Die Company to finish the apprenticeship that I had begun at the Volkswagen factory in September of 1945. My goal was to finish my apprenticeship by 1949 and then work for a year as a journeyman die maker to save money for a car and tuition to study at Lawrence Institute of Technology in Detroit for a degree in Mechanical Engineering. I was on my way.

Four weeks later, after having arranged to stay with the Pauluses, I thanked the Weidle family for taking me in and we said our goodbyes. Even though they lived in one of the hundreds of thousands of Cape Cod style bungalows built to house the many GI's returning home from the war to start a family, I had no trouble finding the Paulus's house. These track homes had sprung up like mushrooms on the outskirts and suburbs of cities all over the country. No wonder

there was a baby boomer generation. They all adhered to the basic two
-bedroom floor plan with a full basement and an attic where one or
two rooms could readily be added. A family had a choice of different
front elevations as well as a clapboard or brick exterior.

Mr. Paulus was a tailor and the only one in the circle of my
parents' friends who did not work in the automotive industry; all the
others were engineers, designers, tool and die makers or machinists.
One of the men, Mr. Huepel, had wanted to open a tool and die design
shop with my father before the war started. Mr. Huepel's business had
flourished. In fact all of them owned their own homes ranging in price
and size from the luxurious Weidle's home to the more modest but
still upper middle class Paulus'. All drove expensive cars, like Mr.
Paulus' big Oldsmobile.

The Pauluses always took me with them to picnics and other
outings with their circle of friends and before long I became good
friends with all my parents' old friends. They took me under their
wings, especially since I spoke fluent German; most of them liked that.
They could freshen up their German, which was forbidden to be
spoken in the U.S. during the war. But I could not link up romantically

with any of the eligible daughters. I just wasn't one of them. I had no high school diploma, I was poor, and I had no car.

A few months after moving in with the Pauluses, I received great news in a letter from my mother; my father would soon be able to get a new passport and come back. Being eligible for American citizenship meant my father would need a permanent address. We'd finally be an American family again.

We'd been back in the U.S. for about six months and, between my mother's house cleaning jobs and my apprentice work, we had enough to rent a small house. But housing in Detroit was still scarce for a family of five. I traipsed around neighborhood after neighborhood until finally after a couple of weeks, found a bungalow where the owner had added two rooms in the attic and a small kitchen in the basement. That would suffice for a permanent address for the four of us for at least awhile. My mother, brother and sister moved back to Detroit from Chicago. No sooner had we settled we then started looking for a bigger house, one that would work for all five us when father returned.

Eventually I made enough money, even after paying the household expenses, to mail the first check to the United States Treasury Department to pay back our loan for our passage. A letter from the government arrived shortly thereafter stating: Dear Mr. Esfeld, We thank you for your payment. However the amount is less than what we can accept for payments toward your loan according to your wages earned. Therefore we will be increasing your payments by ten dollars.

"Mother, we have to watch every penny from now on. I will make a budget allowing so much for food, clothing and the absolute necessities--and nothing more."

I remember seeing my little sister roll her eyes when I said that. She and my brother had just begun middle school in an upscale neighborhood. Already they both were getting acclimated to the latest fashions worn by the rich kids and they, too, wanted to belong and impress their peers.

"Herman, your younger brother is sick," my mother said shortly after.

"What's wrong with Ronald?"

"He has a high fever. Go over to Mr. Paulus and tell them. Hurry."

Mr. Paulus immediately took us to the emergency room at Deacon Hospital where my sister had been born in 1937.

"I'm sorry, but you will have to pay fifty dollars before we can admit him," said the emergency administration clerk.

We were shocked. "What? Fifty dollars?" I said "We don't have fifty dollars! What now?" All I could think of was all the years in a war without a scratch between us.

"Frieda, I will pay the fifty dollars and you can pay me back later," offered Mr. Paulus. Rescued again by the kindhearted *Mr. Paulus*.

"Bless your soul," I said.

The doctors made a brief examination and then announced Ronald would have to be rushed into surgery. After hours of waiting for my brother's diagnosis and condition, the doctor came out and told us, "He is doing fine. We found a badly infected testicle that we removed."

"What caused this?" my mother asked, dumbfounded.

"Most likely from drinking unpasteurized milk from a cow infected with tuberculosis."

"From a cow? Oh my *Gott*," my mother said. "I do remember the kind wife of a farmer who had given him milk back in Wolfsburg shortly before our trip back to the States."

"Well, we believe Edsel Ford, Henry Ford's only son, died from the same disease a few years ago," the doctor told us. My brother soon recovered--but he could never have children. Considering what my family had gone through for eight long years, this news seemed mild at the time. We were lucky again.

With the good references my mother had received from her employers in Chicago, she soon found work as a personal maid to Mrs. Skelton, wife of an executive with Chrysler Motor Corporation. They lived in a stately house in upper scale Grosse Pointe, a waterfront suburb of Detroit. This job was a far cry from the position she'd held as a legal secretary when she was a young woman in Germany before she left for the U.S. to marry my soon to be father in 1925.

While we waited for my father to arrive, I kept accounts in a black booklet, tracking everything we earned and spent. One day as I made an entry my mother glanced over my shoulder and, a slightly agitated tone, said, "Herman, do you have to write down everything to the last penny?"

"Muttie," I continued to call her, "as temporary head of the family I feel responsible for the well-being of the four of us and I feel this strict budget keeping is necessary." I watched my little sister roll her eyes again.

One afternoon in March of 1949, after I had finished my apprenticeship, Mr. Drettmann, my ex-employer, and his wife invited all of us over for coffee and cake, a German custom. Like the Skeltons, they too lived in a luxurious mansion in Grosse Pointe Shores. Mrs. Drettmann was a very attractive American with long brown wavy hair that she wore down to her broad shoulders; her figure was superb and she had the perfect shape: 36-24-32. Her German husband was a handsome blue-eyed blond with neatly parted straight hair; he stood six feet tall and had the slim build of a baseball player. We sat and small talked until the conversation turned serious.

"So, how did you come to all this when Henry had a good job at Ford Motor Company?" they asked my mother. She proceeded to briefly describe the highlights of our life under Hitler's' regime, then changed the subject. "I'm acquainted with your brother's wife. We were schoolmates in my hometown."

Mr. Drettmann nodded in interest and then stood, cutting short our visit. He led us out the door. I'm not sure exactly why the Drettmans had us over that day other than to find out if his brothers went through as much as we did. But while we were there, my stomach did not feel right and my hands had started to sweat. I was relieved I didn't have to divulge any of my experiences.

A few weeks later the unionized tool and die makers in Detroit went on strike. I pleaded financial hardship so that I could be granted permission to work and be excused from picket duty. The union found a job for me at the Schmidt's Brewery where I did odd jobs. The company allowed their workers to drink free beer but only during our breaks and after quitting time. One day before leaving the plant I hastily drank a bottle. When I jumped on the streetcar home I missed the handle and fell off. It took twice as long to get home. "No more beer before going home," scolded my mother.

After three weeks the strike ended and my mother received the wonderful news that my father had been granted his re-entry permit and he would be joining us in May. In the meantime I had started night classes at Northern High School to obtain my diploma.

"Herman, we have to find a bigger home now," my mother said. "Henry is coming home! Let's see about getting one that can accommodate the five of us."

We found a bungalow to rent with the kitchen in the basement again. It was just outside the city limits, which made access to public transportation time consuming. One Saturday my mother and I went to buy bedroom furniture on a payment plan. Friends of my parents gave us furniture and household items they no longer used, and with that and our purchases, my mother transformed the little house into a cozy and comfortable home just in time to welcome my father.

Mr. Paulus kindly went to pick him up at the airport in his big Oldsmobile. It was a joyous moment when my mother, brother, sister, and I greeted my father in front of our house. Twelve years had gone by since my family had left for Germany. Now a new life would begin for us; especially for my parents who literally had to start over.

1949. Right after my father re-joined us back in the US.

A renewed life for the Volkswagen factory in Wolfsburg had been saved by the British: 37,500 Beetles were exported by them in 1949.[6]

The Beetle, the name Americans would soon nickname "the people's car," was still alive with a new head executive at the helm from Opel Motors, a subsidiary of General Motors. Of the original German-American engineers Dr. Ferdinand Porsche had contracted for hire in 1937, only my father returned to the United States after the war: the others had escaped. And, he had ten dollars left in his pocket, given to him with best regards from the German government.

---

[6] *Thinking Small* by Andrea Hiott.

Chapter 35

Black Sunday

*"I don't measure a man's success by how high he climbs, but how
high he bounces when he hits bottom"*
--General George S. Patton

"I never want to go back to Germany again," my father said

when he arrived back in Detroit. But I knew that there was a part of

him that wanted to stay and continue with what he helped start: the

VW factory. He had a glimpse of what the Volkswagen could become

the year he had to stay behind in 1948-1949. During this time billions

of dollars in aid had already started to turn around Germany's

reformed economy. There was a free market in Germany now. Empty

storefronts were quickly filled. The Volkswagen plant and offices

were repaired and expanded with even more space. My father watched

as the factory started to roll Beetles off the assembly line one after

another. It became the first industry to be put back into production in

postwar Germany while the rest of the country still lay in ruins. And my father would have had a big part in that place. But his family came first.

Once again Mr. Weidle came to the rescue, helping my father find work. But there were no opportunities at Ford Motor Company for my dad, just as there hadn't been for me. Many of the job relief programs that came about through The New Deal, the program by President Franklin D. Roosevelt formed during the Depression in the 30s, had ended along with the war. So my father had to travel to and from work by public transportation, as did I and the rest of my family. Getting anywhere took a long time. As summer neared, the travel time took a toll on us all. Time became a precious commodity. Besides, my parents wanted my sister and brother to attend better schools. We were house hunting once again.

By the time high school started in September 1949 for my younger brother Ronald and sister Norma, we had moved into a newer modern apartment complex in the waterfront suburb of St. Clair Shores. The area grew into an upscale development. Three to five bedroom homes were being built with red brick on large parcels with manicured lawns beside a shallow lake filled with yachts and pleasure boats that were shadowed by small hills with access to clean sandy shores. Canals were made for beachfront properties. The area was bustling with new residents eager to start big families.

What wasn't bursting with enthusiasm was the Beetle. At this time Americans were enamored with the big boat-styled automobiles, like the wide chrome-bodied Cadillacs, Chevys and Fords. When the VW arrived, no one took notice or warmed up to the funny curved-shaped little car. In fact, a negative connection became attached to the Beetle because of the place and time it was born.

I didn't talk to my co-workers or any friends about my experience during the war. Even though I had witnessed the black VW roll off the assembly line in Wolfsburg a couple of times, all that was on my mind was being back in the States and getting my lost U.S. citizenship back.

Soon my parents were fortunate enough to buy a used 1942 black Plymouth sedan with whitewall tires and shiny chrome. It belonged to my mother's childhood friend whose husband had just passed away in Chicago. It had been kept in their garage most of the time so the chrome did not have any rust. And it wasn't long after that

when I bought my first car; a brand new 1949 4-door Ford sedan.

"Herman, how can you afford a brand new car?" my mother

asked.

"Muttie, I saved enough money for a down payment and I

don't have to pay off the balance for another two years."

"Why couldn't you buy a used one? We bought our Plymouth

used and it works just fine."

"Most everything we have comes from your friends. I wanted

to buy something completely on my own," I said defiantly. "I'm

saying goodbye to the busses and streetcars. I took out a membership

with the Automobile Club of America." She just nodded in agreement.

I drove my gleaming white streamlined Ford to work, night school and

everywhere I wanted. I was independent now.

One Friday night I drove to a friend's wedding clear across the

city on the west side, about twenty-five miles from home. I had a good

time, danced with a few girls and had a few drinks. I left late, tired and

too tipsy. By the time I got into the city and was about halfway home,

I couldn't' keep my eyes open. I pulled over to the curb, turned on the parking lights, turned the engine off, locked all the doors, and dozed off. At five in the morning nobody was around. Detroit had virtually no crime rate at that time, a fact unknown to me. I napped for about a half an hour, and then figured it was time to move on. At the eastern city limits Jefferson Ave becomes a tree lined boulevard that snakes along Lake St. Clair through the chic neighborhood of Grosse Point. Gliding along these gentle turns in the dim early dawn, there was a sudden crash. I jumped the curb with my right wheel. The car hit a wooden post head on, catapulting the metal mailbox over the car and barely nicking the roofline above the windshield of my car. I heard the loud noise of my hubcap clanging up the lawn.

I panicked and sped on, bumping along, not even thinking about the fact that I was leaving the scene of an accident. Riding the rim on a flat tire, I found a gas station, thankfully in a familiar area near where I lived. It was seven o'clock on a Saturday morning and the attendant had just opened the station.

"What happened to your wheel?" he asked sheepishly. I told him and asked if he could help me.

"The rim is gone. It's useless. All I can do is put the spare on."

He had just begun putting on the spare when a car slowly drove by the station. It backed up and stopped in front of the open garage. A young man in his late teens emerged and walked towards my open door. He had my hubcap in his hand. Stunned and a bit embarrassed, I could only watch in silence as the young man walk around my car. He turned towards me and asked, "Is this your car? I believe this hubcap belongs to you."

Frightened, I said, "Yes sir. I am the one who drove into your mailbox. I'm really sorry."

As I explained what happened, a half smile came over his face and he said, "You're not the only one who has knocked over our mailbox. That's why my Dad decided to mount the mailbox on a wooden post, so it would be less expensive to replace. You're the first one to knock that over." Just my luck, I thought, as he continued. "Give me your name, address and phone number and my dad will mail you the bill. You can send him a check or put the money into an envelope and put it in our mailbox. You know where it is now," he laughed.

Touched by the young man's mannerism, I grabbed his hand and thanked him profusely.

The mechanic, who had by then mounted the spare wheel on my car, said, "You know, you were very lucky. The father could have called the police and had you arrested for driving under the influence and leaving the scene of an accident."

While I slowly drove the short distance back home I thought of how kind and generous I had been treated by this American family whose mailbox I had knocked over without even stopping and ringing their doorbell.

In order to receive my high school diploma I had to take one last semester of night school at Cass Technical High. Then, in early June of 1950, I would participate a formal cap and gown graduation at Northern High School. In one of my classes I noticed two women in their late teens who were together all the time, like glue. Every day after school someone would come and pick them up. One of the women was a nice looking brunette named Brenda. The other woman Frances, blonde and prettier, attracted me. One evening during a break, self-conscious of my German accent, I gathered enough courage to start a casual conversation with them.

"Where are you from?" asked Frances.

"Detroit. But I went to Germany when I was ten and stayed for eight years during the war."

Eventually they knew more about me than I did about them.

A few weeks later Frances showed up alone at class. So I took the opportunity and bravely asked her out to a movie the next Saturday night.

"You have a car, don't you?" she asked.

"Yes I do," I answered with pride. "I have a brand new Ford."

She thought a moment and said, "But I have to bring my girlfriend, otherwise my parents won't allow me to go out."

"Oh, that's fine," I said quickly.

"I'll let you know tomorrow in class," she replied.

The next evening both girls were at class again and Frances looked at me and said, "Next Saturday would be fine with both of us. Here is our address." Sheepishly, she handed it to me.

Wow, I thought, I have my first date with an American girl, two in fact!

Frances lived in an upscale neighborhood next to Grosse Point. I pulled up slowly and punctually in front of her house. But before I could step out of the car Frances and her friend Brenda quickly strode up to me.

"Sorry, Herman, but my parents will not let me go out with you after all. I will explain why at school on Monday," Frances said, clearly disappointed. She abruptly turned around as they both ran back into the house.

I was flabbergasted and disappointed. What had gone wrong? I could hardly wait for the explanation Monday evening, which came at the first class break.

"My parents are from Holland and, like you, I was born in Detroit. During the war, when Holland was occupied by the Germans, my close relatives were treated badly by them. Some of their stories are so severe…we were afraid that my going out with you would open up wounds. That it would create bad feelings between me and my family."

I listened to her in astonishment and let her know that I had not heard of any stories like that before. "I'm sorry for your parents," I finally said. We remained on friendly terms for the remainder of the semester.

At last, just before my twenty-third birthday, with a high school diploma in my hand, I went to the admissions office of Lawrence Institute of Technology in Detroit to apply for the fall semester 1950. Shortly after my graduation day, Mr. Drettmann asked to see me in his office. After small talk and congratulations on the completion of my die making apprenticeship, he said, "Herman, I would like to start you out as an assistant plant manager at the stamping facility I own just north of Detroit on Lake Michigan."

My mind drifted toward my father and the position he had held at the Volkswagen factory. I adjusted myself in my seat while Drettmann continued.

"In a few years that plant will be too small to handle the increased business I am expecting. My plan is to build a new factory. By then you will be experienced enough to take over as plant manager. I like your work ethic and feel you are the right man for the job. Next weekend we will drive up there and I will show you around. In the meantime, think it over and keep it under your hat."

I was so surprised that all I could mutter was, "Thank you for your confidence in me, Mr. Drettmann." This was not the time to tell him that I planned on going to college to get a degree in mechanical engineering.

I never made that weekend trip with Mr. Drettmann.

On June 25, 1950, a day after my 23rd birthday, communist North Korea attacked South Korea. The next day an order came in the mail to report immediately for a physical examination at the local military office. In spite of my seventy percent hearing loss and the constant ringing I experienced in my left ear, I passed the exam. I was told to expect to be drafted in about three months and to get my affairs in order because I would be serving in the U.S. Army for two years. I could not believe it.

The world began to shake under my feet. My well-laid plans for a college education would have to wait. But more daunting was the prospect of being sent to Korea to fight in another ugly war. Surely somebody in Washington must know that I had combat experience when I served in the German Army. Was this a chance to redeem myself? After a few days I came to grips with my feelings, resolved to do whatever was asked of me, and that I would do so to the best of my ability and serve my country faithfully.

Several weeks later I received greetings from Uncle Sam--my draft notice. On September 25, 1950 I was to report to the Michigan Central Railroad Station in Detroit.

I said my goodbyes to Mr. Drettman, who responded, "Herman, good luck. And I want you to know your job will be waiting for you when you return."

My father and I agreed on a selling price for my Ford. I signed the title over to him and he took over the loan payments, putting the equity into my savings account. My brother Ronald was happy to have a car now since he was seventeen and a senior in high school.

Saying goodbye at the train station was easier for me than it had been six years ago in Wolfsburg where only Ronald went with me and helped push our bicycles through knee deep snow in the bitter cold. Now my whole family was there on the platform together with hundreds of others draftees and their loved ones kissing and hugging each other goodbye. We embraced with tears in our eyes and then, finally, one last wave until the platform went out of sight.

Black Sunday came on September 24, 1950, the day I boarded the train to Kentucky. A large forest fire from our northern friend Canada had spewed so much ash and smoke into the skies, as far as Pennsylvania, that it became pitch dark in the afternoon. The Tigers lost their pennant race to the Yankees in the glaring lights at Tiger Stadium in Detroit that Sunday afternoon--and "Beetle mania" was born.

1950. L-R, My brother Ronald, Muttie, with her fox fur stole, my younger sister Norma, and Vati in our St. Clair Shores home soon after my receipt of my high school diploma. I was 22 years old.

Chapter 36

743rd Ordinance-Maintenance-Company

The train rolled lazily through the Ohio countryside and almost lulled me to sleep. Then I heard a voice calling out, "Hear ye, hear ye, get your ham and cheese combo!" What is he saying, I wondered. I had never heard that expression before. I figured he was trying to sell something, but what? I wanted to ask the fellow sitting next to me but I was too embarrassed. So I waited patiently until the vendor with a large tray hanging around his neck stacked with sandwiches walked down the aisle right up to my row. Then I knew. I saw a slice of ham with a slice of cheese on top sandwiched between two slices of white wonder bread. Clearly, I was still a greenhorn.

A railroad spur took our train right into the Fort Knox, my destination and home base of the 3rd Armored Division, near the Kentucky hills and forest with rushing waterfalls. It felt like in the middle of nowhere to me. The farthest south I'd been before was

Chicago. The military base had become permanent back in 1932 and established the Armor Branch of the U.S. Army armor in 1940. It was filled with many training schools, tanks and civil war armory and was an impressive site for a young draftee. Here many of us twenty-two to twenty-four-year olds would be processed, receive our uniforms, and be assigned to various army units for basic training.

We were marched to barracks that dated back to WWII. What struck me immediately was that there was no yelling or loud shouting of commands or cursing by the NCO who led us. It remained like that the entire time I went through my training. Later I heard that the cadre and officers dealing with us draftees were to handle us older draftees more kindly and respectfully than had we been seventeen and eighteen year old recruits during WWII. Many of us have gone through apprenticeships, had some formal education, and worked in respectable jobs with good pay. This type of atmosphere made the transition from civilian life to military life so much easier than my first training and battle field experience in Germany.

One morning on a cold, brisk day I overheard a few fellows moan and groan. "Oh no, not powdered eggs again?" Sometime later that evening, someone said, "We're having shit on the shingle." That was a new one for me; I had to find out what the saying meant. "Shredded beef in a cream sauce on top of a biscuit," bemoaned one of the guys. "Doncha know, my wife can make a plain hamburger that'd put this shit to shame. And she can't even cook!" And a lot of guys moaned again.

But I loved all the stuff they served. So when I asked the cook for a little bit more, I got it. When the cook saw me coming he yelled out, "Get the frying pan out! Four eggs for Herman!" At the end of every meal if there was food left over and he called out for seconds, I was first in line. "Hey, there goes chowhound," the other guys would holler at me--another new expression that became my nickname.

The second day, while I was waiting to be processed, rumors started to fill the stale air inside the building. "The only American infantry division helping the South Koreans defend their territory is being pushed down south to the Pusan area, the only port city left from which to evacuate our soldiers that was not in the line of fire. There's desperate fighting going on," claimed a recruiter. Stateside I heard that our government had federalized the National Guard units of four states. "Four divisions are being put through basic training to be brought up to strength with you draftees and then deployed," the recruiter continued. In that moment I realized I would be among those first in line to be sent to Korea.

At the end of my processing there was one last question: "What branch of service do you want to serve in?" an officer asked bluntly.

I was taken by complete surprise. The thought of my proficiency in mastering the German language raced through my mind. "An interpreter," I answered instinctively.

The young clerk looked slightly taken a back. After a short pause he asked, "And what language?

"German," I answered.

"I have to check with my superior and find out how to handle this." Without excusing himself, the clerk got up from his small desk and disappeared. After a while he returned and said, "We are not set up here at Fort Knox to give an interpreter test in German. The material for that will have to be delivered here from another facility. I will summon you when we are ready."

I reduced to waiting once again. After all, I was used to that.

I decided to visit the Patton Museum located on the base. I had read the impressive story of the Third Armored Division and its campaigns under General Patton. The museum displayed several German tanks and tracked armored vehicles from WWII. Among them was an 88 mm anti-aircraft gun fitted with a frontal shield used as an artillery piece, the very weapon that I once used. Because of its high velocity the gun was especially effective against tanks. My eyes lingered on the number one gunner stool mounted along the barrel where I, as a sixteen-year-old, had sat as a German high school flak helper. The words came stinging back into my mind: "Fritz, it's a clear blue sky without a cloud coming, perfect weather for an air-raid." "Herman, do you always have to paint the devil in the sky?"

I brushed the sweat off on my forehead and walked over to observe several train loads of draftees pulling out. They were headed for Korea, a place where I had no idea what I would be assigned to for another three long weeks.

Finally they called me to the orderly room for my language test. The next day they called me in for the result. An officer sitting behind his desk glanced up from my test papers and said, "Recruit

Esfeld, you did quite well on your test. You passed it. However we do not need any German interpreters. We need Korean interpreters!" His voice grew loud. He paused a few seconds and continued, "Recruit Esfeld, what branch of service would you now like to serve in?"

Inwardly, I smiled to myself, refraining from jumping up and down. I had plenty of time to prepare for my answer so I promptly answered, without a hint of my German accent, "Sir, I would like to serve with your Army Ordinance-Maintenances Corps."

The officer started to leaf through my papers and said, "Yes, I see here you recently completed your tool and die making apprenticeship and you would qualify. Let me check the roster of the 743rd Ordnance-Maintenance company which is to support the 43rd Infantry Division. We are just now bringing that division up to strength."

The officer had the roster of the ordnance maintenance company brought to him. I felt myself perspire through the thin army T-shirt as he checked it over slowly. I flashed to the anti-aircraft gun and stool I had to sit on as a German flak helper. My breathing became so fast and loud in my head, I almost didn't hear the officer when he exclaimed, "Yes, we still have an opening as a machinist in the Service and Recovery section. I will assign you to the 102nd infantry regiment for your fourteen weeks of basic training, after which you will be transferred to the 743rd Ordinance-Maintenance-Company. The two units are located together with the headquarters of the 43rd Infantry Division at Camp Picket near Blackstone, Virginia. Be prepared to be called on in a moment's notice for your rail transportation. Good luck, soldier. You are dismissed."

"Thank you, sir." I almost shouted. I executed a smart salute that evoked a brief smile from the officer. I made a perfect about face and left the orderly's room, something I had done a thousand times as a German soldier.

Outside, with a feeling of immeasurable relief, I reflected upon the friendly and helpful way I had been treated by the officer. No one here knew I had been in the German army and I didn't want to tell anyone, though I didn't feel guilty about it. How could I? I was brainwashed, a method the Chinese had used on young American POWS. Now I felt I could redeem myself. I vowed to do my utmost during my American military service, even if it meant fighting in

Korea.

While I waited to be shipped out I heard through the grapevine

that the numerous troop transports I had seen leaving the railhead went

to two of the four National Guard divisions where by now they would

be taking their basic training and then immediately shipped to Korea.

That dimmed the prospect of me being sent to Korea any time soon, I

thought. It reassured my family too.

Chapter 37

Basic Training, the American Way

Other than learning a few things like the use of the American submachine gun, which was lighter in weight and more accurate than the one I was accustomed to, basic training seemed routine. The self-powered semi-automatic guns were equipped with thirty rounds of ammo concealed in a magazine and snapped into a chamber underneath the gun, unlike the German guns into which I had to feed belts of ammunition. No screaming or humiliating drill sergeant type of treatment. It may have been tough at the beginning of my training but it was conducted in a professional manner, which pleasantly surprised me.

One day after settling into a comfort zone with my training I got the courage to ask my sergeant, the teacher at the time, how to hit the ground from a running upright position to a prone position and be ready to fire a weapon. He was happy to accommodate: The sergeant took my rifle, gripped it with both hands, dropped down on his knees, and dug the butt into the ground. He pitched his torso forward flat onto the ground and swung the rifle around into firing position.

After the demonstration I asked, "And would it be alright if I showed you how a German soldier did it?"

A little shocked the drill sergeant hesitated a moment and then he said, "Go ahead, soldier."

I gripped my rifle firmly, took a few running steps, and then slid to the ground like a panther, pulling my rifle up from along my side and into the firing position.

"Well, soldier that was an interesting comparison," he said.

I did not wait for him to ask me how I knew the German method nor did he or anyone else ask. WWII was still too fresh in my mind.

Only one tragic incident marred my time in basic training. Time and time again we recruits were warned not to bring back any live ammunition from the range. But one soldier did just that. Lying in my barrack one afternoon I heard an explosion followed by the screams of "get the medics. Call an ambulance!" I rushed outside toward the noise. It came from the barrack next to mine. I was stopped at the entrance at ground level. What happened, sergeant?" I asked quickly, my heart pounding loud and fast.

"I'm not really sure," he replied. "The medics are up on the second floor waiting for an ambulance."

Dark smoke and the smell of burnt powder drifted through the area. Then the ambulance came. Three bandaged soldiers were carried out and whisked away in one of the ambulances. Then a body covered with a white sheet was slowly carried down the stairs on a stretcher and loaded into the ambulance. It drove away slowly. There had been a fatality. A young soldier killed. But how, I wondered. Soon a weapons inspection team arrived and started to gather up the evidence. The soldiers who had been on the second floor when the explosion occurred were detained and questioned.

Later that evening the mess hall buzzed with all kinds of rumors. I knew from others that the dead recruit had been in a group using live ammunition on the firing that morning. They fired 50 caliber machine guns and practiced throwing hand grenades and rifle grenades. I went up to one of the recruits who had been on the second floor when the explosion happened.

"Yeah, I knew the guy. I saw him pick up a rifle grenade on the range. But I didn't see what he'd done with it. Obviously he concealed it pretty damn good 'cause he'd brought it up to the barrack. Some are sayin' that the guy reached the top of the stairs and stumbled or dropped the grenade, setting it off," he said.

I went to the charred spot in the floor; blood was still visible. I would never know what the poor fellow intended to do with that projectile.

My basic training ended right after Christmas so nobody got to go home for the holidays. Then I was transferred to the 743rd Ordnance Maintenance Company along with three other soldiers: Bob Whitney and Leonard Kunz, both from Michigan like myself, and Bruce Taylor from the state of New York. We were classified as machinists assigned to the machine shop truck in the Service and Recovery section. All four of us were either young journeymen or tool and die makers.

Shortly after I transferred to the 743rd I heard reports from our commanders that a large number of infantrymen with whom I had just finished taking basic training were being shipped to Korea as replacements. Now the rumor mill heated up again. Heavy fighting in Korea and the casualties among the newly trained and inexperienced two National Guard Divisions were terrible. Would I be next?

Then I heard a rumor that our division would be sent to Germany, but not before the 102 Infantry regiment had been replenished and its new recruits finished with basic training. It seemed that being with the 743rd was keeping me out of harm's way for the time being. At least I hoped so.

I adjusted quickly to military life in the American Army. In spite of my German accent, I got along well with my section leader, James Baker, a Sergeant First Class and a National Guardsman from Rhode Island. I vowed I would serve to the best of my ability and be the first one in line for a promotion, should one come up.

On my first 72 hour weekend pass I drove to Washington D.C. with Len and Bruce, my first time in our nation's capital. We visited the Smithsonian and went to a show starring the Andrews Sisters. We went dateless. Back at the base I spent my free time indulging in a weekly quart of ice cream I'd gotten at the PX (Post Exchange) or reading about military history at the library. I started to enjoy an occasional cheeseburger, but I didn't frequent any bars in town or look for the company of women. I did not smoke, gamble or learn how to play poker with the guys. What did I do? I stayed out of trouble and saved my money. I became so dependable a few card players would come to me shortly before payday to ask for a few bucks to hold them over. I scrutinized each one before handing over my loot. I always got paid back. I knew how to pick the right hotshots.

Every Sunday afternoon there was a dance in the social hall. The young women were bussed in from Richmond, forty miles away. Although I could dance well and liked dancing, I only went a few times. I would rather take in a movie but my buddy Bob Whitney went every Sunday and eventually he swept a southern belle off her feet and married her.

Every Saturday morning we had a GI party or barrack inspection followed by an inspection of our weapons, beds, lockers and foot lockers. If you failed you didn't get a day pass. One Saturday morning the officer of the day, with my company sergeant in tow, stepped up to my locker. When he saw how orderly I had arranged my clothes he turned to the sergeant and said, "This is amazing. I want everyone here to look at this. Call them all over." Back in Germany, when I turned sixteen and before my compulsory service as a flak helper, my mother showed me how to neatly fold and stack my shirts, underwear and socks. She also taught me to mend my socks, sew on buttons, stripes and patches. Those habits and skills sure came in handy now.

The top sergeant yelled out, "Listen, soldiers, I want every one of you to come over and look at soldier Esfeld's locker. That's the way the officer of the day wants your lockers to look," he commanded while he pulled out a note pad and jotted something down. All my comrades started milling around my bunk. When the inspection was over, I felt embarrassed and wondered if the other guys saw me as a hero, or if I had made any enemies. I couldn't tell --but no one got a demerit.

Sure enough the first promotions came through and I got my first stripe. I was now a Private First Class (PFC) in the United States Army.

One morning a Corporal of the Guard came to awaken me before anyone else at four in the morning. I was on KP duty—kitchen police. I was to help the cook, prepare and serve breakfast. Then, afterwards, I had the tedious job of scrubbing and washing the dirty pots and pans. That's where I met John Campbell, who was singing and cracking jokes and being jovial as can be–a far cry from the strict discipline of a German soldier. His jovial mood made the sweaty work much easier and the time went by fast.

While we peeled the potatoes one day, Campbell said, "I'm from Margate City, near Atlantic City, New Joisey. I learned to be an auto mechanic by helping out at 'da fillin' station my family owns." I drifted for a moment, wondering if he'd ever seen a Volkswagen. He continued in his Jersey accent, "And ya' know, I sure miss the smell of 'da salty Atlantic and 'da taste of ah red lobsta' we'd catch off 'da coastal wautas. Have ya' eva' tasted a red lobsta' befo'?" I shook my head no. "Well, ya' have ta come to Joisey fo' a visit. We'll catch some lobsta' an' ya' can try it. Right now just glad I got a jab woikin' in da automotive section witcha, Hoiman."

"Okay, John." I too was happy that John and I were in the same platoon. He played the trumpet and practiced during his time off. It sounded darn good. Over time John and I became good friends. We both felt the same about going into town chasing girls, coming home drunk or gambling. To me it seemed like a waste of time and money. Our friendship felt like family.

In the spring my company went on a field trip. We slept on cots in tents and our service and recovery section practiced retrieving and loading disabled Sherman tanks on the tank transporter. A few of my buddies who were in sheet metal work and plumbing rigged up a shower. "What a godsend," I exclaimed. "A cold shower is just what I need in this hot and humid climate of southern Virginia!" I admired the ingenuity and skill among the soldiers in my outfit.

One night we were startled by a noise followed by the bellowing order of the guard, "Halt, who goes there? What's the password? Identify yourself or I'll shoot!"

"Don't shoot. They're raccoons who get into our garbage cans," answered the cook who had his tent next to the kitchen. I felt tiny beads of sweat on my forehead. As a German soldier I had no time or place to relax. The constant daily fear of being shot by my own commanders or the enemy was frozen in my blood. I couldn't wait until morning.

1950-1952. Me in the 743rd Ordinance Maintenance Company division.

Chapter 38

American Soldier

Right after my promotion to corporal toward the end of our bivouac I prepared to go on my first furlough, after which I was to report back to my barracks at Camp Picket, Virginia. Since my leave started on a Saturday, my brother Ronald agreed to pick me up. A junior in high school now, Ronald was going to pick me up in the Ford I had surrendered to my father. He said he would bring my younger sister Norman along as a traveling companion.

Norma had just turned fourteen. I found out later that my tomboy sister had an ulterior motive behind coming along all the way from Detroit; she was anxious to get her driver's license the next year. So she persuaded my brother to let her practice driving on the long straight stretches of highway.

On the day they arrived I was in my tent packing my duffle bag and getting ready to change into civilian clothes when I was told to go back to the orderly tent and wait. But one of my commanders directed Ronald to my tent. There, one of my buddies walked up to him and said, "Gee, Herman, I never saw you in civilian clothes, let alone change into them so fast."

My brother laughed. "Oh, I'm not Herman. I'm his brother Ronald."

"Boy, you sure had me fooled. You two look like twins!" my buddy exclaimed.

The drive to Detroit, four hundred miles away, would be the fastest and wildest automobile trip of my life. We raced through the Smokey Mountains where dangerous stretches of hairpin curves were often blanketed with blinding fog and fish-tailed on some of the wet pavement. We stopped only for gas and food. The little over six hour drive took us five and half. I never gave thought to how reckless and stupid my brother and I were being, especially in front of our little sister who was soon to get her driving license.

When we arrived, Mother and Father greeted us all with open, grateful arms, like so many times back in Wolfsburg. When we sat down for dinner one night, I broke the news. "I might be sent to Germany," I said to my father.

He reflected a moment and then gave me advice. "Herman, whatever you do in Germany, don't marry a German girl and bring her back to the United States. She'll just get homesick and will want to go back to Germany."

I knew what he was talking about. Just after I was born, Mutti took me back to Germany. But a few months later she decided to come back to join her husband.

In just a few months I would be twenty-four and the thought of my father's warning brushed through my mind. Germany seemed a whole lot better than the war going on in Korea.

When I reported back to training at Camp Pickett, my entire division was sent on maneuvers to North Carolina in the midst of the humid summer. My Jersey buddy Bruce Taylor and I were driving a machine shop jalopy of a truck in a convoy down south when suddenly the truck dropped its drive shaft and came to a screeching halt.

"What on God's earth happened?" screamed Bruce. He climbed out and noticed the universal joint had broken.

1950. My 1949 Ford 4-door white sedan that my brother and sister drove to pick me up in Virginia.

1950 Christmas. My first furlough home in Detroit in an American military uniform.

"Looks like we might be wolkin' to Carolina," he said. I figured World War II had worn out the rolling stock in our division.

Fortunately, mechanics from our automotive section pulled up, removed the driveshaft and hooked the truck to one of the wreckers. We got a free ride the rest of the way.

The hot weather hit us like after a tropical hurricane upon arrival at Southern Pines, our training ground near Fort Bragg. The air was thick and it was unbearably sticky. A nearby farmer kept us supplied with fresh watermelons at a reasonable price. They were a welcome respite in the heat, but no match with the fresh cold water produced for us by the division's water purifications section.

We were immediately warned not to jump into any of the overgrown foxholes left behind by previous units without first checking them out. "You could be landing on top of a bunch of rattlesnakes," said my superiors. They love to preach.

Shortly after getting back to Camp Pickett I received the news we would be shipped out. The 43rd Infantry Division, along with the supporting 743rd Ordinance-Maintenance Company, would be stationed somewhere in southern Germany. We would sail sometime in September. The daily fear I'd been living with that I still could be shipped to Korea was over! I wanted to be through with fighting.

I immediately wrote to my parents to tell them the good news. I mentioned my new military duty as a mechanic in the maintenance division of the army. We would be shipped out soon to Germany to keep the peace. I knew they would be ecstatic to hear this.

Now a flurry of activity began as we prepared the vehicles and weapons for shipment overseas. All exposed metal surfaces and weapons, such as the machine gun MIA1 and even the Thompson submachine guns, a one-man operated machine gun popular in the prohibition era, were covered with heavy grease to protect them from the elements. The old WWII trucks had been replaced with new REO trucks equipped with engine snorkel and hydrodynamic transmissions.

I flashed back to Germany when delay in equipment for the VW factory before the war broke out had made my father somewhat impatient. He thought he would be building an economical, affordable car, massed produced like no other in the U.S. Instead he had been directed to repair German war planes and the *Kubelwagon* along with a few other war machines.

Before shipping out I was promoted to sergeant and put in charge of the machine shop truck with three machinists; they were my army buddies and family now, Whitney, Taylor and Kunz. As the embarkation date approached General Eisenhower held a review of our division and explained that it was our mission in West Germany to be a deterrent to Joseph Stalin so that he could not a make a grab for West Berlin, which now was occupied by the United States, Great Britain, and France; the Soviet Union had control of East Germany.

I stood quietly and listened to the General's speech. Then, after a parade through downtown Norfolk, we boarded the Victory class troop transports and sailed out of Hampton Roads Naval Base to the port city of Bremerhafen. Three and a half years later, I found myself back in Germany--but this time in an American uniform.

Chapter 39

The Unofficial Interpreter

When my unit got off the ship at Bremerhafen, the old familiarity did not have a chance to sink in with me because we immediately boarded a train that was waiting near the pier to take us to the city of Darmstadt, just south of Frankfurt.

On the passage over, I had written a letter to my grandmother because I had learned that our route would stop in Achim, ten miles south of Bremen, where my mother was born and my widowed grandmother lived. My grandfather had passed away just the year before.

"Hey, Herman, you got a bottle for that letter?" joked my buddy Whitney as the ship roiled.

"Yeah, Herman, gotta genie in there?" teased Taylor.

As the train rolled through the station I tossed the letter addressed to my grandmother out the window and watched it swirl to the ground next to the tracks. My buddies laughed and we all looked down the tracks for long while.

"Ha, Herman. Do you really think she'll get it?" my buddies teased.

Miraculously, four days later, my cousin found it and delivered it to her. It wasn't long before I received her reply telling me how happy she was to hear from me. That shut my buddies up for a short while.

When we arrived at Achim we had to wait for our truck to catch up from port delivery. This gave me a chance to observe the city in the near distance. The landscape was made up of moorland and dark green manicured farmland. I was amazed at how quickly the devastation from the war had been rebuilt and cleaned. There were freshly red-bricked buildings and new cobblestoned streets where craters, left over from bombs, had been; it helped make up for the ghastly war pictures in my head. Too soon, our truck arrived and, loaded, we continued on the train to take us to our final destination south to Augsburg.

At the next few station stops my buddies and I leaned out the window to search for a *fraulein* to have small talk with. But all I was doing was interpreting. Then I had an idea; I told my buddies, "All you have to say is, '*Ich Liebe Dich*' (I love you)." They mastered it quickly, though each did so with very comical (to me) pronunciations. The responses we got were sometimes in English or a shy smile on the women's fresh young faces--and of course a flood of questions.

One elderly German lady shouted to me hastily from the train station, "Will there be another war?"

"No, we will keep the peace," I answered back in German.

She nodded her head and replied, "*Das ist gut* (That's' good)."

The first day at our camp in Darmstadt we were told that half of the troops could go out that night for some entertainment and free German beer and the other half could go out the next night. I'd had German beer before and knew how potent it could be. "German beer is three times stronger than American beer," I pumped into my buddies. "If you drink it like you're used to drinking at home, it'll floor you in short order." Despite my warning, I expected the worst and somehow felt obligated to stay in camp and help the unfortunate ones find their tents and cots when they returned and help put them to bed. And so it was.

The new REO trucks, 2 ½ ton all-wheel drive 3-axel cargo trucks with 10 tires and, Frank said, nicknamed "deuce and a half," arrived and our 743rd Maintenance Company started its drive through the beautiful rolling countryside of southern Germany to our final destination, the city of Augsburg. I was sitting in the cab next to the driver from our automobile section mechanic, Frank. He turned to me and said, "Sergeant, would you like to have some fun?"

"Sure," I snapped back. "Anything to break up the monotony. What do you have in mind?"

"Wait and I'll show you." As we rumbled through the next town on a downgrade and approached a few pedestrians my buddy turned off the ignition and then immediately turned it back on again. Suddenly an earth shattering explosion followed by a reddish colored tongue of flame and then black smoke shot out of the tailpipe. I looked out the window back at the pedestrians, who had jumped a few feet, covering their ears.

"They're scared out of their wits," I hollered and laughed. The cab driver jinked the prank a few more times.

"Hey, I think we better stop this business," I said to my buddy Frank. "Not only could we cause an injury but also we could get in trouble by being reported. The name of our outfit is stenciled in white letters on the front and rear bumpers. Besides, the Germans will think we're just a bunch of Wild West cowboys. We need to make a good impression. After all, we are still their occupiers. Let's smile and wave at them instead."

Frank thought a moment, then nodded. "Yeah, I guess you're right, Sergeant."

When we arrived in Augsburg the MPs led our convoy onto the grounds of the Patch Kaserne barracks, named after the general who served both in the South Pacific and Germany during the war. These barracks were formerly the home base of a German Panzer grenadier division. The soldiers were housed in solid masonry buildings with an outside stucco finish. They had three floors plus a finished attic with dormers. The complex had a theater, separate clubrooms for officers, NCO's, and enlisted men, and separate living quarters for officers. To my amazement the place had survived the allied bombing raids unscathed.

The many garages of various sizes for vehicles, artillery pieces, tanks and miscellaneous rolling stock, spare parts, and a repair shop made it quite suitable to house the 43rd Division's tanks, artillery and our Ordinance Company. The four of us machinists were assigned to a separate room. It was cozy and a lot less noisy than the larger dorms. Luckily none of us snored heavily.

Bob Whitney's shoulder had a tendency to dislocate during the night and his scream of pain would awaken us. We usually managed to pop it back in place except on this one hair-raising occasion when Bob was howling in pain. It took the four of us to pull him from his bed while still on his mattress, which we dragged down the hall, down a flight of stairs, through the entrance, and into a jeep where we had to place poor Bob on a stretcher for the ambulance ride to the infirmary. He didn't stop howling the entire way. The next day Bob came back with a contraption to wear that would immobilize his arm during sleep.

A day or two later, after we had settled into our new home, I was ordered to report to the company commander. The captain had his office next to the orderly rooms. On the way there I wondered why he wanted to see me.

When I arrived the top sergeant announced me to the captain, "Sergeant Esfeld to see you, sir."

"Send him in, Sarge," the captain said.

I entered and came to attention with a smart salute and said, "Sergeant Esfeld reporting as ordered, sir."

"At ease, Sergeant. I'll come right to the point. Your section leader Sergeant First Class Baker tells me you speak German, and from your records here quite well. Is that so?"

"Yes, sir," I said.

"Well then, I will give you an assignment as unofficial interpreter for our company."

My head started to spin. I'm going to be an interpreter after all!

The captain continued without hesitation. "I received permission from division headquarters allowing us to keep a tailor and a barber in the building to attend to the men's needs. You will request a list of candidates from the German Employment Office. No doubt the German officials will recommend one or two of each. Start with them first."

I silently stood, remembering the reprisals back in the German army. I hoped this wasn't a repeat.

He went on. "Visit their place of work and interview them. When you've made your choices, show our new employees where they will work, which will be up in our finished attic. Check it out yourself first. Then arrange for the moving of their equipment. You have my permission to use any suitable vehicle from our motor pool." He held out his hand with an envelope. "Here is my authorization for you to show to the German officials, the guard office or any MPs that ask you what you are doing. Make a German translation of it and have the orderly clerk type it up and I'll sign it. Do you think you can handle this, Sergeant?"

"Yes Sir, Captain." My mind was swimming with it all, but I had not wanted to interrupt.

"You are dismissed."

I took the captain's authorized paper and went out to the orderly room where I sat down to translate it. While the clerk typed it up I ran up the stairs to check out the attic. Except for sweeping up the floor it looked perfect to me. There was plenty of daylight coming in through the dormer window.

I quickly returned to the orderly room, picked up the captain's authorization papers, now in German and English, and reported back to my section leader, F.C. Baker. I explained to him what the captain wanted me to do.

"I'll need some help, especially in carrying equipment upstairs," I said.

"Go ahead, Sergeant. I'll give you all the help you need. Good luck now," he said.

That evening I made sure my boots were shined and that I had a crease in my brown gabardine pants. I buffed my insignia buttons until they shined, cleaned my field jacket, and polished up my holster, which carried a 45 caliber pistol devoid of any bullets. Soldiers were not allowed to have live ammunition in their weapons except when on guard duty.

Chapter 40

The German Barber and the German Tailor

The next morning I checked out a jeep from the motor pool and drove into the city to find the German employment office.

"Excuse me, please, could you give me directions to get to the employment office?" I bravely addressed a policeman in perfect German.

"*Ja.* If you go three blocks down, make a right, and then in four blocks you can make a left," he replied in a surprise tone as he looked me up and down.

Upon entering the lobby I straightened up and, in a military stride, approached the front desk. Noticing the name plate on the receptionist's desk, I said, "*Guten Morgen, Frau Schneider.* "*Wie geht es dir* (how are you)?"

Startled she took the paper I held out and mumbled, "*Guten morgen, Herr....?*"

As a government employee she wasn't used to being greeted with such familiarity by a stranger, especially by one in an American army uniform who spoke German. After reading my captain's letter she smiled and directed me to an office. I hesitated upon seeing so many people sitting on chairs along the walls waiting to be called up.

At the far end of this large room I noticed a desk with another woman sitting behind it; she was talking to a client in front of her. There was no way I was going to wait with all these people staring at me and wondering what a soldier of the U.S. Army was doing in a place like this. I made up my mind. As a person of authority I had to be assertive. Before the official behind the desk could call the next person, I rushed up to her desk where I again noticed the nameplate. "*Guten Morgen Frau Frohlich, ich bin* Sergeant Esfeld," I bellowed out. I went on to tell her the purpose of my being there and handed her the captain's letter of authorization.

Reading the letter Frau Frohlich said, "Obviously we can help you and I will gladly do it. I will assign you one of my assistants, who will help you from start to finish. Wait just a minute and I will get him for you."

As I waited curiosity must have caught the best of her. She stopped to turn to me and said "Are you German? You talk with such an accent-free German."

"*Nein,* I am American born of German parents," I answered without any further comment.

"That is very interesting," she said.

By then her assistant had arrived, an elderly man, short and balding but fit and dressed in casual clothing. She briefed him on my orders and then reached out to shake my hand. "Here is Hans. *Aufwiedersehen,* Sergeant. Lots of luck."

"*Aufwiedersehen, Frau Frohlich.* Many thanks for your help."

Her assistant took me into his office and pulled out a list of available tailors and barbers. After some searching he picked out one of each, men who didn't live too far from our barracks, and said, "I will contact these two men and make sure they are available for an interview with you. They will make a trip to your barrack to inspect the place where they will be working. Is this okay with you, Sergeant?"

"Yes. I'll meet you in the lobby at one-thirty this afternoon. *Aufwiedershen*," I said.

Hans shook my hand with a quick smile. I sensed relief in his grip since I spoke fluent German. I was amazed how smoothly things went. Typical Prussian-type thoroughness, I thought.

On the way back to my barrack the smell of fresh baked goods made me stop at a small bakery just outside the gate to my base. As I peered through the window I remembered how I had to witness the young German soldier, a so called defector who stole from a bakery, fall to his death by execution from a firing squad ordered by my own commanders. I reassured myself: I'm an American G.I. now. I walked in and ordered a bag of freshly baked jelly donuts for me and my buddies. I left a big tip and said thank you in German. When I returned my buddies eyes grew big. With our mouth's watering we devoured the twelve Berliners donuts. We all just loved them.

After I briefed my captain on the day's progress, I ate lunch and then headed back to the employment office at one-thirty sharp. Hans, the assistant employee, was already waiting for me. "Everything is okay. We'll see the tailor first," he said, greeting me with another firm handshake as he climbed into the jeep.

I etched the drive to the tailor in my mind in case I had to drive back to pick up his equipment. The tailor stood outside his front door to greet us. He was a diminutive man in his forties with a grayish receding hairline. He led us into his workroom. His agile movements and the twinkle in his eyes reminded me of a character out of one the Brothers Grimm fairytales. As we spoke, I sensed a desire in him to always please his customers. Although he only knew a few words in English, his animated speech would help in conversing with my buddies. I liked him and I wanted Hans to tell the tailor he got the job so that Hans could take some credit. I liked being in charge for once.

The tailor, who had been sitting cross-legged on his work table, jumped up and called his wife into the room to tell her the good news. His wife was a small, pleasant looking woman with dark brown shoulder length wavy hair, also with a touch of gray. She rushed up to me, shook my hand, and said excitedly, "*Danke schon, danke schon.*" She must have overheard me speaking German.

"You are welcome," I replied.

I wanted to impress my captain so I instructed Hans to tell the tailor to be ready with his equipment the next morning. Hans and I then drove to the barber's apartment with the tailor bouncing in the back seat of my jeep. A man in his fifties opened the door. He had a full head of well-groomed black hair; I took that as a good sign. He took us into the *Wohn kuche,* a living room-kitchen combination that was quite popular in apartments in Germany. A sofa sat against one wall with the kitchen table in front of it.

"My wife is at work," he said, taking a photograph off the wall.

Noticing how spic and span the place looked, I wondered whether this was his job while his wife was at work.

"We are displaced people from an eastern part of Germany that now belongs to Poland. We lost everything, including the barbershop I once owned."

He showed Hans and me the black and white crumpled photograph that was saved from his bombed out shop. I looked carefully at the words *Herr Fiseseur* (men's barber). I barely made out his name, painted on the shop's window.

"It's difficult to start over in this city or in any other city in Germany because of the lack of suitable buildings due to the heavy bombings during the war," he explained, his tone a little louder. He chose his words carefully and spoke slowly. He then showed me the makeshift chair he used to cut hair in the neighborhood. I nodded my head to signify my approval to Hans.

"Okay, you must be ready tomorrow afternoon with your equipment. We will pick you up then," instructed Hans to our new barber.

"Now I'll take you with our new tailor to my barrack to show you your new workplace," I said.

With Hans in the front seat I raced all of us back to my barrack to show them their new workplace. The smiles on their faces showed that they liked what they saw.

"Thank you," they both said with grateful and long handshakes.

I drove them back home and then I dropped off Hans at his office. Before leaving, he turned to me and asked, "Can I help you tomorrow?"

"Yes, you can," I answered without hesitation. "I'll pick you up in the morning."

And I roared off to make it in time for chow.

Chapter 41

The Sake of Giving

The next morning I chose a more suitable vehicle, a small sized truck from the motor pool that could accommodate equipment and furniture and four medium sized men. I drove to the employment office where Hans was already waiting. We hightailed it over to the tailor's place where the smell of freshly brewed coffee percolated through the front door. The tailor's wife let us in and, before we could protest, handed over two black coffees.

With the help of Hans, a few kind neighbors, and two of my buddies, we managed to load, then unload up the three flights of stairs by noon chow. I invited Hans and the tailor to join us for lunch, but the tailor declined. His wife had supplied him with his own hot meal and he wanted to clean and set up shop.

Afterward we drove off to pick up the barber. As we moved the barber's chair and a table into the dormer room next to the tailor I noticed him sitting cross-legged on his table, diligently sewing an American uniform for his first customer. Evidently, word had spread quickly that a tailor was ready to do business up in the attic.

After I made sure the barber was settled in I went downstairs and reported to the captain. "Sir, mission accomplished as ordered, sir. One tailor and one barber now working up in the attic, sir."

"Thank you, Sergeant. A job well done. I am amazed at how fast you accomplished this."

"Thank you, sir. I had good cooperation from *both* sides," I emphasized with an accent on both.

"That is good to hear. I'll call on you again when I'll need you."

Having been dismissed, I took Hans back to his office and thanked him for his help.

"Thank you, too, Sergeant. I am happy and thankful that two unemployed qualified people are off the city's dole and can once again provide for their families," he exclaimed.

"Hans, I might need your help again."

"*Ya*, Sergeant. *Aufweidersehn*."

In spring of the following year, 1952, not much had changed at our base in Augsburg. We played baseball or tried miserably at soccer, the main sport in Germany and throughout Europe and other countries, but hardly known in the U.S. With the Korean War still raging across the Pacific, rumors started to spread about murderous treatment of our POWs in the communist prison camps. And in the world of the Volkswagen, sales in the U.S. were under a measly one thousand, yet nearly 180,000 had been produced in Wolfsburg. The VW drew international attention, with importers as far away as Morocco.

I received another order to report to my captain's office.

"Sergeant Esfeld, I have another assignment for you. Our division commander, the General, will be here for an inspection of our Ordnance Company. I thought this would be a good opportunity to have a group picture taken of our company with the General. I asked for his approval and he agreed, but he stipulated that the divisional Signal Corps not be involve with the arrangements. That's where you come in."

I nodded my head in a sigh of relief. The Signal Corps was needed more than ever to develop modern techniques to fight against the enemy's mortar and aerial attacks. This had become more and more apparent during the Korean War. The corps had grown quickly in size and in importance. I figured their existence was probably top secret.

"I want you to organize the event and arrange for a German photographer," the captain continued. "Keep in mind there will be about three-hundred fifty personnel in our company present. We are more than half the size of a regular infantry battalion. I know you will do a good job, Sergeant. You have three weeks' time."

Realizing what a formidable undertaking I'd been assigned, I left the orderly room with my head spinning. This would require a photographer experienced in taking pictures of large groups, I thought, but I have Hans to help me.

Sure enough Hans and I found a photographer who photographed the company in sections and then spliced the negatives together. The final result was a photograph of the 743rd Ordnance Maintenance Company of the 43rd Infantry Division over two feet long. It came out perfect. I had a copy of it that hung in my basement for twenty-five years.

One more assignment would come to me toward the end of my two-year service in the U.S. Army. In the meantime, business was flourishing for the German tailor and the German barber. Every morning I took a jeep and drove the short distance to the bakery to buy freshly baked Berliners for my buddies and me. We were hooked. I made plans on which European countries I wanted to see on my first furlough. But first and foremost, I wanted to see Helga.

1952. L-first row standing me; L-behind me Page and third man from left Leonard Kunz; on his left is my buddy Bruce Tailor with the big ears; Second row from top, 2nd man from right buddy Bob Whitney; First row kneeling with the pendent my section leader, sergeant first class James Baker, with the 743rd Ordnance Maintenance Co., Service and Recovery Section of the US army in Augsburg, Germany. Courtesy of the German photographer I rounded up.

Chapter 42

Helga

Helga, the little girl who lived next door to us in Stuttgart back in 1938, should now be a young woman, I imagined while writing a letter to her for the first time. I told her I was stationed in Augsburg.

Dear Helga,

How are you? I hope you remember me, the little American boy next door to you. I hope you are well. I am now an American soldier stationed here Augsburg. I have my first furlough and I would like to come visit you on a weekend. Would that be alright?

Yours truly,

Herman Esfeld.

She replied a few days later saying yes, but it had to be on a Sunday. She was now a student at the University of Stuttgart and had classes on Saturday mornings. I was thrilled. She had just turned twenty. It had been thirteen years since we saw each other. But then I got an idea, so I boldly wrote her back right away.

Dear Helga,

Thank you for your quick reply. I wonder if it would be alright if I brought one of my suitable single buddies with me. Could you arrange a blind date for him?

Again, yours truly,

Herman

She wrote back and, to my utter surprise, she said yes, that would be fine. She had already asked one of her classmates named Doris, who agreed to come along. But I had to scramble to find that suitable buddy. I could not ask Bob Whitney, he was married; so I asked Bruce Taylor and Leonard Kunz, my other two roommates. They liked the idea of going to Stuttgart with me but suggested just the three of us guys go some other time. I had almost come to a dead end, but then I thought of my new friend Ted Kirchberg; he was from Chicago and of German descent. He even spoke some German, had a sense of humor, and was never a loss for words. I approached Ted, a tall, lanky brown haired guy with bushy brows and big brown eyes; he said yes.

Helga had told me where in the city we would meet. I admired the courage of these two German women going out with us uniformed American soldiers in public. A lot of Germans were disdainful of their young girls and women going out with GIs. Some forbade their daughters entirely and others wouldn't talk to us or even make eye contact. But not these two, I thought as I pulled on my freshly shined boots .They were more open minded and curious. What their countrymen thought didn't bother them.

It took only two hours to drive to Stuttgart in a U.S. Army jeep; we could have made it in less time by train, but then we wouldn't have had a vehicle. Helga recognized me right away, even though I too, despite my thinness, had grown and was dressed in a U.S. military uniform. I was just under the average height for an adult male, but my shoulders were filled out and I was well fed, thanks to our local bakery.

Helga had grown into a fine, petite woman with long blonde hair. This young, vivacious student was a far cry from the six-year-old girl with whom I sneaked a kiss sitting in my father's car in our garage. She now stood over me a little, whereas before I stood over her.

"Helga, you have grown into such a beauty! And how surprised I am that you could recognize me in an American uniform," I exclaimed. This was my first real date. I was excited, but finding the right words felt awkward.

After a light lunch at a German *Kaffeehaus* and a short stroll sightseeing, Ted and I took Helga and Doris to the afternoon dance at the American Servicemen's Club. They loved to dance to the American tunes of the big bands. Later we had a meal with typical American fare.

Ted and Doris got along just fine. In spite of the mixture of German and English, we had interesting and animated conversations. The day ended with an early evening at a cozy *Weinstube* (wine cellar) with the romantic sounds of soft music playing in the background.

"*Aufwiedersehen*," we all said to one another when the evening was over. It had been a wonderful day that felt more like a day and a half, with all we had packed in. Building up my courage, I murmured to Helga, "I would like to see you again. But this time I would like to visit with your parents."

She laughed and said, "*Das konnen wir machen* (we can do that)."

Helga was still as lively and exuberant at twenty as she had been when we played together as neighbors over fourteen years ago before the war broke out. She had blossomed into a tall and slender, attractive woman with dark eyes like her mother and a jovial, pleasing personality like her father. He owned a chemical factory and was now busy manufacturing house paints, which were badly needed for the repair and replacement of the damaged and destroyed housing from the bombing during WWII.

"Hello, Herman. It's good to see you again. How are your father and mother?" Helga's father cordially asked. Because Helga's parents were prosperous and part of the upper middle class, I knew I was not deemed suitable marriage material for their daughter. But because of the contribution my father made to the creation of the now flourishing Volkswagen factory, they treated me warmly; in fact, so warmly that when Helga asked if we could borrow his car, an older model Adler, he obliged.

I liked Helga even though I soon realized that, because of her status, my pursuit of a serious relationship with her would not get me very far. Her bubbly personality, adventurous spirit and intellect that radiated like a high school girl on her first date mesmerized me. Together we went to the theater, museums and the cozy wine cellars. It couldn't get much more romantic.

The day that we took her father's car, a fine leather two-seater with a sleek long and narrow front body and bug-eyed lights perched on front fender wings, I had bought gifts for Helga and her mother. I had gone to the PX earlier and picked out a lace nylon slip for Helga. When I was growing up in Detroit my mother always took me shopping and with her I watched her pick out all the pretty clothes for women. For her mother, I purchased a large can of pre-cooked chicken.

When they opened their gifts there was a moment of silence followed by an embarrassed smile on their faces. Or maybe they were holding back a laugh; I couldn't tell.

"*Danke schon,* Herman," squeaked Helga.

"*Danke schon*," Mrs. Gronwald said politely.

I was baffled by their lack of any joyful response. What had I done wrong?

Later on Helga explained, "It is not appropriate for a man to give a lady who he hardly knows such an intimate garment. But I do like it." And she gave me a peck on the cheek. "As for the chicken? Those hunger years for the upper crust Germans are far gone. We look at American canned goods with disdain. A nice bouquet of flowers would have been a better choice."

I felt like crawling into a hole.

The Gronwalds graciously recognized my good intentions. "Herman, what would be one of your favorite German dishes that I could prepare for you?" the kind Mrs. Gronwald asked me later that day.

"*Swiebelduchen* (onion cake)," I said rather loudly. I learned to love this Swabian specialty at my grandmother's house. Right after my stint in the German anti-aircraft artillery duty my brother and I walked into her back kitchen, which faced the barn, to the smells of chopped onions being fried together with bacon bits and sour cream, all splattering in the skillet. I thought I had died and gone to heaven.

"It is not quite done yet, Herman," grandmother had said as my mouth hung open in anticipation. "I have to pour it over yeast dough and then I bake it to a crisp brown." Standing at my grandmother's side as she cooked, the looming thunder of enemy fighter planes embedded in my mind dissolved. That day in my grandmother's kitchen, only my hearing still suffered from the anti-battery guns I'd had to man; my sense of smell and taste were one hundred percent.

"Oh, onion cake; I'll gladly make it for you. We will have it for lunch," Mrs. Gronwald said with a smile, which I returned with a broad one of my own.

After the debacle with the ladies' gifts earlier in the day I came to doubt if Mr. Gronwald would trust me with driving the 'old Adler,' his gem.

He looked at me for a moment. "The car has a manual transmission and has to be double-clutched when shifting gears. Can you do that?" he asked.

"*Ja*," I answered. "I have that with our old army trucks." I thought about the Volkswagen and the Kubelwagon, its predecessor. What would my father think of me driving an Adler, a British upper class sensation?

"Well, then, let's go outside and give it a try."

When I passed the test, Mr. Gronwald grinned. "Okay, you two can take the car."

So Helga and I drove into the city to see a concert, Helga laughing at me all the way as I feverishly tried to master double clutching again. The car would stutter and then strut and then stutter until I got the hang of it. After the concert I drove us to our favorite weinstube, a cozy wine bar that had managed to escape the bombing during WWII. We both ordered a glass of wine.

The pub was busy and loud. The local patrons drank and talked about their less fortunate neighbors or asked questions about lost loved ones and what would happen to the German working class now. When we walked in, heads turned to look at me and it got quiet for a second or two. I drank my wine quickly as Helga sipped on hers.

We stayed for two glasses each, then I asked, "Helga, how about we go for a ride into the country?" I thought for sure she would say no since we had her father's car and it was already dark outside. But my double clutching had considerably improved by now. On the way out of the city I passed the street where I should have turned. "Where are we going?" asked Helga, sounding a little surprised.

I had not socialized with a girl, not even attended dances or gone on dates, since carrying their books home from school back in Detroit. As I drove down what I thought to be a lovers' lane, all the lost time of my adolescence went out the window. I turned slowly onto a furrowed dirt road. There had been a cold and steady rain the past two days, but this day the white snow clouds crowding the sky were all that was left. I didn't go too far for fear of getting us lost, especially in Helga's father's car.

As I drove up a slight rise I finally answered her in English: "Lovers' lane." I looked desperately left and right for a wooded area. There was nothing but dark open farmland. Finally at the top of the hill I turned left onto a short dirt road.

"For heaven's sake, what is lovers' lane?" I could see Helga's eyes open wide.

"*Liebhaber* Lane," I translated literally. By then I had turned left again onto a dirt path that the farmers used to get to their fields. I stopped the car with one of the front wheels resting on the edge of a freshly plowed field illuminated only by a half moon. The stars were out, twinkling in full force. I turned to Helga. "Lover's lane is where a boy and girl try to make out or kiss," I explained.

"Herman, please don't make it so suspenseful," Helga said impishly.

"Then let me demonstrate." I lowered my voice like a chemistry professor addressing his students. I leaned over and kissed her lightly on the lips. She reciprocated and I took her in my arms and kissed her a few more times, the way I thought it should be.

Breathlessly she pulled away from me and whispered, "Now I know what 'making out' means."

"Do you remember when I gave you your first kiss in the back seat of my parents' car parked in the garage?"

"*Ja.*"

"But this is so much better!" we both blurted.

Emboldened from the excitement, I took off my gloves and placed one hand carefully over the place where I imagined her left breast would be. It felt firm and round. Helga sat still with her head back while I fumbled for her coat buttons. I wondered what she was thinking when suddenly I noticed something.

Through clenched teeth I hissed, "Helga, we must get out of here."

She straightened up with a jolt. "What's the matter?" She was just as startled as I was.

Even though we'd been there for just a few minutes, I realized that all four wheels of the car were sinking deeper and deeper into the muck. "Holy cow! We might be stuck, Helga. Your father will be furious with me. This is his car!" I said aloud in perfect German. I had to get out of there before it was too late. I shifted the car into reverse and backed out slowly, but the tires would only spin. I peeked out the window and saw all the tires half covered in muck.

"The car is starting to sink into the soil on your side!" I panicked and grinded the gears.

"Oh my Gott," cried out Helga.

I frantically rolled the car back and forth a few times until the tires grabbed and we started to move backwards. The training I had in the American Service and Recovery section with vehicles sliding off icy roads or parked on soft ground kicked in. My heart pounded faster than a jack hammer as I slowly backed the car uphill hugging the edge of the path until I got on the pavement of the road that led to the highway. I looked over to see Helga's bare white knuckle grip on her door handle.

We raced down the hill for the short distance to Helga's home.

She let out a sigh of relief. "Herman that was a close call. You did a wonderful job of driving," she said, laughing hysterically.

"Thank you." I thought, so much for a romantic interlude.

We made it back past the midnight hour. Quietly Helga and I entered the house--but sure enough, her father had been waiting for us at the front door.

"I expected you to be back an hour ago. Now it is midnight. I worried about you. Where were you?" he asked with a frown.

Helga had a ready answer. "I am sorry, father. Herman and I stopped at this wienstube for a night cap. It was so cozy in there, with the dim light and musicians playing softly in the background, we just lost track of time." Helga gave her father a hug and a peck on the cheek.

Satisfied with the explanation, her father said with a smile, "I am glad you two had a good time and are back safely." We shook hands and said good night in the German custom. I retreated to the room they had made up for me for a one night stay. As I lay in bed I wondered how Mr. Gronwald would react when he discovered the two whitewall tires on his Adler covered with mud. There must have been at least six inches of dried mud and manure caked on the wheels.

I no longer saw Helga as I had before thirteen years of war, as only an intelligent, studious, yet outgoing and fun loving girl. Her father doted upon her and was, perhaps, overly protective. She had told me she'd never had a steady boyfriend, in spite of being an attractive young woman. I saw her in a different light now, as if touched by a magic wand: her openness, especially toward my GI uniform and how she appeased her father by stretching the truth about our date. That endeared her to me. I was enamored by her. An angel must have been guiding me to her.

To this day I don't remember if Helga's father ever found out how his tires got muddied. I don't recall the excuse Helga gave him, but he never said a word. All I know is, for a fleeting moment, there in that muddy farm field, I was in heaven. And I sure learned a lesson about giving gifts to women. So much had changed from our first kiss in Wolfsburg.

I had to return to the barracks back in Augsburg the next day. I thanked the Gronwalds for a wonderful weekend at their home and their warmhearted hospitality. I turned to Helga and said, "Merry Christmas, Helga. Can I see you again?"

She smiled and said, "*Ja*, absolutely. Just let me know ahead of time."

I hugged her, said, "*Aufwiederschen*" softly, and left for the train station. I never saw Helga's parents again.

Chapter 43

Die Goldene Gans (The Golden Goose)

"When it's time for love, we know it's time."
--Edna Esfeld

That Christmas season of 1952 I felt homesick. Helga informed

me that her family would spend Christmas at home and then leave for

a ski vacation, which added to my melancholy. At the end of January

she would visit her grandmother in Heidelberg. In Michigan, during

the holidays, my mother would always take me into Detroit, holding

my tiny hand as we sludged through burnt-colored snow into the toasty

warmth of department stores for gift shopping. When I was in military

training camp in Virginia a speck of light snow here and there

camouflaged the spirit of Christmas for me. But now, stationed in

Germany, with all the Christmas decorations the spirited Germans

created and displayed, I was more than ready for a little adventure.

A few buddies from my ordnance company, sensing I had the

holiday blues, approached me a couple of days after Christmas.

"Herman, why don't you come with us out for dinner? You can choose the restaurant since you speak the language. We would like to try some typical German food," they said.

"Well, you're in luck," I told them, having agreed. "I have found the right place. It's in the city but off the beaten path, a cozy feel, and they serve good home cooked food. It's a *Gasthuas* (guest restaurant) that belongs to the local brewery right next door. Convenient for them to sell their beer in the restaurant. It's called *Die Goldene Gans*," I told them. "In English, The Golden Goose."

They laughed.

I made reservations for an evening right after New Year's. Smartly dressed in our pressed American uniforms, six of us entered the noisy, smoke-filled, beer smelling *Gaststube* (dining room). I could see the curious eyes of the German patrons upon us as the *Wirt* (host) led us to a long table in the far corner all neatly set with dinnerware on a white tablecloth. Shortly a pretty young waitress with a frown on her face stepped up to our table and handed us the menus. She stood stiffly.

"*Fräulein,* please give us a few more minutes. I will be ordering for my buddies if you could give me a little more time," I asked her politely in my perfect German.

With a sigh of relief in her voice she said, in a fast southern German accent, "I am so glad you speak German."

From then on my conversation with our waitress was kept strictly to business. My comrades enjoyed their selection of German food, washing it down with plenty of German beer. We left the place happy and satisfied. And I became smitten with the petite *Fräulein* who served us, and grateful she hadn't asked any questions about me. Her wavy light brown hair that hung to her shoulders and the bright smile flashed at us once or twice intrigued me so much that during the ensuing weeks I pursued her. It was practically forbidden for a German *Fräulein* to go on a date with an American GI or even be seen with him. She reluctantly turned me down each time.

But after a few weeks my persistence paid off. I courted Ida for about two months. When we went out to dinner, the only thing we did on our dates, Ida would walk ten steps ahead of me so no one would see her out with an American GI. It wasn't long before we fell in love—and then it was time to meet her family.

Ida's mother had perished from American bombs in February 1945 while she worked at a restaurant. Ida had no siblings, so the only family member I met was her friendly uncle. After I explained my background to him, he was open to us getting married. But when a priest found out Ida was going to marry an American, he paid her a visit. He berated my fiancé in front of me. Ida's uncle almost threw him down the stairs of the apartment Ida had been living in since she was eighteen. With her mother gone and so little family left, Ida was willing to move to the United States with me as soon as possible.

On the 22nd of September 1952 I asked to be discharged from the army. The military would not wait for the paperwork for Ida's passport so that we could be transported back to the States together. And the army would only pay for my overseas trip if I used army transport, though they did pay for rail within Germany and transport from New York to Detroit. If I wanted to be with my bride, a discharge from the army was my only option.

The Italia, built in 1909, was touted as an elegant ship by fancy brochures distributed throughout Europe. I thought taking this ship over to my homeland would be a good introduction for Ida and maybe a nice honeymoon for us. I scrambled like hell to make arrangements for our passage overseas. I didn't have money for a diamond ring until many years later. But I set our wedding date for mid-August, eight months later, and paid for a sail date in early October from Hamburg to New York City on the exquisite ocean liner Italia, as shown in these pictures.

At the end of a bitter cold January, I called Helga in Heidelberg. I knew I had to tell her in person about the sudden change in my plans. My military buddies teased me for weeks because they knew I had stayed a weekend at Helga's.

After an exchange of cordial pleasantries on the phone I asked her if I could spend the next weekend with her in Heidelberg. "Ja, we can take a stroll across the bridge over the Neckar River and up a hill to a little park where we can plan what to do," she said.

"That sounds great. See you then." I hung up quickly, thinking "Keep it short. The enemy is listening in." I heard those words constantly during wartime. Giant size posters stuck to public phone booths in Germany warned Germans to keep telephone conversations short and to the point. I had become obsessed with the propaganda. This time I did not want to elaborate over the phone what I needed to tell Helga in person.

We greeted each other warmly with a light kiss on the lips. We started on our walk with Helga doing most of the talking about her Christmas and skiing in the Swiss Alps. As we crossed the Neckar Bridge I noticed an American couple approaching us arm in arm. The man wore an officer's coat and hat but I could not make out his rank just yet. I got ready to salute when I glanced at the striking blonde young woman on his arm. In disbelief we both called out each other's names and greeted each other.

"Helen? Helen Eckhart from Detroit? I can't believe it!" I recognized the silver bar on the officer's shoulder pads. He was a First Lieutenant. Awkwardly I fumbled for a salute, whereupon he laughed and waved it off.

"That's alright, Sergeant. With the way my wife and you greeted each other, you two must go back a long way."

"Yes, sir. Our fathers worked together as design engineers at Ford Motor Company in Detroit back in the '30s before I came to Germany with my parents in 1937." I hardly remembered Helen then until we met a few more times after I returned from the war to the United States in 1948.

"We are married now and my husband is stationed here in Germany," Helen said.

After I introduced Helga we shared a few niceties and said goodbye.

Now I dominated the conversation with Helga as we went up the hill to the park.

When we reached the top of the hill we stood quietly for a moment and enjoyed the beautiful view of the university town of Heidleberg. We looked across the Neckar River to the hills on the left where the Schloss castle lay in partial ruin. I was desperately trying to think of how I could tell Helga what I had to tell her.

We took a few snapshots of each other and sat on a bench.

With an expectant look in her eyes I began. "Helga, you are such a beautiful and wonderful young woman. During my last visit with you and your family I realized how many things we enjoy doing together and felt I was falling in love with you. But common sense also told me that the disparity in our situations could not be bridged and would not allow me to further advance our relationship to the next level. Oh, how I would otherwise have loved to do that. But something else happened in the meantime. That is why I am here to tell you personally. Shortly after Christmas I met a girl. I have already taken her out a few times. I would like to take her out more often. Therefore, Helga, I will not be seeing you again."

By now she was looking at me with glistening eyes. "Herman, I understand, but we will remain friends won't we?"

"Of course we will," I said and grasped both her hands, giving her a kiss on the cheek.

Helga and I continued to write each other every Christmas for ten years until she married a medical doctor and started a family. She abruptly stopped writing me without telling me why.

Chapter 44

Home Again

I filled out my application to marry Ida. Shortly afterwards we both were interviewed by the Division Chaplain. The paper mill processing my application ground ever so slowly. It seemed like forever before I finally I received permission for us to marry, but it was too late for me to participate in the military's large scale maneuvers at Grafenwhoehr, only a few hours away from the magnificent Bavarian Alps. Consequently I had more time to spend with my fiancé and making marriage arrangements. My luck prevailed when I found out it was too late to ship me back to the U.S. for my discharge out of the Army on September 25th, 1953; instead I was advised I would be discharged from Augsburg on the same date.

I arranged for a church wedding and a carriage drawn by a white horse that took us from the civil ceremony at City Hall to the church and from there to the reception hall. I invited my German relatives on both sides of the family but only my seventy-one year old grandmother was able to make the four hundred mile train trip. I also invited twelve of my comrades, including John Campbell. I arranged for a sit-down dinner and a three piece band for music and dancing. Champagne was served along with an open bar. Ida wore a beautiful, flowing white lace wedding gown and I dressed in my U.S. military inform. My grandmother smiled and laughed the whole while dancing with John Campbell through half the wedding and having the time of her life! Only one black and white picture was taken of us standing together; our wide smiles of happiness reflected our absolute joy.

Before long, I was honorably discharged. I donned the expensive suit, coat and hat my mother had picked out and sent to me to come back home. I took my bride to the railroad station and said goodbye to a group of my buddies. They whistled and hollered at me in my civilian clothes.

"Look at Herman. Woo woo, nicely dressed."

I smiled and waved as Ida and I climbed aboard the train to Cuxhaven, the port city where we would be boarding the ship that would take us to the United States. On the way we stopped off to say goodbye to my relatives. At my mother's sister's home my *Tante* Katie and her husband gave us a surprise farewell party that lasted late into the evening.

The next morning the doorbell rang. *Tante* Katie, still in her housecoat, answered.

"Hello, is Herman here?"

"One minute please," my aunt said flustered. She ran up the stairs to the bedroom where Ida and I were still sleeping.

"Herman, someone is at the door for you," she called out.

"What?" I replied sleepily as her footsteps loudly crept away. After a long night of celebrating and a huge hangover the two of us were not in any condition to receive guests. I managed to peek through the curtains with half an eye open. To my amazement there was Henry Drettmann from Detroit with his wife waiting in their pink Cadillac at the curb! I felt somewhat at a loss and rather chagrined. Henry Drettmann had made good his stated intentions of visiting his home country for the first time since he emigrated to the U.S. in the early twenties.

1953 August 9th. Ida's and mine wedding day in Augsburg.

After all, it was through the efforts of my father's former colleague from the 30s that Vatti got a job as a tool and die design engineer at Ford Motor Company's rear axle plant in 1950. Working once again for his old employer enabled my parents to buy a modest bungalow in the middle class suburb of St. Clair Shores while I was on active duty in Germany. When we arrived in September 1953, Henry Drettmann had my old job waiting for me, as promised.

I quickly threw on some clothes and went downstairs. "You must have heard I was getting married here in Germany," I said to him. I explained to him the circumstance of that fortunate encounter with Ida at the Golden Goose restaurant.

He just laughed and said, "I took a long shot and almost made it."

My brother and sister were living at home when we arrived in Detroit that summer of '52. They both were attending high school and were making good grades. One night, at one of our family dinners, they both took me aside.

"Herman," they said. "We noticed lately our father is acting withdrawn, even a little depressed. Perhaps it's what they call a 'midlife crisis'. He's almost fifty-three years old. But we think our father feels he let us all down, even endangering our lives by his decision to go to Germany to help create a factory to build the Volkswagen. Now he sees how his former colleagues and friends all prospered through the war years here in the States. We feel the three of us should encourage him and tell him we love him in spite of everything."

I nodded in agreement. We sat our father in front of us and I began.

"*Vati,* Ronald, Norma, and I know how difficult it must be for you to start all over. But we want you to know that we don't feel badly towards you for making the decision to go to Germany. We are old enough to understand what it meant to you. We are thankful for having survived those war years and for you to be able to come back to the United States after us and keep the family intact. Now we are all off to a fresh start and we want you to know that we support you and love you."

Seldom did I ever see my father become emotional. With tears in his eyes, he stood and silently thanked us each with a hug. He continued to help each of us as best as he could. He taught me die stamping and let me design my own dies while he moonlighted at home. He introduced me to one of his apprentices, who eventually became my boss. He took me out of tool-making and into engineering; he mentored me for many years. When I retired in 1990, I was manager of manufacturing and engineering.

He helped my brother Ronald with an apprenticeship in tool-and-die making and after that as an apprentice product designer. My father and brother ended up working in offices right next to each other at Ford Motor Company until my father retired in 1966. He put my sister Norma through Wayne State University in Michigan, which enabled her to attend her junior year at the University in Munich, Germany. She became a teacher and worked as such most of her life. My father served us well.

Sometime during the mid-1950s news broke out that some of our GIs who had been held as prisoners of war by the Chinese had defected. These P.O.W.'s openly recanted their oath of allegiance to the United States and its armed forces. They wanted to live in China under communistic rule. This shocked not only me but the rest of America as well as the Pentagon. It was surmised that the change in thinking of those GIs was the result of the consistent and intensive propaganda the P.O.W's were subjected to by the Chinese communist government. That was when the word "brainwashing" was coined.

1954 Detroit. Below: My father moonlighting for Ford Motor Co. before being re-hired. Above: Me working as a tool and die maker. Ida and I lived with my parents for six months before moving into our first home in the Mark Twain area of Detroit.

I knew too well how effective it could be on the brain of a young person in his or her formative years. Had I not experienced it myself under the rule of the Nazis in Germany? I blocked the answer to that question for the next seventy five years of my life.

I bought a VW in 1969, a brand new tan one. I was the only member of my family to park one in the driveway. It had black vinyl seats, white wall tires and a fancy sunroof that manually opened and closed. I taught both my daughters how to drive the stick shift during winter and summer weekends when their local high school and college parking lots were empty. I even bumped it a few times pulling out of the garage with my boat size car. Eventually, I handed the bug down to my eldest daughter for her high school graduation gift after a couple of years. She drove it to work and school; then sold it before going to Michigan State to live in a dorm. Nora sold it to a high school friend of Edna's. It became her first car too.

Chapter 45

Freedom is Not Free

"Success is not final; failure is not fatal; it is the courage to continue, that counts."
--Winston Churchill

I never said anything about my experience in World War II. The only thing I ever said about my war experience was that I had served in the American army as a drill sergeant during the Korean War, but had been stationed in Germany, thereby eliminating the danger of fighting for my life in the Korean War, known as the forgotten war. Even though the Korean War lasted just three years-- half as long as World War II--there were over one million casualties from all sides in that short period. And tens of thousands still carry the physical and emotional wounds from which they were impacted in the swamps and cold winters in which they had to fight.

After twenty-seven years of marriage, my wife Ida and I divorced in 1980. It was a sad occasion. Afterwards, I kept the house in which we raised our children, two girls, Nora and her younger sister

Edna. Nora, the more studious and out-going, married before our divorce and going on thirty years now, bared two beautiful children of her own, Krista and Matthew, my only grandchildren and three great grandchildren. Edna, adventurer and athletic one, moved out to California two months after her high school graduation in 1977 and started her own business which she still owns. And for the first time in my life, at the age of fifty-eight, I lived alone there. I didn't know how to cook or clean or wash clothes. I bought a microwave, which took care of most of my cooking. The house went months without cleaning unless my daughter Nora came by. I took most of my clothes to the cleaners. An ex-German-American soldier has got to do what he's got to do.

A year after our divorce in 1981 I visited my close friends Trudy and Willie Timm, originally from Germany, who lived near me. "Herman, sit down. I am writing a birthday card to my girlfriend in Germany,'' Trudy said.

"Oh, is she married?" I quipped.

"Yes. Her husband is a German baron and my girlfriend is the baroness vonEyss. However she is filing for divorce."

My ears perked up. I was free and flying over to Germany soon to spend the holidays with my relatives. Trudy continued. "Ruth and I grew up together as children in Germany. Herman, I know you two will fit perfectly together," Trudy said in her German accent.

"Besides you are going on vacation over there, anyhow. She could show you around a little bit," Trudy persisted.

"I'll look her up. I'll be spending a lot of time with my aunts, uncles, and cousins whom I haven't seen in forty years, since after the war. And it will be Christmas."

"Ruth doesn't have much family left because of the war and her daughter is now living in New Zealand. I will tell her you will be giving her a call when you are in Germany."

And that was that. I'd fly over to Germany, visit with my family, and on the way I'd pay Ruth a visit. I had no expectations of Ruth and I.

Sure enough the moment I laid eyes on Ruth it was love at first sight. And now, Ruth and I are now going on twenty-eight years of a wonderful marriage. Right after we were married I told her about my time during WWII and how my father managed to bring us to

Germany to build the VW factory before the outbreak of the war.

"Herman, have you ever been back to the Russian front where

you fought for your life?" she asked me in German one day.

It was 1986 and we had been married for just a year and were

living in Jackson, Michigan. Ruth no longer worked and I was coming

close to retirement. Her question surprised me. I didn't know what to

say. I had not been back; I had no intentions of retracing my childhood

as a Hitler youth and a German soldier. I never ever thought about it.

"I think it would be helpful for you," she insisted.

So, in 1999, my second wife Ruth and I traveled through

Germany on a vacation. We had breakfast in the village of Kremmen

where the SS General Steiner and remnants of his SS Panzer Division

had made their breakout from Berlin. We drove over the bridge

crossing the Ruppiner Kanal and parked our rental car on the side of

the tree-lined road next to the little farmhouse that was still standing.

We slowly walk backed to the bridge. Standing on that bridge, gripped

with emotions and memories that flooded back to those ten days in a

foxhole in April of 1945, I explained to my wife the events that took place. The farmhouse that had been almost completely demolished by the 88mm anti-aircraft guns now stood beautifully restored with modern picture windows. On the other side of the road I noticed a nicely tended vegetable garden still surrounded by an even higher hedge. I would not be able to spot the Russian soldier crawling behind it now.

Looking down the canal from the bridge I could hardly recognize the embankment behind where our platoon had dug in. It was overgrown with twenty-foot high deciduous trees. But where had my foxhole been? Before I could try to find it, my wife and I would have to ask for permission, since the pathway leading to the area looked like private property. So we walked up to the farmhouse and knocked on the door. I noticed a few pockmarks still left in the soft brick wall made by fragments of the exploding Russian mortar rounds.

The door was opened by a middle-aged man with a curious look on his face. I introduced ourselves and told him why we were there. His eyes grew wider and wider in astonishment as my story unfolded.

"At that time I was not yet born but my parents told me there had been some fierce fighting in our village," he explained. He went on to say that I was the first one to revisit the area. He told us we could walk along the path and stay as long as we wanted.

We thanked the nice man and my wife and I went on in search of my foxhole. However, the entire area had been filled in and covered with grass. But I remembered that I had made a landmark with a concrete electricity pole which I figured to be fifteen feet in front of and a little bit off to the left of my foxhole (ten days in a foxhole and the mind can do a whole lot of wandering). Sure enough, the pole was still there. I could look through trees on the embankment over the canal to the other side where Ivan had been dug in. With all those trees, Franz would have had a bad "field of fire," and Ivan a good cover for a sneak attack.

Fifty-four years later I found myself standing at the exact spot where my foxhole had been: the fresh smells of fields of grass, well plowed farmlands, and the mountainous backdrop of a lively green forest, clearing my senses, like on deck of the ship to Germany in 1937. Now I was no longer a young, brainwashed soldier for the

Fuhrer, but a loyal American citizen who had served my country of origin in the US army. And I was a tourist. How lucky we were.

JUNI, 1990

Wanderwege und gemütliche Gaststätten vermißt er in den USA

Hermann Esfeld: Erst deutscher Soldat, dann amerikanischer GI

Halle (Fe). „Ich freue mich schon jetzt auf unseren nächsten Urlaub in Deutschland!" Interessanten Besuch hat Käthe Schwede aus Halle, Oststraße 6: Ihre Schwester und deren Mann, Ruth und Hermann Esfeld aus Detroit/Michigan sind wieder einmal hier in „Old Germany". Hermann Esfeld ist von Geburt her waschechter Amerikaner, ist aber in Deutschland aufgewachsen und sieht deshalb hier seine zweite Heimat. Ein Kuriosum, über das er aber erst heute lachen kann: Innerhalb von fünf Jahren hat er erst für die Deutsche Wehrmacht gekämpft, war dann in Deutschland als „GI" stationiert!

1927 wurde er als Sohn deutscher Eltern in Detroit geboren. Sein Vater war Ingenieur für den Autobau, war 1925 aus der Bremer Gegend nach Amerika ausgewandert. 1937 wurde der Vater von Professor Porsche dann nach Stuttgart geholt, um dort als Spezialist das Volkswagenwerk mit aufzubauen.

Vom 2. Weltkrieg überrascht, mußten erst der Vater und dann auch Sohn Hermann in der Wehrmacht dienen. Und so bekam Hermann die deutsche Staatsangehörigkeit, verlor die von den USA, wurde Flakhelfer. Nach der Gefangenschaft ging er 48 wieder in die Vereinigten Staaten, bekam dann auch die amerikanische Staatsbürgerschaft wieder zurück und wurde so 1950 beim Ausbruch des Koreakrieges eingezogen. Hatte dann aber noch Glück im Unglück und wurde in Deutschland in der Nähe von Augsburg stationiert.

Beruflich trat er in die Fußstapfen seines Vaters, wurde auch Ingenieur, und ging jetzt mit fast 63 Jahren in den Ruhestand. Neben einer einheitlichen Staatsrente von etwa 900 Dollar im Monat bekommt er noch eine Betriebsrente, das ist „drüben" so üblich.

Nach einer halben Weltreise ist er jetzt mit seiner Frau wieder in Halle gelandet und freut sich, mit dem Mietwagen durch die deutsche, ihm so liebe Landschaft zu fahren. Wenn auch auf den Autobahnen fürchterlich gerast wird, so hält er doch die Deutschen für disziplinierte Autofahrer. Die gepflegten Wälder und Wanderwege, gemütliche Cafés und Gaststätten, das vermissen sie in den USA - und deshalb werden sie auch immer wieder nach Old Germany reisen.

„Old Germany" ist ihre große Liebe - von links Käthe Schwede aus Halle und ihr Besuch aus den USA, Hermann und Ruth Esfeld.
Foto: R. Feldkirch

1990, June. L-R: With Ruth's older sister Kathe, visiting my foxhole and the farmhouse across from the *Ruppiner Kanal*, me, and my 2nd and present wife Ruth.

1947 October 10. Letter of gratitude from Volkswagenwerk's CEO thanking my father Henry Esfeld for his ten years of service, mentioning in particular his loyalty, enthusiasm and reliability.

The End.

Made in the USA
Charleston, SC
27 May 2015